Practical Cyber Security
for
Extremely Busy People

Protect yourself, your family, and
your career from online exploitation

2021 Edition

Daniel Farber Huang

Practical Cyber Security for Extremely Busy People
Protect yourself, your family, and your career from online exploitation
2021 Edition

©2020 Daniel Farber Huang

All Rights Reserved.

No part of this book shall be reproduced or transmitted in any form or by any means, electronic, mechanical, magnetic, and photographic, including photocopying, recording, or by any information storage and retrieval system, without prior written permission of the publisher.

No patent liability is assumed with respect to the use of the information contained herein. Although every precaution has been taken in the preparation of this book, the publisher and author assume no responsibility for errors or omissions. Neither is any liability assumed for damages resulting from the use of the information contained herein.

Published by Princeton Studios

ISBN: 9798573431413

Cover Design by Alexander Huang-Menders

To Theresa, Quincy, Christian, Alexander, Celeste

Always.

Contents

Topic	Page
Introduction	i
Section I – At a Minimum, Do This	1
Encryption Explained in 20 Seconds	3
Chapter 1 – Secure Your Assets	5
Chapter 2 – Some Common but Important Terms	15
Chapter 3 – Secure Your Pipeline	17
Chapter 4 – Email Safety	25
Chapter 5 – Is That Really Your Password?	47
Chapter 6 – 2-Factor Authentication	57
Section II – Protect Your Privacy	61
Too Long; Didn't Read	63
Chapter 7 – Why Your Privacy Matters	67
Chapter 8 – Browsing	81
Chapter 9 – Mobile Device Safety	97
Chapter 10 – Tried-and-True Phone Scams	115
Chapter 11 – Encrypt Your Devices	133
Chapter 12 – Block, Remove, Backup, and Restore	137
Chapter 13 – On the Road	145

Section III – Online Self-Defense 151

    Chapter 14 – Social Media Discretion 155

    Chapter 15 – Defend Against Trolls 179

    Chapter 16 – Non-Consensual Pornography / Revenge Porn 239

    Chapter 17 – Protecting Teens and Children...259

    Chapter 18 – Removing Your Personal Info from the Internet 277

    Chapter 19 – Identity Theft 285

Section IV – Protect Your Career..291

    Chapter 20 – Separate Your Work Life from Your Personal Life 293

    Chapter 21 – Job Searches and Career Tools 297

    Chapter 22 – Online Meetings..301

The Wrap Up 309

Appendix 311

    Identity Theft Recovery Action Plan 313

Acknowledgements...331

About the Author 333

Bibliography 335

Index..345

Introduction

This book was written to help protect every person who uses a computer, mobile phone or tablet. Cyber security is not only about protecting governments or companies from spies. It's so much more, and also so much more personal. Cyber security is about:

1. stopping trolls from stealing you or your loved one's intimate photos and posting them online without your consent,
2. protecting your family from bullies, predators, and stalkers,
3. stopping thieves from draining your bank accounts or stealing your identity,
4. preventing companies from secretly tracking your online activities because they want to make money off of you,
5. securing your home WiFi so hackers can't break in and steal your valuable personal information,
6. creating safeguards to protect both your expensive physical devices and the precious data and files within,
7. stopping scammers from damaging both your home life and your career, and
8. much, much more that protects innocent victims from online crime.

Simply put, this book was written for You.

I appreciate that you're extremely busy, and have written this guidebook as clearly and concisely as possible to get to the point. Real-life case studies will bring you into the mindset of both cyber criminals and victims to help you protect what's most important and valuable to you.

In the year 2021, millions of people will continue working remotely or going to school either partially or completely to fulfill their responsibilities. The need for individuals to take proactive steps for personal cyber security is more important than ever.

Practical Cyber Security for Extremely Busy People is designed to provide you with a clear, achievable action plan to:

1. Secure your physical assets,
2. Protect your personal data online and in the real world,
3. Protect you from phishing attacks, malware, and other exploitation, and
4. Defend you against targeted attacks by online harassers and trolls.

This guidebook was written to help aware individuals like yourself make actionable steps to protect you, those you care about, and your career from cyber threats and online exploitation. While movies often portray cyber criminals as edgy, sometimes well-dressed, sometimes slovenly individuals, or hodgepodge collections of misfits, in reality much of today's cybercrime is run like a day-in, day-out business with management structures, standard operating procedures, and motivated employees all looking to advance their careers. Cybercrime is a lucrative industry that continually is developing new and clever ways to target, exploit and steal from millions of honest individuals, legitimate companies, and other marks every single day. So, what should you do?

Comprehensive cyber security doesn't happen overnight (usually), but the good news is that taking the actionable steps outlined in this guide will rapidly and cumulatively put you in a more secure, better prepared position to live your life, protect those you care about, and manage your career safely.

Included throughout the book are screenshots, graphics and other visuals to provide a clearer picture of instructions, websites and apps that you may consider using. The intention is to make the cyber security steps you personally take less intimidating, more transparent, and more efficient. You'll know what to expect beyond the pages of this book.

Sources are noted with online link addresses where available. I encourage readers to do their independent research to strengthen their cyber awareness even beyond this book, as continual awareness is a healthy habit to build upon, similar to exercising or learning a new skill.

I provide instructions for many of the most popular devices and apps. If you have a device or app not specifically discussed, the concepts are still the same, and steps you would take for your specific device or app are likely similar to the ones discussed in these chapters.

My cyber security experience is built from multiple areas. Firstly, for several years I have worked closely with numerous federal, state, and local law enforcement agencies across the U.S. on providing solutions to their mobile technology requirements. I have focused on providing hardware and software solutions to federal field agents, investigators, the police, and other authorities to support them in performing their duties. I am a strategic consultant helping a wide range of companies in different industries reduce risks at all levels of their organizations. Experience has taught me that the most common cyber risks to a company aren't usually its hardware or software. Bad things usually happen because of something that someone in the company did or didn't do. It might be caused by a part-time, temporary worker or the CEO, often unsuspectingly but sometimes intentionally. Either way, the damage can be devastating. I try to help prevent that from happening.

Secondly, my work as a journalist, documentary photographer and independent humanitarian advocate has required me to evaluate my personal cyber security from a different angle. I have traveled to nearly 40 countries, often to document and photograph humanitarian crises or politically-sensitive situations. I have worked in locations where there have been covert or visible threats against foreigners or, more specifically, journalists from oppressive governments, military, local authorities, organized crime, and even disorganized street criminals. Often I work with a team I organize. In addition to my personal safety, I am responsible for the on-the-ground safety of other individuals. I need to ensure my teams have the necessary gear (computers, phones, cameras, and other equipment) to accomplish our reporting. I need to ensure the sensitive information we are collecting (photos, videos, interview notes, and evidence) are securely stored as quickly as possible to prevent seizure, theft, or even accidental data corruption. I need to consider if crossing international borders may present additional risks to our team, such as the possibility of having our mobile phones inspected or confiscated. Authorities have the ability to copy a cellphone's contents – photos, contacts, messages, call and browsing histories, account logins, everything – without the owner's consent. Our cyber security planning and execution are extensive, every single time.

And thirdly, I earned my Master's degree in Journalism and Certificate in International Security from Harvard University. During my studies I gained perspective and insight into the ways governments, non-state actors, corporations, and even lone individuals are using cyber warfare not only against each other but also against unsuspecting civilians. When I earned my MBA from The Wharton School, I was trained in efficiency, so throughout this book I will get right to the point. You're busy, I get it.

Let's get to it!

Section I – At a Minimum, Do This

Section Table of Contents

Topic	Page
Encryption Explained in 20 Seconds	3
Chapter 1 – Secure Your Assets	5
Possession is 9/10s of the law	6
Make it personal	7
Mark your equipment	8
Webcam security	9
Microphones	10
USB thumb drives	11
U.S. military hacked with free thumb drives	12
Charger cables and charger plugs	13
Device startup passwords	13
Mobile phones	14
Computer and phone repairs	14
Chapter 2 – Some Common but Important Terms	15
Things to avoid in cyberspace	15
And some tech terms clarified	16
Chapter 3 – Secure Your Pipeline	17
Consider doing these 7 important steps	17
Bluetooth security	22
Secure your Apple AirDrop	24
Chapter 4 – Email Safety	25
Phishing	25
Breaking: Nigerian prince disables autocorrect	26
Spear phishing	28
Scamming the eager-to-please employee	28

Urgent request from a distant friend	*31*
Whaling	34
Thar she blew	*34*
Fearware – Welcome to the new world	35
Fearware – A message From HR	*38*
Don't get hooked by phishers	39
Extremely encrypted email	43
If you get scammed, call the Feds	45
Chapter 5 – Is That Really Your Password?	**47**
Have you been pwned?	47
How common is your password?	*50*
Use a password keeper	51
The 50 Worst Passwords	*53*
Don't use Facebook or automatic logins for other sites	54
Secret questions	54
Don't use public computers	55
Chapter 6 – 2-Factor Authentication	**57**
2-factor authentication – You Be You	57
The Bank of America text verification scam	*58*

Encryption Explained in 20 Seconds

Encryption is just a fancy word for scrambling your data so it's unreadable to prying eyes. We'll be using the word "encryption" in this book, and I don't want the jargon to confuse or intimidate any reader.

If someone steals your computer or phone but doesn't have the startup password to access your data (the way you typically turn on your device), they could still physically plug into your hard drive (similar to the way someone can plug in a USB thumb drive or portable disk drive) and try to access the contents. Encrypting your hard drive(s) prevents a thief from reading your memory as a standalone device. If someone were to steal your encrypted device, take out the hard drive, and try to access the files and information stored on it, encryption makes the data scrambled and unreadable.

Similarly, encrypted communication, such as through internet browsing, messaging apps or text messaging, prevents hackers from intercepting and reading what information you send and receive. Unencrypted connections leave you open to surveillance by outside actors, which can range from run-of-the-mill hackers to government agencies.

A little further in this book we'll show you how to encrypt your own communication and devices to protect your privacy.

Chapter 1 – Secure Your Assets

First and foremost, before securing yourself in cyberspace, let's work on protecting yourself in real-life. While digital theft is rampant, there's also countless reasons why thieves would be more than happy to physically steal your laptop, mobile phone or any of your expensive accessories. Let's take some important (but also inexpensive and low-tech) steps that will immediately improve your resilience from theft.

Laptop security

When was the last time you read the information etched on the bottom of your laptop? The correct answer is "probably never" because why would you? Nobody does. Although the bottoms of laptops are smooth and sleek, mostly like the laptop covers, they're just wasted real estate.

Writing in permanent ink or a paint marker is a more bulletproof method to identify your assets. Name stickers are another option, but they can be peeled off or defaced and are a less-permanent solution. I write my name, email and cell phone number on the bottom of my laptops using either a black Sharpie marker or a fine point white paint marker depending on the color of the laptop. I also write "Reward if found" to encourage the finder to contact me and the recovery amount will depend on the circumstances, but I'd try to be generous to get my digital tool back.

Although this simple step would be invaluable in recovering a lost or stolen laptop, I am amazed at how often I get pushback from people to do so.

"It's too pretty" is one of the most common rationales. Again, it's on the bottom, nobody will see it. Until you need it.

"It's my work computer" is another excuse, but realistically I don't think companies actually care that much. When it's time to give your laptop back to your company's IT department because you either broke it, are getting an upgrade, or are leaving the company, the person checking it back in won't care.

In the event you plan to resell your devices at some point in time, and keeping your items in their best condition is important for resale value, then labeling your devices with stickers will still help identify your possessions to a certain extent.

Possession is 9/10s of the law

Legally that's not true but, in practice, it works sometimes.

I once read a news article about a woman flying on a commercial airline who, during her flight, casually placed her laptop on top of her bag on the floor. The flight wasn't extremely crowded and the row behind her was unoccupied. At some point her computer slid under her seat and ended up at the feet of a man seated further behind her. Once she realized her computer had moved, she went back to find it and saw the man had it. She asked for it back but he said, No, it was his computer, a truly underhanded move on his part. They got into an argument (not surprisingly) and by the time they landed the airport police were summoned to the plane to resolve the dispute. The man told the police it was his computer. The woman told him to turn it on to prove it was hers, as she could enter the password, but the man refused to do so. The airport police did not have the authority to force the man to power it up or to let her touch it even if he did. The man kept insisting the laptop was his and, with no way to prove otherwise, he was allowed to walk off the plane with his newly stolen prize. The woman had no recourse, her computer was stolen in front of her.

While the man couldn't be forced to turn on the computer, he probably could have been impelled to flip it over if the woman insisted her name was written on the outside.

Make it personal

If a thief saw these two laptops left unattended, which one would they more likely steal? (Photo by Imgix on Unsplash)

Making your important devices and equipment easily identifiable by personalizing them with stickers and labels also provides something of a psychological deterrent to would-be thieves. While stickers with your name aren't the most secure method of tagging your gear, they still help to personalize your assets and make them less attractive to thieves should they fear being caught with something that is easily identifiable. Pilfering a black, nondescript laptop from an unaware target? No sweat. Pilfering a black laptop covered in graphics, logos and other visual markings? Hmmm... maybe I'll look elsewhere.

I happened to obtain a roll of reflective orange tape (the kind used on vehicle graphics that's hard to peel off) and I put it on everything I own. I mean everything, from laptops to under my mouse to small gadgets to phone charging blocks (which are the things I used to lose most often). I even wrap a short piece around my phone charging cables when I'm procrastinating at my desk. All in all, marking up my equipment makes it clear which items are mine.

At a minimum it prevents my pieces from being confused with others when working with colleagues around a conference table or in a classroom.

The best part about personalizing your assets is it is up to you to decide how creative you want to be, with the benefit of reducing the attractiveness to a thief of walking away with your items. It's form and function combined.

Mark your equipment

1. Laptops
2. Cellphones
3. Cellphone cases – I write my name and alternative phone number on the inside of the case
4. Expensive gadgets
    a. Webcams
    b. Wireless mice and keyboards
    c. Bluetooth headsets
    d. Wireless headphones
5. Easily-lost items
    a. Laptop power cords and power bricks
    b. Phone chargers
    c. Phone cables
    d. Stylus pens

Webcam security

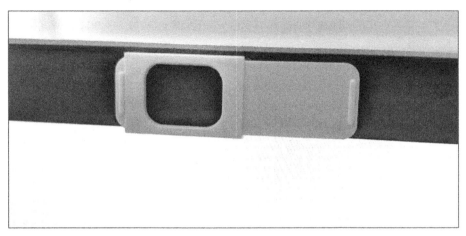

A webcam cover can shield your view from unwanted surveillance.

Webcams are great to have, when they're not being terrible. Before the 2020 pandemic, the in-the-office joke used to be "this meeting really could have been an email." Now, with remote work the snark has evolved to "this video call really could have been an email." It's important for people to feel connected to their colleagues, customers, friends, and families (usually). Video calls are only going to become even more intrusive and constant than 2020 has found them to be.

Social media has been more than gleeful to broadcast to the world the momentary yet hugely embarrassing missteps unwitting Zoom users have made on video calls, ranging from not wearing pants in view of the camera (to either the dismay or laughter of the other participants); using the bathroom; talking to their parents, pets, or plants; to any number of other previously unimaginable faux pas. In some well-publicized incidents, the meeting participant's behavior was so out of line the person ended up getting fired.

What's more, some malicious cyber criminals may have the ability to turn on and monitor a victim's webcam (and microphone, more on that below) remotely, often without the victim even knowing they are on display. The technology to do so has existed for years.

When a webcam is not being used, users (that is, YOU) should cover the lens with something opaque, which can be something as simple as a Post-It Note, piece of masking tape, or, if you want, get a fancy sliding plastic cover.

If you're using an external webcam, a best practice would be to unplug the camera from the USB slot entirely. That's the most reliable way to ensure you don't broadcast yourself unaware from that device (but it's important to still leave your laptop's built-in webcam covered). Just plug it back in before starting your next video call and you're good to go.

Microphones

Similar to webcams, covering the hole for your laptop's built-in microphone with a tight-fitting piece of thick tape (even just double-layer or triple-layer of tape from your desk dispenser) will help in muffling your microphone from unwanted listening.

If your computer has an auxiliary microphone jack (it's usually the small 3.5mm jack similar to earphones), a simple but effective way to protect yourself from unauthorized listening is to cut off the jack from unused earphones (I have a couple of random ones from airplane flights cluttering my desk drawer) and stick it in the microphone jack. By inserting the jack into the socket, the computer should default to thinking there's an external microphone plugged in. You can verify this in your computer's audio settings. Since you physically cut the jack's wire, there's no recording device to connect to should someone try to listen in on you. Unplug the jack when you need to use your real microphone.

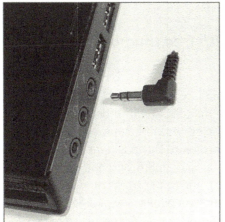 

Temporarily disable your built-in microphone with a disconnected earphone jack.

USB thumb drives

Similar to the idea that you wouldn't just eat anything without knowing what it was or where it came from, what you stick into your computer should be treated the same way. USB thumb drives are portable storage devices that can hold documents, photos, movies, programs or other files, and are never around when you need one. Depending on what business conferences or events one may attend, oftentimes companies are freely giving out USB drives with their company logo on it, which are useful swag to take home. It also makes USB drives perfect delivery devices for spreading and installing malware, or programs that may steal data, monitor activity or leave a computer open to manipulation, hidden in executable or root files on a thumb drive's memory.

Bottom line, even if they're free, colorful or stylish-looking, do NOT use USB thumb drives if you do not know where they came from. Fortunately, the price of memory continues to decrease. Purchasing new thumb drives made by major manufacturers is the prudent thing to do.

U.S. military hacked with free thumb drives

Back in 2008, the U.S. Pentagon discovered their classified SIPRNet computer network, which connects the military, senior officers in the White House, and U.S. intelligence agencies, was infiltrated and being monitored by Russian intelligence. According to David Sanger in his fascinating book, *The Perfect Weapon*, Russian operatives had left USB thumb drives littered around the parking and public areas of a U.S. base in the Middle East. Someone picked one up, and eventually plugged it into a laptop connected to the military's SIPRNet network. According to Sanger, "In short, if the Russians were in that communications channel, they had access to everything that mattered." To keep a similar breach from happening again, USB ports on Department of Defense computers were eventually sealed with superglue.

Around the same era, U.S. and Israeli intelligence were trying to infiltrate the Iranian government's computer network used for its nuclear program. Sanger notes the Iranian system was "air gapped," meaning it was not connected to the internet or the outside world. It was an independent, standalone system that was supposed to be impervious to hacking since it couldn't be accessed online. The U.S. and Israeli forces sought to cross the air gap by inserting code on USB keys, as well as other techniques. Eventually they succeeded.[1]

[If you're interested in this fascinating story, I highly recommend reading *The Perfect Weapon* for deep insight into the use of cyberweapons and the mischief or havoc nations and other actors can wreak upon each other.]

---

[1] David E. Sanger, *The Perfect Weapon: War, Sabotage, and Fear in the Cyber Age* (Broadway Books, 2019).

Charger cables and charger plugs

If I wanted to target an unsuspecting victim and install malware on their phone or laptop, I would build a small memory chip into the plastic housing of charger cables or charger plugs that would launch a covert program once plugged in. Just saying. Think that sounds far-fetched? The National Security Administration's (NSA) Advanced Network Technology division (ANT) has been making these gadgets available to its employees since at least 2008, if not longer. They were being sold through a now-public, formerly classified NSA ANT catalog.[2]

So, the same advice for USB thumb drives goes for charger cables and plugs that are randomly given to you or which you don't know where they came from. It's a minor but necessary cost to keep yourself more protected in our ultra-connected world.

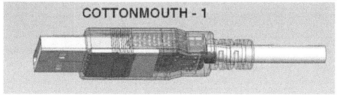

A now-public National Security Administration catalog of monitoring tools includes a USB cable with covert surveillance technology built into the housing. (National Security Administration ANT Catalog)

Device startup passwords

Even if you are working 100 percent at home where, at present, you might be the only person with access to your computer, tablet, or phone, adding startup passwords is one of the simplest but most effective steps you can take to protect your work, data and files. Many computers allow you to set a password with as few as four or six characters or sometimes a PIN code

---

[2] "NSA Ant Catalog - USB," IC Off The Record, https://nsa.gov1.info/dni/nsa-ant-catalog/usb/index.html.

with a mere four digits, but having a more complex password here (that, alas, you'll have to remember) is worth the miniscule amount of extra effort.

Fingerprint readers and facial recognition are also reasonably secure methods to protect your computer. Whichever option you choose, this initial layer of security can prevent much more significant attacks from being directed at you.

Mobile phones

On the inside of your phone case, write your first name and the initial of your last name (for example, I would be Daniel H.) and a trusted, reliable family member's or friend's phone number that can receive text messages on your behalf. You may also want to write "Reward if found", and "Please call or text." Do not add your main email address(es) as that can be used to override any 2-factor authentication you'll have installed to protect your accounts (we'll cover this topic in Chapter 6 – *2-Factor Authentication*). Should your phone be lost (actually lost, not left in your car or other pair of pants), you can lock or remote delete its contents immediately. You can still have the wiped device returned to you and then reinstall your data from the cloud (more on this later).

Computer and phone repairs

I don't like paying full retail price for a new iPhone screen any more than most people, but I would feel more confident that my phone was not maliciously tampered with by the Apple employee than a random repair store. The same goes for my laptop repair on the rare occasion I run into a problem.

If you require technical service or hardware repairs to your technology, always get your devices serviced from authorized repair facilities, even if a local shop is willing to service your problem for a lower price. There is little industry oversight of repair shops to protect consumers and their data. The vast majority of independent repair shops are trustworthy and provide the services they advertise. However, should an untrustworthy repair person choose to install spyware onto your device while it's in their hands, you'd likely never know about it and continue using your newly-repaired device as usual, all the while leaving yourself vulnerable.

Chapter 2 – Some Common but Important Terms

As we're about to dive in, let's take a quick moment to clarify some of the terms you'll encounter as we take action steps to secure your online security. There will not be a test on this, but it's good context to help you implement the recommendations in this book more easily.

Things to avoid in cyberspace

Fearware – phishing attempts that take advantage of stressful situations and play on human emotions

Malware – disrupts, damages or permits access to a device or entire system

Phishing – the fraudulent act of sending emails, links or other communication pretending to be from a legitimate sender

Ransomware – blocks access to a computer or device until money is paid for its release, with the risk that ransom gets paid but no release is made in return

Spoofing – impersonating the identity of something else, such as a person, group, website, email address or phone number.

Spyware – malware that monitors a user's activity and transmits data, including personal information or usernames and passwords, covertly to an unauthorized user

Virus – spreads from computer to computer, installing code that will affect how your device operates, potential to cause serious damage such as corrupting important data or destroying files.

And some tech terms clarified

Algorithm – a set of computer instructions for solving problems

Bot – an autonomous program (like a digital robot) that can interact with systems or users

Cookie – Small pieces of data that are used to identify your computer and used to either track or remember your activity on websites.

http – the communications protocol used to connect to servers on the internet and send pages back to the user's browser. HTTP stands for HyperText Transfer Protocol.

https – HTTPS Secure is the encrypted version of HTTP.

IP address – stands for Internet Protocol address, and is a series of numbers and periods that identifies individual computers

Tracking pixels – Tracking pixels are embedded in images and work similar to cookies to track a user's activity, location and other information.

URL – the address of a web page, such as https://www.redcross.org

Chapter 3 – Secure Your Pipeline

Nobody likes dealing with their WiFi issues. I get it. It seems like the last thing phone companies, cable companies, and router manufacturers care about is making products and services we actually want to use. Easy-to-understand, intuitive user interfaces are not high on their list of priorities, and it shows. We'll go through these important vulnerabilities as quickly and painlessly as possible.

Now that you've gone over your physical assets – your computer, cell phone, and all the expensive add-ons, the next piece of your cyber armor to consider is the way you connect to the outside world. WiFi connections are getting faster and faster, and 5G speeds at home are readily available to allow you to read emails faster and perhaps more noticeably (and some would say more importantly) stream Netflix without lags.

A weakly-protected WiFi signal is also a welcoming entryway for hackers to gain access to your computers and mobile devices. What's more, there is a rapidly growing population of other types of connected gadgets that are creeping into countless aspects of our daily lives. These smart gadgets are as diverse as security cameras, body-fat scales, smart refrigerators, and light switches. These and other types of smart, connected devices are generally categorized as the Internet-of-Things. Hackers and other bad actors are continually finding new ways to infiltrate Internet-of-Things devices. As consumers continue to add smart (or smarter) gadgets to our homes and workplaces, new opportunities for mischief or surveillance grow accordingly.

Consider doing these 7 important steps

Here are the 7 key steps you should take to secure your WiFi against intruders, some of which may already be set up for you. (Fear not, it's a little time-consuming once but worth the effort for the significantly increased protection you will create for yourself.)

Fix your most basic settings

Depending on who you're paying for internet connection service, the way to access your wireless router will vary. Search your provider for instructions to get into your router setup software program.

Network Name. Once you are in, you will have the ability to change the name of your router from the default to something customized. You should change the name because the default name can provide hackers with information on the make and model of the router you are using, which would help them exploit known vulnerabilities with that type of equipment. Your new router name should also be anonymous, not your home address or anything that makes it obvious that network is yours. [My niece's WiFi name is "FBI Surveillance Van" which I find amusing.] Whatever you name yours, make it something that strangers won't associate with you or your family.

Network Password. I've seen demonstrations by cyber security experts where they cracked WiFi passwords using off-the-shelf programs in literally seconds. Scared the heck out of me when I realized how easy it can be. Having a complex WiFi password is beyond important. This is one of those passwords where it should be annoyingly long to enter, since it should not need to be entered that often.

I set my WiFi password to the longest string my router will allow – 64 characters. Granted, I drove my wife and children crazy for about 3 weeks as they had to update their passwords on their laptops, phones, and videogames. But then again, I had to do the wireless printers, security cameras, smoke alarms, and other smart devices. It was a bother for a while, and I received a lot of grumbling but, seriously, I watched a password get cracked in seconds.

Router Name. If your router allows, change the router login name to something besides "Admin" so it is harder for hackers to determine.

Router Password. Whatever your login name, absolutely change your router password from the default "Admin" or whatever it came preprogrammed with. Make it something long and memorable. It doesn't have to be as crazy long as your WiFi password, but should still be meaningful to make it difficult for hackers to figure out.

In *Chapter 5 – Is That Really Your Password?* we'll get into password keeper programs that will remember your different passwords securely so you personally don't have to remember all the different passwords you create.

Good news! If you've completed Step 1, you're way ahead of countless others out there who haven't done anything to secure their WiFi lifeline beyond the default settings. Well done, You!

Turn on the router's firewall

Chances are this is already turned on by default, but it's an important feature worth checking. Firewalls typically have different levels of security you can choose to allow information coming into and going out of your network. The range may be described as Low Security, Typical Security, and Maximum Security, or variations thereof. Maximum security sounds good, but in practice it is highly restrictive and will prevent you from surfing easily, so I recommend setting yours to Typical/Medium/Standard levels.

Set up WPA2 encryption

This step sounds scarier and more difficult than it really is, so apologies for the technical jargon. When you set up your router you have the option of setting the strength of encryption you want to use. WPA stands for WiFi Protected Access. WPA2 is the current highest standard available to protect your network. So, select that. Here's what the options look like on my router setup:

Basic Security Settings >					
Advanced Security Settings >	2.4 GHz Wireless: ● On ○ Off		5 GHz Wireless: ● On ○ Off		
Wi-Fi Channel Settings >	2. Change the SSID setting to any name or code you want				
Guest Wi-Fi Settings >	(SSID is the same thing as the name of your Wireless Network.)				
Wi-Fi Protected Setup > (WPS)	2.4 GHz SSID: [████████]		5 GHz SSID: [████████]		
Logout >	3. Wi-Fi Security				
	Securing your Wi-Fi traffic as it transmits through the air, we recommend you use WPA2 security, unless you experience compatibility issues.				
	Risk Level	2.4 GHz Security		5 GHz Security	
	Low	● WPA2		● WPA2	
	Medium	○ WPA2/WPA mixed mode		○ WPA2/WPA mixed mode	
	High	○ WEP			
	High	○ None		○ None	

Set up a Guest WiFi

If your router offers this feature, a Guest WiFi allows visitors to use your WiFi without giving them access to your home network of connected computers and devices. If a visitor connects to your primary WiFi with a malware-infected computer or smartphone, that malicious program can spread across your home network. By providing them access to a Guest WiFi, you are able to give them internet connectivity while keeping you both safely separated.

When you set up the Guest WiFi in your router's settings, be sure to create a Guest WiFi password that is different from your primary WiFi password so they can't accidentally (or intentionally) access your primary WiFi network.

Set up automatic updates

      Check to see if your router's firmware is updated automatically by your service provider or if you have to set it up in the device's settings. Either way, it is important your router stays current as new fixes and patches are rolled out as new vulnerabilities are discovered. A few months ago, news articles came out saying three "serious vulnerabilities" were found in the router my internet provider uses. Fortunately, the proper fixes were sent to my device automatically, no effort required on my part. Check to ensure your device is also automatically updated.

Reboot your router regularly

      You can reboot your router by either using the reboot button in the router's software settings, by holding down the device's power button, or simply unplugging the power cord and plugging it back in a few moments later. I recommend rebooting your router once or twice a month, which will help with automatic updates and possibly improve your overall connection speed.

Move your router to the center of your home

      A scammer trying to crack into your home WiFi needs to have access to your WiFi signal, so the more you concentrate your WiFi inside the walls of your home the better. WiFi signal spreads out from the device like water ripples from a stone dropped in a pond. There are two main types of WiFi signal frequency available: 2.4GHz (the most common available) and newer 5GHz frequencies. 5GHz frequencies are faster but have shorter reach than 2.4GHz. If you have signal extenders around your home, think about their location and how easily your WiFi can be picked up beyond your walls.

Speedtest

One way to test the strength and speed of your signal is to use a broadband testing app such as Speedtest by Ookla, a free app available for your computer or mobile device. You can use it to walk outside your home and see how easy or difficult it would be for a hacker to connect with your network signal from the street. If the outside signal is strong, consider where your router or extenders are located inside your home and consider moving them somewhere more protected.

Bluetooth security

Bluetooth is another pipeline hackers can exploit to gain access to your devices and information. The best rule for using Bluetooth is

Turn off your Bluetooth when not using it.

Bluetooth's hands-free technology for headphones, navigation, electronics and Internet-of-Things is a great convenience but it is also open to significant security risks. Flaws in some Bluetooth headsets and hands-free car kits have allowed hackers to turn those devices into mobile bugging devices, letting attackers listen in on conversations.

New versions of Bluetooth continue to be developed as devices get more sophisticated, and each version will naturally have some new, as-yet-undiscovered vulnerabilities that may expose you, your devices or your data.

Bluetooth is often marketed as a short-range signal, perhaps no more than 30 to 50 feet in effective range. In reality, with signal boosters and enhanced antennas (and depending on the sophistication of the hacker) the working range to access your devices can be much greater.

Here are some of the ways bad people exploit Bluetooth devices.

BlueJacking – Bluetooth hijacking where spam advertising or other intrusions are sent to a target device. BlueJackers may impersonate a trusted entity like a bank, phone company or other known entity (such as Amazon.com) to trick a target into clicking a link or entering personal data.

BlueSnarfing – More dangerous than bluejacking (which sends data to a target), BlueSnarfing steals data from a target's device, such as photos, emails, text messages or the device's unique identifying information, which can be used for more harmful cyberattacks.

BlueBugging – BlueBuggers insert a backdoor into a victim's phone or laptop, allowing them access to the device to spy on the target's activity. Hackers may be able to impersonate the victim on social media or online banking.

BlueSmacking – BlueSmackers overwhelm a victim's device by sending too much information to it so the device is unable to operate. Usually this can be overcome by rebooting the targeted device. [3]

---

[3] Kim Crawley, "Bluetooth Security Risks Explained," *AT&T Cybersecurity* (blog), June 11, 2020, https://cybersecurity.att.com/blogs/security-essentials/bluetooth-security-risks-explained.

> ### *Secure your Apple AirDrop*
>
> Apple's AirDrop turns your phone into a Bluetooth peripheral, which can allow nearby unauthorized individuals (i.e., creepers, hackers, troublemakers) to connect with you anonymously. Troublemakers have used Airdrop to send unwelcome and/or distasteful images to nearby devices. To protect yourself when you are not actively using AirDrop, you should either disable AirDrop or allow "Contacts Only" to reach you.

Here are three steps you should take to reduce your exposure to Bluetooth hacking.

Upgrade your gadgets. There have been many Bluetooth versions over the years, ranging from Bluetooth versions 1.0, 1.1, 1.2, 2, 2.1, 3+, 4 and the newest version 5 (introduced in 2016). All versions have their own security weaknesses to knowledgeable hackers. If you have devices that are more than four years old (and likely running the older Bluetooth versions), it's a good idea to phase them out for newer devices that use Bluetooth version 5.

Change the default PIN codes. Headset PINs are (almost) always "0000," which opens the door to attack. Change your default PIN codes where possible on your Bluetooth devices to something hard to guess.

Turn it off. Again, the safest way to protect against Bluetooth exploitation is to keep it turned off when you're not using it.

Chapter 4 – Email Safety

According to online security company Retruster, as of 2019 phishing accounted for 90 percent of data breaches. What's more, 15 percent of people successfully phished were targeted at least one more time within the year. Phishing attempts grew 65 percent in 2019 from the prior year. And according to Verizon, 30 percent of phishing messages get opened by targeted users.[4]

Phishing

Phishing is a broad brush, shotgun approach to scamming. It's not very sophisticated but still effective when sending messages out to hundreds of thousands or millions of people. Phishing is when scammers send out emails pretending to be from a reputable company and try to get the recipient (otherwise known as the Mark) to click on malicious links or reveal personal information, such as passwords or credit card information. We've all received them, whether it be from a fake Ebay, fake Paypal, fake Apple or other fake company informing us that we need to update our password, or a purchase (that we didn't make) has been approved, or endless variations on these themes.

Email lists of individuals or organizations of all types (such as companies, schools, and even police departments) are easily purchased on the black market as well as legally. Often phishing links will send an unsuspecting victim to a cloned website of a real company, where the victim provides their information thinking they are protecting themselves in some

---

[4] "Protect Your Users against Phishing Emails, Ransomware & Fraud," retruster, https://retruster.com.

manner. Instead, they are providing their valuable data directly to the bad guys.

Other phishing scams will send the victim to Google Forms where the target will be asked to enter their information, thinking it will be used for legitimate purposes.

Unless you really do have a relative who is a Nigerian prince, be skeptical of all unsolicited emails you receive.

Breaking: Nigerian prince disables autocorrect

There's a good reason why so many Nigerian prince/recent widow/exiled political despot scam emails are poorly written with typos and incorrect grammar. According to Steven D. Levitt and Stephen J. Dubner in their book, *Think Like a Freak*[5] (a follow up to their wildly popular book *Freakonomics*), sending out phishing emails is easy but actually working through the long con to the point where a victim is separated from their money takes time, sometimes weeks or months. The typical sales funnel for businesses goes like this:

1. Leads
2. Sales Calls
3. Follow-up
4. Conversion
5. The Sale

Phishing scams are no different. In this case, the Leads are the initial email list. The Sales Calls are the initial email ("Hello and Blessings My Love…"), the Follow-up are the initial responses and banter that the scammers hope to engage in with the mark, the Conversion is where the tale is told offering unimaginable wealth, and the Sale is where the

---

[5] Steven D. Levitt and Stephen J. Dubner, *Think Like a Freak: The Authors of Freakonomics Offer to Retrain Your Brain* (William Morrow Paperbacks, 2015).

victim wires over thousands of dollars (or more) to secure the promised transaction, which – any day now – is supposed to result in millions of dollars being sent to the mark as a finder's fee or commission.

Now, the vast majority of people who receive these emails immediately disregard them knowing they are a scam. But there is some portion of the population who might be intrigued and respond. (Sadly, I personally know one older woman who was ready to send her meager but precious retirement savings to one of these cons. Fortunately, her diligent son was able to intervene and prevent disaster from happening. Good job, Andrew!)

The longer a scammer works on converting a potential victim who somehow wises up during the process and fails to close the deal (that is, get suckered), the more time, energy and resources the scammer has wasted, which would have been more productive focused on an easier target.

According to Levitt and Dubner, the scammers were wasting time on "false positives," or people who initially appear to be prospects (by having responded to the scammers) but don't ultimately pay off. Somewhere along the conversion process they wised up and realized it was illegitimate. Rather than identify these false positives downstream, it's in the scammers' best interest to eliminate them as early as possible. That's where the sloppy email proves its worth.

Many people would immediately reject a well-written, polished email from Nigerian royalty seeking a business partner. Emails with typos and grammar errors would turn away targets who might be initially curious but are unlikely to be suckered all the way through to closing the sale. The sloppy solicitation email would only hold credibility with the most gullible people, who are exactly the targets the scammers are searching for. The poorly-written email is a self-filtering mechanism to weed out those annoying, unprofitable false positives.

Be skeptical. Be a false positive.

Spear phishing

Spear phishing targets a specific individual, organization, or business. Rather than taking a broad-brush approach and sending out thousands of generic emails, spear phishing requires the scammers to do some level of research and reconnaissance on a mark.

Scamming the eager-to-please employee

"You working today?" the email from my boss said.

"Yes, I am. How's it going?" I replied.

"I need you to help with something ASAP," came the terse reply.

"Sure, what do you need?"

"I need you to buy 10 $100 gift cards and email me the card numbers right away."

What the hell? That's an odd request, although not entirely out of the realm of reason from my boss at the time. Maybe he wants to give them as gifts to clients or something. My boss, a small business owner, was prone to bursts of inspiration and frenzy. This might be another of his pet projects coming to life. Upon closer inspection of the emails, however, I realized the sender's email looked like my boss's proper work email, but clicking on the details showed it was actually coming from a different account. It was an imposter trying to scam a quick $1,000. Dirtbag.

Our company website at the time listed the names and roles of our small team. Finding the actual email of the owner was easy with an online search. And then using the same format (Initial of first name followed by full last name @ companyname.com) the would-be thief emailed me, pretending to be the owner in need of some ASAP gift cards. The same thief tried the same scam on other employees over the coming weeks, hoping to trick an eager employee trying hard to cater to their boss. Fortunately, nobody fell for it, but I am sure it's worked elsewhere, otherwise the thieves wouldn't keep trying it.

In another instance, at a different company I'll call "Keystone" for this discussion, a malicious actor gained access to a vendor's email and quietly diverted an actual email conversation with Keystone's accounts payable person (that is, the person who cuts the checks or sends out ACH electronic payments to vendors). The scammer had been able to see the email history with Keystone, including large, frequent purchase orders in the tens of thousands of dollars. Their first action was to take an email conversation about a pending invoice (the scammer was able to learn the exact dollar amount from prior emails), and forward the chain to a dummy email that looked like the vendor's except it was subtly changed by one letter, a change not easy to spot unless you were looking for it.

Using the fake email address, the scammer continued the friendly back and forth with Keystone's A/P person. "Happy Friday, have a great weekend!" and so forth. Then, soon enough the scammer sent their invoice with – of course – payment instructions to a "revised" account.

Keystone was a small company that runs lean with a small staff. Employees are often shifted from their current office role to take on additional responsibilities to fill staffing shortfalls. In this case, the A/P person was fairly new in the role and, fortunately, she asked the question, "How do I change a vendor's bank account number?"

"Why" was the logical response from Keystone's finance manager. Upon review, the scam was discovered before any money was paid on the fraudulent invoice to the fake account. Looking back at the email conversation that spanned about 2 weeks, it was fascinating to see how the scammer slid into the emails, with the actual vendor's accounts receivable person not knowing what was happening. Keystone notified the vendor that someone was impersonating their accounts receivable department. If the scammer(s) were trying to con Keystone they most likely were doing the same to the vendor's other customers.

Running a con is in certain ways like making a diamond. With enough time and pressure in the right places, a lump of carbon (or in this case, an unsuspecting customer) can turn into a highly profitable payday. In this scenario, after gaining access to the vendor's emails, the time and effort the scammers put into playing Keystone were negligible (reading the email history then diverting the conversation) for a potential payout of tens of thousands of dollars. And the vendor had hundreds of customers, all ripe for targeting. It's a numbers game for the scammers, only one or two have to hit to make it worthwhile and profitable.

A variation on the above theme, where scammers gained access into a company's emails, was to try and hijack payments for invoices that had already been sent out to customers (rather than issuing a phony invoice as was the case above). I've had clients whose accounts payable departments have received imposter emails (otherwise known as "spoofing") where a scammer impersonating a vendor wrote, "Our bank is doing their annual audit over the next few days so I'll need you to send payment to our other receivables account. Here's the wiring details... "

Fortunately, I caught that one too. Working together with this rapidly-growing client, we immediately instituted standard financial operating procedures requiring multiple safeguards and approvals before entering or modifying any vendor details, including bank account information.

The following is another real-life example of an unsuspecting individual having their email hacked and their contacts being hit up for money...

Urgent request from a distant friend

As I was searching my own emails for phishing examples, I came across the below message from one of my very infrequent contacts, whom I'll call Barney in this discussion. Identifying information and email addresses have been redacted for privacy.

Because we don't speak very often, the urgency from Barney's message was an immediate tipoff that this was phishing or another scam, so I looked at the sender's name and email. Both looked legitimate when I clicked for details compared to the contact information I had on file for Barney. Often spoofed emails are immediately identifiable but the details here showed the same comcast.net account.

To probe a little deeper, I hit "reply" to see where the email would be sent and it was being directed to an outlook.com account and not the comcast.net account shown. It used the same name format for Barney's name, but to a different email service (outlook.com). This was a fairly clever misdirection, successfully spoofing the first layer of identification.

I called Barney, the victim, to alert him someone was impersonating him. He was already aware of it and informed me the hacker broke into his email account, sent the above message to probably his entire contact list, and then (in a move that's both damaging and just plain mean) deleted the victim's entire contact list of over 1,000 people so he could not alert his contacts that his account had been hacked, and that he was not in distress or in need of emergency money. Comcast was unable to retrieve his contact list for him, so he was out of luck. Turns out, according to Barney, the scammer was located in Niger, which was discovered thanks to his attorney daughter's research.

Fortunately, Barney did not use his email password for any other accounts, which limited the potential damage the hackers could inflict upon him. He changed his email password, which, according to Comcast, would automatically log out any of his open email accounts. Hopefully was able to prevent the scammer from playing inside his email any further. However, the initial damage had been done and the misdirecting emails already disseminated to Barney's wide range of contacts.

Barney said that one of his contacts did respond to the fake email out of immediate concern and the scammer then provided a phone number for the worried friend to call. The friend actually did place the call. The person on the other end sounded so excited to have actually received a call the friend immediately grew suspicious and hung up. Then he called Barney directly and realized it was a scam.

If I were to grade the above attempt, I would give the scammer a point or two for doing a decent job of masking their spoofed email address, at least for a first layer of scrutiny. Often you can click to see the details of an email sender and the redirection is easily viewable, although I am sure this will be phased out over time to more devious and sophisticated methods of identity masking. Here, the outlook.com email was masked until you hit reply and it showed up more clearly, but it would still require a closer look by the recipient being targeted.

If I were to do something nefarious like this, I would take a slightly slower approach to warm the marks up. First, to make this more believable the scammers could have easily set up their own comcast account, and create a name that very closely resembled Barney's. For example, changing a letter "n" to "m", or a lowercase "i" to a lowercase "l" or substituting a capital letter "O" for a zero "0".

Second, instead of putting an urgent message out to an entire list, I would have considered easing in gently. Instead of asking for a favor immediately, perhaps sending a message saying "Hey, hope you are well. I was thinking about you the other day so I just wanted to check in and say hello." Then see who responds with a "Thanks, you too!" or whatever innocuous response might be sent. Or some variation thereof. And then work the marks for whatever con the scammer was hoping to pull.

The reason I'm detailing alternatives to the above is not because I am recommending you consider doing these (and I want to state clearly here: Don't do these things!), but because I hope they will resonate with you when you receive slightly curious or suspect emails in your inbox. And you'll most certainly be receiving them at some point, if you haven't been deluged by them already.

Whaling

Whaling attacks are like spear phishing but in more expensive zip codes. While spear phishing often targets individuals working in a certain category or function (such as accounts payables staff or purchasing agents), whaling attacks target business executives such as CEOs, CFOs or other high-ranking individuals (including politicians and celebrities). The payoffs to the scammers can be staggeringly large. Criminals will go to great lengths to collect as much information on the target as possible, often drawing data from social media and other sources to gather personal information, which makes the attack seem even more authentic.

Thar she blew

According to Emsisoft, a software protection company, some highly notable whaling attacks include:

Seagate releases copies of 10,000 employees' W-2 tax forms

In 2016, the HR department of data storage technology giant Seagate received an email that appeared to be from the company's CEO

Stephen Luczo. The email asked for copies of employees' 2015 W-2 tax forms and other personally identifiable information, including names, social security numbers, income and home addresses. HR dutifully fulfilled the request, which resulted in the personal details of almost 10,000 current and past employees being sent straight to the cyber criminals.

Snapchat hands over payroll information

Snapchat is no stranger to cyberattacks, but in 2016 the social media platform yet again found itself at the center of a data breach when an employee was tricked into releasing payroll information about some of its employees. In the attack, a member of the payroll team received an email from someone claiming to be Snapchat CEO, who made a request for employee payroll information. The data was duly handed over to the attacker and the information was leaked shortly after.

FACC CEO loses job after company wires $56 million to fraudsters

FACC is an Austrian plane manufacturing company whose customers include Boeing and Airbus. In 2016, it emerged that the company had been the victim of a successful whaling attack, which led to the finance department wiring $56 million to the fraudsters. While the full details of the attack were never publicly released, FACC's CEO was fired as he had "severely violated his duties," followed with the CFO being terminated soon after the attack.[6]

Fearware – Welcome to the new world

COVID-19, climate change, political elections and any other number of current events provide unscrupulous actors enormous opportunities to exploit people's concerns on an issue. Just as quickly as the coronavirus

---

[6] Jareth, "Phishing vs Spear Phishing vs Whaling Attacks," *Emsisoft* (blog), February 19, 2019, https://blog.emsisoft.com/en/32736/phishing-vs-spear-phishing-vs-whaling-attacks/.

pandemic spread around the world, fake websites popped up by the hundreds of thousands with either misinformation, phishing scams, product offers or a combination of all of these.

According to the cyber security firm Zscaler, during the beginning months of COVID-19 (January to April, 2020), more than 30,000 suspicious, COVID-related **newly registered domains** (NRDs) were created. The keywords for the suspicious NRDs included words commonly connected to COVID-19 including test, mask, Wuhan, kit and others.

COVID-19 phishing campaigns target both consumers and companies. At **companies**, some phishing attempts that Zscaler documented looked official, sometimes supposedly coming from the company's own IT or payroll departments. Some even included CAPTCHA screens to look legitimate.

It's not hard for determined scammers to appear legitimate to unwitting victims, for example by adding verification steps like this popular CAPTCHA feature, to mask their online scams.

On the **consumer front**, Zscaler identified emails asking for personal information purporting to help individuals get their government stimulus money or for COVID-related charitable causes.

With so many people working from home, the demand for **VPN security** grew accordingly so guess what the bad guys did. Zscaler reported some cyber criminals developed fake VPN software intended to fool users into downloading and installing even more malware by pretending to be a legitimate VPN client.

A **fake mobile app** pretending to track coronavirus and alert users of nearby COVID-19 patients was actually ransomware designed to lock a victim out of their phone and demand payment to unlock the device.[7]

Another fake COVID app offered to send users a "Coronavirus Safety Mask" after installing their app, but after installation the app searched the user's contacts. The app then sent mask offers to the contact list, and could continue to spread exponentially from there. Upon installation, the app had to request user permission to read contacts and send text messages. "This is a huge red flag for the user to immediately discard the app," Zscaler wrote in its blog.[8]

Malicious documents such as **Excel spreadsheets and PowerPoint presentations** containing COVID-19 data but embedded with hidden malware were prevalent as well. Fake emails supposedly coming from Johns Hopkins University with Excel documents attached had titles such as "WHO COVID-19 SITUATION REPORT," but would contain code that would install remote desktop access onto the unsuspecting victim's computer.[9]

---

[7] Deepen Desai, "30,000 Percent Increase in COVID-19-Themed Attacks," https://www.zscaler.com/blogs/research/30000-percent-increase-covid-19-themed-attacks.

[8] Shivang Desal, "Android App Offers Coronavirus Mask, Delivers Trojan," *Zscaler* (blog), https://www.zscaler.com/blogs/research/new-android-app-offers-coronavirus-safety-mask-delivers-sms-trojan.

[9] Brendan Hesse, "Beware Coronavirus-Themed Malware Disguised as Excel Spreadsheets," *Lifehacker*, May 22, 2020, https://lifehacker.com/beware-coronavirus-themed-malware-disguised-as-excel-sp-1843613107.

Fearware – A message From HR

A particularly cruel scam being pulled during the COVID-19 pandemic is the **You're Getting Fired Scam**. According to an April 21, 2020 blog post by Abnormal Security, a corporate cyber security firm, some scammers are sending out emails supposedly sent from a Human Resources department, insisting the recipient join a Zoom call (in a few minutes, naturally) for the purpose of discussing "Contract Suspension / Termination Trial."

The sender's email was made to look like it came from Zoom customer service. The body of the message read:

Meeting Reminder with [Company Name] Team on Zoom!

This is a reminder that your scheduled zoom meeting with Human Resources and Payroll Administration Head will start in a few minutes. Your presence is crucial to this meeting and equally required to commence this Q1 performance review meeting.

A link to "Join this Live Meeting" was conveniently supplied, which would have led the panicked recipient to a fake but believable Zoom site, where the recipient would enter his or her Zoom credentials on the fake site, exposing their login details. Next the hackers could log into the victim's actual Zoom account and take any other information stored there. Abnormal Security estimated that this phishing attempt was sent to more than 50,000 recipients.[10]

---

[10] "Zoom Phishing," *Abnormal Security* (blog), April 21, 2020, https://abnormalsecurity.com/blog/abnormal-attack-stories-zoom-phishing/.

Don't get hooked by phishers

Here are some immediate steps you can take to strengthen your email resiliency from unfriendly or malicious actors.

Does this smell funny to you?

An overabundance of skepticism is a healthy habit when it comes to your cyberlife. Be suspicious of any message that asks you to do something quickly and unexpectedly. If the message comes from someone you know, send them a text or call them to verify it's them asking. You can also use the excuse, "Rather than emailing back and forth I figured this was faster since you said it was a rush." If it was them, you should be commended for being responsive. If it wasn't them, you should be commended for catching a scam before it became a crisis.

This next one has been said a million, probably a billion, times but it always gets ignored. *Beware of anything that sounds too good to be true.* Plain and simple, no matter how desperate one might be feeling at that moment for more money, less weight, better looks, better romantic partners, whatever. (Face it, your life isn't that bad that you truly need to click a random link that gets sent to you offering an easy answer to problems. And that's a good thing! 😊)

Even if it does sound *pretty good* to be true, don't click that link.

Report and delete suspicious emails

If you receive a suspicious email on your work email account, you should contact your company's IT department and inform them of such, and ask if they want you to forward the questionable email to their attention for review. It's important to raise the flag on suspicious, potentially damaging emails to the appropriate individuals in your company because if you are being targeted there is always the possibility that your co-workers are being targeted as well. And they may not be as diligent as you.

Deleting a suspicious email protects you individually, while reporting one protects everyone else in your organization.

Fortunately, the most obvious spam is automatically screened

Built-in spam filters are good at catching the most obvious detritus (including the lose weight fast, get rich in real estate and start a side hustle emails I seem to attract. And apparently hot singles in my area are really interested to meet me, so I'm told.) Some built-in spam filters also disable any links in emails marked as spam to prevent a user from accidentally clicking a potentially malicious link.

Set up easy email filters

Focus on what matters. One problem with email today is the sheer volume of new "stuff" flowing into inboxes every single day.

It helps to sort your email automatically between direct emails from actual people versus mailing list distributions such as newsletters and promotions. I created filters in my Gmail and Yahoo accounts to move any email with the word "unsubscribe" into a separate folder away from my Inbox, which bumps up my productivity and reduces hourly distractions as daily newsletters and promotions no longer clutter my main inbox. It's a clean and easy way to prioritize incoming messages and allows me to focus on emails that may require a response versus those to be read at my leisure. By reducing the noise in your email traffic, it also may help you spot suspicious emails more easily.

The following instructions to create an email filter are for Google's Gmail but similar steps would apply for other email services.

Step 1: Go to your email's **Settings** option. In Gmail, next select **See all settings,** then select **Filters and Blocked Addresses**, and then select **Create a new filter.**

Step 2: In the new window that opens up, indicate you want to filter all emails that contain the word "unsubscribe" and then select **Create filter.**

From				
To				
Subject				
Has the words	unsubscribe			
Doesn't have				
Size	greater than	▼	MB	▼
☐ Has attachment	☐ Don't include chats			
			Create filter	Search

(The "Has the words: unsubscribe" row is circled.)

Step 3: Note that Gmail organizes messages by labels, rather than folders. Your email provider may use folders, labels, or something different but the concept is the same. In the next screen, Gmail indicated I could choose an existing label or create a new label. I created a new label called "Newsletters and Stuff" and clicked the option to **Apply the label**. I also clicked **Also apply filter to matching messages** to label existing messages that contain the word "unsubscribe." Now when I use Gmail, all existing and future filtered emails will be out of my Inbox and in the category Newsletters and Stuff, which helps unclutter my inbox substantially.

41

[Form screenshot showing Gmail filter options with checkboxes:
- Skip the Inbox (Archive it)
- Mark as read
- Star it
- ✓ Apply the label: Newsletters and Stuff
- Forward it to: Choose an address... | Add forwarding address
- Delete it
- Never send it to Spam
- Always mark it as important
- Never mark it as important
- Categorize as: Choose category...
- ✓ Also apply filter to matching messages.
- Learn more | Create filter]

Verify the sender's address versus their display name

An email display name is anything you want it to be, whereas the email address should show where the email is actually coming from. Email display names are arbitrary, and scammers rely on our tendency to trust what's in front of our eyes. That's why using "customerservice@apple.com" or "service@paypal.com" as a display name is so effective for scammers, if even for a moment, when sending you messages.

If any email you receive is suspect, confirm that the sender's address is in line with the display name and is coming from a legitimate organization's website address. More diligent scammers will spoof both their display name and email address in the email they send you. If you choose to reply to a questionable email, double check the reply address that shows up in your response email. Sometimes you will see your reply being directed to a different email than the original sender's, which is a more clever and robust spoofing effort. Don't reply!

Practice "hover hands" on links

Before clicking on any link in your email, take a moment and let your cursor rest on the link or button before clicking. In the lower left-hand corner of your browser window you should be able to see the real URL address that the link will take you to.

Right clicking on the link will also allow you to see the real URL address that the link will direct you to.

Will it direct you to a real company website (e.g., www.bankofamerica.com) or to a URL that may be questionable (e.g., www.bankofamerlca.com). Did you notice the difference in these two addresses? If Yes, good on you. If No, look again.

Enable automatic updates

Automatic updates help keep your computer current with upgrades, patches, and fixes against known vulnerabilities to prevent older malware from exploiting you. The speed and frequency of upgrades across all your programs and apps are more than most humans can (or would want to) maintain, so make your update settings automatic and as frequent as the settings will allow.

Block email images from automatically displaying

Companies, advertisers, and less savory actors often embed tracking pixels in images. Tracking pixels are invisible pieces of information inside email images that alert them when you open the image and can collect information on your computer and even your location. You don't even have to click on the image for the tracking pixel to activate, the image just has to load on your screen for your information to be collected. To prevent prying eyes, you should set your email settings to prevent automatic display of images. Doing so will also speed up your ability to review your messages without having to wait for images to load. There will be options inside each email message to allow you to view the blocked image if you want to.

Extremely encrypted email

When It comes to email security, not all emails are created equal. For example, Google's Gmail is enormously popular and extremely convenient, but its millions of users trade off convenience for privacy. Because it's owned by Google (which is no stranger to digging into your privacy), Gmail views your data and can share it with third party companies for targeted advertising. Gmail also logs every one of your logins and can access every single email in your mailbox. Other popular email providers also have some level of access into your email.

Protonmail

https://protonmail.com/

One widely-accepted solution for extreme email privacy is Protonmail, which offers end-to-end encryption, self-destructing emails, and other features for your privacy. Emails sent to other Protonmail users are automatically encrypted, and non-Protonmail recipients can receive a link to their encrypted message. Because of its encryption standards, even the people who work at Protonmail can't read your emails. The company is also based in Switzerland, which has some of the strictest privacy laws in the world.

Protonmail offers free and premium versions for all platforms.

If you get scammed, call the Feds

https://www.ic3.gov

If you believe you have been the victim of an Internet crime (or if you want to file on behalf of another person you believe has been a victim) you can file a complaint with the FBI's Internet Crime Complaint Center, or IC3.

The IC3 defines internet crime as any illegal activity involving one or more components of the Internet, such as websites, chat rooms, and/or email.

Internet crime involves using the internet (such as websites, chat rooms, or email) to communicate false or fraudulent representations to consumers. These crimes may include, but are not limited to, advance-fee schemes, non-delivery of goods or services, computer hacking, or employment/business opportunity schemes. If either the victim or the alleged scammer is located within the United States, you can file a complaint with the IC3. The victim does not have to be a U.S. citizen to file a complaint, as long as either the victim or alleged scammer is located in the U.S.

After a complaint is filed with the IC3, the information is reviewed by an analyst and forwarded to federal, state, local, or international law enforcement or regulatory agencies with jurisdiction, as appropriate. The IC3 does not conduct investigations and does not provide the investigative status of a previously filed complaint. Investigation and prosecution is at the discretion of the receiving agencies.

Chapter 5 – Is That Really Your Password?

I have a terrible memory. For names and faces I'm the worst. For passwords as well. Short ones, long ones, whatever, for whatever purpose. Most other people are probably the same way when it comes to passwords.

Online thieves and malcontents have the tremendous advantage over the general population in that they know millions of people use easily crackable passwords. What's more, countless people use the same username and password across accounts, whether it be their Facebook or credit cards.

Nimble password breakers also have ample tools at their disposal, including lists containing thousands or millions of password combinations, often using automated programs to enter password guesses using variations around common words (with numbers or symbols at the beginning, mixed in the middle or at the end of the string). And the automated cracking tools often work.

Other times, thieves may gain access to a single one of their target's accounts, and use that password as a starting point to gain access to other of that target's accounts, trying variations on a theme. For years, I made the poor choice of using the same username and password on dozens of online accounts, from my frequent flyer numbers to news sites and everything in between. It took a decent amount of time to undo that vulnerability by resetting my duplicate password across my important accounts.

Have you been pwned?

According to UrbanDictionary.com, "pwned" is a variation (albeit a poor one) of "owned." The term originated from a typo in the online game Warcraft, where a designer misspelled "owned." When the computer beat a player, the game was supposed to announce the loser "has been owned." Instead it said the player "has been pwned."

Why does that matter here? Well, it basically means to be owned or dominated by an opponent or situation. According to HaveIBeenPwned.com, the largest data breach to date, according to the site, exposed over 772 million unique emails alongside passwords those addresses used on other breached services, totaling 2.7 billion records. The data from that particular breach was made available on a popular hacking forum.

Use either of the below sites to see if your email(s) and passwords have been exposed in known data breaches. I discovered that a number of my emails have been involved in multiple breaches. Bummer. These sites provide information on which accounts were specifically exposed so I went to each one listed and changed my passwords.

HaveIBeenPwned

https://haveibeenpwned.com/

HaveIBeenPwned contains databases of known data breaches in which victims' emails and passwords were stolen. Importantly, it's a repository where people can check to see if their emails are among the more than 10 billion (Yes, billion) user accounts stolen from (as of the date of this guide's publication) 481 breached websites.

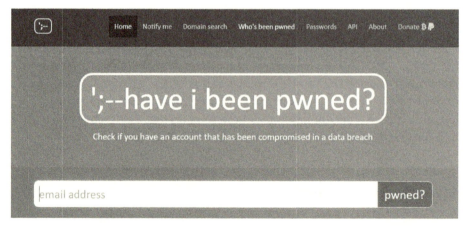

Firefox Monitor

https://monitor.firefox.com/

Firefox Monitor will search for known breaches. You can set up a free Monitor account to be alerted to new breaches involving your email address.

How common is your password?

HaveIBeenPwned also has a feature where you can see how often different passwords were found across the breaches, so you can see how clever or common your passwords might be. Here's an illustration of how longer passwords are better to use, using actual results.

Password	Number of times password was used by breached accounts
password	3,759,315
password1	2,418,984
password12	186,721
password123	123,063
password1234	23,743
password12345	11,696
password123456	7,581
password1234567	5,503
password12345678	5,532 (this is slightly more common than "password1234567")

Use a password keeper

For the last few years, I've been using a password keeper to generate my PWs and store them securely online. I use LastPass Premium, which has proven to be robust and reliable for just a few dollars a month. I share my LastPass account with my immediate family of spouse and teenage children, so they can both access my various online accounts. Importantly, LastPass instills good password habits in their daily activities by allowing them to create and store secure passwords for their ever-growing population of online accounts. When they're older and independent they'll get their own subscriptions.

Here's what a 50-character auto-generated password from LastPass looks like.

BSA334un5FN!qYlDFmH@sfFo3IxJGOckrIveEcz9*R@RhI3b6p

Clearly the above string is too hard for most humans to memorize, but that's really the point. A good password keeper will organize your security information and create robust passwords so you can login to your accounts easily, while making it harder for others to do so.

In *Chapter 8 – Browsing*, we give recommendations on a few browsers you can use that protect your privacy and also include built-in password keepers for you to use.

In addition, here are two password keepers you can add on to your browsers with both free and premium versions. There are countless others, but you get the idea.

LastPass

https://www.lastpass.com/

1Password

https://1password.com/

When I open up new online accounts, I typically use one of my emails as the username (I have 5 active emails that I'll discuss further in this book) and then let LastPass generate a random password using as many characters as the target website will allow. As a default I typically opt for PWs that are 34 to 60+ characters just because I can. A longer password costs nothing more but it geometrically increases the number of possible password choices a hacker (or their automated robot program) will have to attempt to gain access to my account. Now there's no way I would ever remember these extensive character strings but I don't have to, the password keeper does it for me. When I log onto a website, LastPass will either autofill in my username and password or, if there are multiple accounts for a website (such as Facebook) LastPass lets me tell it which account I want to sign in with. It's easy and robust.

The 50 Worst Passwords

SplashData, Inc., a developer of password security solutions for personal and business protection, compiles an annual list of the 50 worst passwords. Here's the 2019 list. Does anything look familiar?

1 - 123456	18 - lovely	35 - freedom
2 - 123456789	19 - 7777777	36 - football
3 - qwerty	20 - welcome	37 - charlie
4 - password	21 - 888888	38 - letmein
5 - 1234567	22 - princess	39 - !@#$%^&*
6 - 12345678	23 - dragon	40 - secret
7 - 12345	24 - password1	41 - aa123456
8 - iloveyou	25 - 123qwe	42 - 987654321
9 - 111111	26 - 666666	43 - zxcvbnm
10 - 123123	27 - 1qaz2wsx	44 - passw0rd
11 - abc123	28 - 333333	45 - bailey
12 - qwerty123	29 - michael	46 - nothing
13 - 1q2w3e4r	30 - sunshine	47 - shadow
14 - admin	31 - liverpool	48 - 121212
15 - qwertyuiop	32 - 777777	49 - biteme
16 - 654321	33 - 1q2w3e4r5t	50 - ginger
17 - 555555	34 - donald	

Interestingly, the password "password" (one of the worst of all bad passwords) has finally been squeezed out of the top 50. SplashData reported it still finds people continue creating passwords using the same predictable, easily guessable words and alphanumeric patterns.[11]

---

[11] "Top 50 Worst Passwords of 2019," *Team Password* (blog), December 18, 2019, https://www.teampassword.com/blog/top-50-worst-passwords-of-2019.

Don't use Facebook or automatic logins for other sites

Nowadays, when creating a new user account, many sites and apps will give you the option of signing in using your Google, Facebook, Twitter or other accounts. I'll call these "primary" accounts for clarification here, and the non-Google, non-Facebook, non-Twitter accounts are "subaccounts" for this discussion.

While using primary accounts to log into subaccounts is much easier and, I admit, tempting because doing so doesn't require you to type in your basic info or creating another password, I recommend against doing so. The downside to this convenience is that if someone gains access to that primary account, they then have access to all of the shared accounts. What's more, all the scammer needs to do is check the messages in the primary account to see which other accounts have been granted sharing permission for a roadmap to your digital life.

It's also easy enough for hackers to create illegitimate websites that allow you to log in with your primary accounts, and the scammer just obtained your primary account's actual username and password.

Although it takes just a few more steps in the beginning setup process, create unique usernames and passwords for all of your accounts.

Secret questions

A few years ago, the socialite Paris Hilton, heiress to some of the Hilton Hotels fortune, had her online identity stolen and an online account breached because the hackers were able to figure out the answers to her security questions, including her mother's maiden name, which was easily searchable online.

Secret questions, or security questions, are a useful layer of verification in theory, but one problem with many of them is they ask questions where the answer can be found with some online investigation. Maiden names, parent's names, grandparents even. Hometown, favorite sports team, and other tidbits of information may be gleaned from social media. Even an inexpensive and completely legal background search that can be performed instantly online will often list the names of relatives and history of residential addresses. With enough time and determination, a stalker or hacker can find ample information about any target.

I recommend using codewords, nicknames, or unrelated but in some way memorable words, names or phrases to answer security questions, rather than the straightforward response. For example, if asked the common question, "What is your mother's maiden name?" Don't actually give her maiden name, but instead type in her favorite dessert, song title, her childhood nickname or something else obscure that you associate with your mother.

Secret questions are a great platform for inside jokes. "What city or town did you grow up in?" Name a faraway land from your favorite story, fast food restaurant, or even your favorite planet if you have one. Do this consistently if you like. You can use the same fake answer for your Mom's maiden name across accounts. Or if you want to be extra, extra thorough, you can give different answers to that question on different accounts, and save the site-specific response in your password keeper notes for such accounts. More power to you should you be that diligent.

Don't use public computers

If you must use a public computer, perhaps at a FedEx Office or hotel business office or even an acquaintance's computer, when you are done and before you walk away do these critical four steps:

1. Log out of any websites and accounts you were using.
2. Delete the complete browsing history of whatever browser you were using. If I'm using a truly public computer, I delete the history until the beginning of time. If I'm using an acquaintance's computer, I'll delete the history going back as far as I used it to not inconvenience them too much.
3. Delete all contents in the computer's Recycle Bin.
4. Restart the computer.

Chapter 6 – 2-Factor Authentication

2-factor authentication – You Be You

More and more websites are giving users the option to use 2-factor authentication (sometimes called 2FA), which requires a user signing into an account to have a secondary means of confirming they are, in fact, the authorized user. Different methods of the second verification include receiving a text message or perhaps an email. Some other methods include using an authenticator app that generates a temporary code which refreshes every minute or so. Other physical authenticators include digital keychain fobs that generate temporary codes, which the user has to have in their physical possession to use rather than a perpetrator in, say, Eastern Europe or Asia. Or Toledo.

Here's the hard and fast rule: Everywhere you can opt for 2-factor authentication, **do it**. Whichever means you choose – text message, email message, authenticator app, key fob or whatever other clever new means gets introduced in the future – 2FA is one of the best ways to prevent hackers and thieves from gaining access to your accounts. And not just your accounts tied to money, such as your bank or credit card accounts, but your accounts for purchasing, services, information, and social media too.

Creative thieves are continually developing new cons and scams to steal money or other valuables from a target or a target's relations and connections. A direct way of stealing is obtaining actual account information and diverting funds out of accounts, taking out loans or credit in the victim's name, or buying things illicitly with the victim's credit cards.

Indirect ways of stealing from a victim including taking on a target's online persona and, perhaps, convincing that target's grandparents to Western Union money because the imposter claims to have been in a car accident or perhaps arrested. While one would think people's scamming radar would pop up and common sense would prevent scams like this from making it to successful completion, the phrase "Please don't tell Mom and Dad," is powerful and can manipulate emotions and otherwise logical minds.

Two-factor authentication is good, but not foolproof. Not because the technology isn't up to the task, but because there are still human beings involved in the process. While the best tech may work well on paper, the following is an example of how thieves figured out how to hack a brain rather than an algorithm.

The Bank of America text verification scam

"Hello, Ms. [insert name]. This is Bank of America Fraud Protection calling. We noticed some suspicious activity on your debit card and are reaching out to you to confirm if these transactions are yours. Before we begin, to confirm that we have contacted the account holder, you'll be receiving a text from Bank of America in just a moment. Please confirm the code in the text."

And with that, the scammer on the phone just bypassed Bank of America's 2-factor authentication and gained access to the target's online bank account. The scammer's immediate steps (which would take only minutes to complete) would be to: (1) change the account's registered email and password and (2) wire all available funds to a dummy or offshore account. Before the target realizes what has just occurred, they'll already have been robbed.

For this scam to work, the thief will need to have the target's online banking username and password. In reality, that's not too difficult for experienced scammers to obtain, either by purchasing personal information on the Dark Web or by relying on the likelihood that people still are very lax with their passwords. (Ask yourself: How many of your accounts use the same or extremely similar usernames and/or passwords?) In reality, this scam is likely to be a coordinated group of people working the operation like an efficient business, targeting hundreds or thousands of potential victims.

In theory, 2-factor authentication prevents unauthorized users from simply obtaining what are often easily-cracked passwords and gaining full access to an unwitting target's account. Thieves, however, remain thieves by blowing up theories like this. It's highly likely that Bank of America customers are not the ones to be targeted by this scam, as 2FA text codes are pretty standard fare. I learned about the BofA situation first, so I am using that bank as an example, but this can be perpetrated across the spectrum of accounts. If there's something to be gained, whether money, personal information or other data, there's most certainly someone who will want to steal it for nefarious reasons.

According to Bank of America's website, "Bank of America will never ask you to provide your Social Security number, ATM or debit card PIN or any other sensitive information in response to an email or text. If you receive an email or text from Bank of America and you're unsure if it's real, don't click on any links."

Easier said than done. So, what do you do to protect yourself? First and foremost, hang up and call back. Politely, of course. In today's world, when any company calls you about an issue, it's best to say you'll call them back. Importantly, do NOT call back the number the "helpful" representative provides you during their phone call. If they are legitimate, they should understand without hesitation. Instead, call the phone number listed on the company's website (for customer service, fraud prevention or whatever department is appropriate). Alternatively, customer service numbers are provided in the billing statements you receive.

Section II – Protect Your Privacy

Section Table of Contents

Topic	Page
Too Long; Didn't Read	63
If you are willing to spend a few dollars:	63
If you want to use free solutions	65
Chapter 7 – Why Your Privacy Matters	67
How much tracking is too much?	*68*
See how much of your data is tracked	71
Request copies of your personal data	78
Chapter 8 – Browsing	81
Browsers vs. search engines	81
Cut down on tracking cookies	81
How incognito is incognito?	83
Use a browser that respects your privacy	83
Extreme browser privacy	87
Use a more private search engine	88
Fix your browser settings for privacy	89
Chapter 9 – Mobile Device Safety	97
Locate, lock, or erase your lost devices	97
Tricking your fingerprints to make purchases	*99*
Keep sensitive photos in a vault	101
7 signs someone is tracking your cell phone	104
Encrypt your chats and texts	106
The most popular apps have some privacy weaknesses	107
Your state's cell phone location tracking laws	109
Extreme privacy	110

Chapter 10 – Tried-and-True Phone Scams 115
    Know thy caller 115
    Phone Scams 116
        Can you hear me? NO! *117*
        The story of Jolene *119*

Chapter 11 – Encrypt Your Devices 133
    What encrypting your devices won't do 133
    Computers and laptops 133
    Phones and tablets 134

Chapter 12 – Block, Remove, Backup, and Restore 137
    The quick and easier solution 138
    Set up automatic backups 141
    What to do if your Windows or MacOS fails 143
    Sanitize your trash 144

Chapter 13 – On the Road 145
    Virtual Private Networks (VPNs) explained in 30 seconds 146

Too Long; Didn't Read

TL;DR If you want to bypass the next six chapters but want the quickest route to achieving privacy and security, you can take the direct route and follow the instructions on this page. It will cost a bit of money to implement but I believe the benefits and peace of mind dramatically outweigh the costs of not doing so. In the following chapters there are options for free solutions but they do require more time and effort to implement. You can decide what's best for your time.

If you are willing to spend a few dollars:

Step 1: To protect your privacy, stop using Google Chrome as your default browser and use Apple Safari or Mozilla Firefox instead. The reasons behind this are detailed in Chapter 8 – *Browsing*, but this TL;DR is briefest summary possible.

Step 2: Purchase and install Norton 360 Deluxe

For comprehensive protection for your online activities, the short answer is to purchase and install Norton 360 Deluxe. Norton 360 Deluxe provides protection for up to five PCs, Macs, smartphones or tablets. It features a wide suite of protections, 100GB of cloud backup, password manager and other useful bells and whistles.

I think this is one of the most robust solutions out there when installed. I personally use Norton 360 Deluxe for my personal and professional lives, as well as my family's online protection. The price for the software subscription is about $40 annually to protect five computers or mobile devices.

Step 3: Subscribe to DeleteMe to remove your personal information from data broker sites

DeleteMe

Data broker sites can reveal your home address, phone number and other details to stalkers, trolls, and generally annoying solicitors. DeleteMe uses real human beings to go through the laborious, time-consuming process of removing your personal data from 41 (and counting) online data broker sites, and does a quarterly review of those sites to remove any new data that might have been added.

The cost may cause someone to pause, but I believe it's well worth it for the privacy it affords. The standard plan for 1 person is $130 per year ($10.75 per month), $230 for 2 people for 1 year ($9.54 per person per month), or $350 for 2 people for 2 years ($7.24 per person per month). Here also is an affiliate link that will apply a 20% off discount from DeleteMe's standard pricing, I hope it helps!

https://joindeleteme.com/refer?coupon=RFR-115917-RMHRRR

If you want to use free solutions

Step 1: To protect your privacy, stop using Google Chrome as your default browser and use Apple Safari or Mozilla Firefox instead.

Step 2: Install an antivirus scanner software

Step 3: Install malware remove software

Step 4: Schedule a backup program to save your data and files

Step 5: Contact the major data broker sites listed in *Chapter 17 – Removing Your Personal Info from the Internet* and have them remove your personal information

There are several other valuable steps you can take to protect your privacy detailed in the following chapters. If you want to do a deeper dive into Section II where we provide specific steps to protect your privacy, bless your heart. If you don't and are satisfied with a reasonably solid (but less than bulletproof) setup above, then you can jump to *Chapter 14 –Social Media Discretion.*

Chapter 7 – Why Your Privacy Matters

Have you ever felt like you're being watched? You most certainly are being monitored online.

Personal information is highly valuable to companies, interest groups, and even entire governments to influence (or sometimes blatantly manipulate) the spending, preferences, and even voting habits of targeted populations. There is an entire industry comprised of consulting companies and data analysts that develop highly-specific profiles of different types of individuals based on a person's browsing activity, buying habits, social media activity, reading habits, and an enormous number of other indicators.

Target audiences can be segmented into smaller and smaller groups using the massive amounts of data being collected about people's online activities. Marketers (in the broad sense of the word) often try to craft different, highly-specific messages that would resonate best with each microtargeted group. Sometimes that microtargeting is used to encourage specific consumers to buy more toothpaste or a particular brand of baby diapers. Other times the objective can be much more manipulative and malevolent.

Unfortunately, in our modern world, misinformation is easily spread through what's called computational propaganda, which uses algorithms, automation, and human input to intentionally distribute misleading information over social media. The propaganda might range from political spin and half-truths to outright lies. The sheer volume of propaganda directed at target audiences over hours, days, and years can be overwhelming. Some messaging may be subtle and nuanced to plant seeds of an idea or perspective in a target audience's thinking. Other messaging may be so triggering that it intentionally pushes the target audience to violence against another group.

According to the University of Oxford's Oxford Internet Institute, social media is actively used as a tool for public opinion manipulation, though in diverse ways and on different topics. In authoritarian countries, social media platforms are a primary means of social control. In democracies, social media is actively used for computational propaganda either through broad efforts at opinion manipulation or targeted efforts on specific segments of the public.[12]

Keeping track of what you do online translates to money in someone's pocket, but it's usually not your pocket. There's a reason why companies like Google, Facebook, Twitter and many others are valued at hundreds of billions of dollars. For many companies, data mining is gold mining.

Consumer privacy laws are evolving in the U.S. and the EU, which is encouraging but companies still have enormous power over our personal data.

In the following chapters we will look at ways to protect your privacy and data. Before we do, it's worthwhile to spend a moment and understand just how much of our personal data is in the hands of companies like Google and Facebook.

How much tracking is too much?

To provide perspective on how much of your personal information and activity Google tracks, you can request they provide you with a download of all the information they have on you based on your email address. Upon request, Google will send you download links to see your records.

---

[12] Samuel C. Woolley and Philip N. Howard, "Computational Propaganda Worldwide: Executive Summary," Computational Propaganda Research Project (University of Oxford, Oxford Internet Institute, n.d.).

I recently requested Google provide my information through their website. They make it easy to submit a data request (instructions are provided further in this chapter). When I received their response, Google informed me they had 1.3 terabytes of data (or 1,304 gigabytes) across 54 of their services or apps connected to the email account I provided.

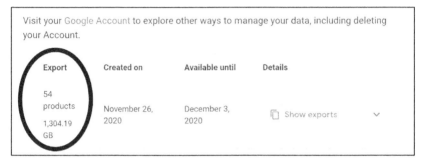

Google has captured 1.3 terabytes of data about me from one email account.

Because their downloads are limited to 2GB per file, I had 632 files waiting for me to download individually if I wanted to retrieve my data. My computer doesn't even have enough disk space to download all that Google knows about me.

> **Download data**
>
> Since this export is too big for a single file, we've split it into 632 packages.
>
> Part 1 of 632 (2 GB)   ⬇ Download
>
> Part 2 of 632 (2 GB)   ⬇ Download
>
> Part 3 of 632 (2 GB)   ⬇ Download
>
> Cancel

What does 1.3 terabytes even look like? According to legal software company Digital WarRoom, for perspective Shakespeare's entire written works can be stored on only 5 megabytes (5MB) of storage. One gigabyte (1/1000th of a terabyte) can store roughly over 15,000 images, almost 65,000 Microsoft Word files, or over 100,000 emails. I do a lot of all of these, so let's use Microsoft Word files as a reasonable middle estimate. If Google has 1.3TB of information on me, that is approximately 84 million (that's 84,000,000) Microsoft Word files of information on my browsing habits, shopping habits, social media, photos, videos, emails, and who knows what other information.[13] How long of a history they have, I have no idea. I don't even remember when I started the Gmail account I tested.

    I have multiple email accounts, each with their own history stored somewhere inside the behemoth that is Google. Not to mention the data tracked by Facebook, Twitter, and countless other platforms.

    I have a public-facing Facebook account that I rarely use. Requesting my data from Facebook showed they had 401MB of data on my rarely-used activity. It's reasonable to assume Facebook could easily store multiples more data on an active user who reads, likes, shares, comments, and posts regularly.

---

[13] Paulette Keheley, "How Many Pages In A Gigabyte? A Litigator's Guide," *Digital WarRoom* (blog), April 2, 2020, https://www.digitalwarroom.com/blog/how-many-pages-in-a-gigabyte.

See how much of your data is tracked

I'm focusing on Google and Facebook in this discussion but be aware that any number of other browsers, social media platforms, and websites will capture your information every time you are online.

Google does have extremely useful products that I use regularly, but I do so knowing that I'm willing to trade some convenience for some privacy. I just don't want to give all my privacy away without limits.

When I requested my data from Google, the company said it had my information across 54 of its products. All those products are listed on the following pages to give you a sense of breadth of information that can be tracked on individuals. I don't even remember using many of the products listed. Facebook's lengthy list of areas where they track its users (i.e., You) is included as well.

I'm not expecting that you'll read all the different categories listed on the following pages, but I hope it illustrates how very much of our online lives are not private.

Instructions for obtaining copies of your data from Google, Facebook, and Twitter are provided further on in this chapter.

Google products capturing your information

Android Device Configuration Service
Android device attributes, performance data, software versions, and account identifiers. More info

Arts & Culture
Favorites and galleries you've created on Google Arts & Culture.

Assistant Notes and Lists
Notes and lists you have in Google Assistant.

Blogger
Your Blogger blogs, including posts, pages, comments and videos, as well as settings and your Blogger profile.

Calendar
Your calendar data in iCalendar format. More info

Chrome
Bookmarks, history, and other settings from Chrome

Classic Sites
The content and attachments of your sites created in Classic Sites. More info

Classroom
Your Classroom classes, posts, submissions, and rosters More info

Cloud Print
Your Cloud Print history and devices.

Contacts
Contacts and contact photos you added yourself, as well as contacts saved from your interactions in Google products like Gmail. More info

Crisis User Reports
Information provided to help others during crises

Data Shared for Research
Responses saved with your Google Account from your participation in Google research studies and projects.

Drive
Files you own that have been stored in your My Drive and Computers. More info

Fit
Your Google Fit activity data.

Google products capturing your information (continued)

Google Account
Data about registration and account activity.

Google Fi
Your Google Fi phone number and voicemails

Google Help Communities
Your ask and reply contributions to the Google Help Communities including text and images posted. More info

Google My Business
All data related to your business. More info

Google Pay
Your saved passes, activity using virtual account numbers, and transaction history from Google services, like Play and YouTube and peer to peer payments

Google Photos
Your photos and videos from Google Photos and from other Google services, such as Google+, Blogger and Hangouts. More info

Google Play Books
The titles and authors of your purchased and uploaded books in Google Play Books plus notes and bookmarks More info

Google Play Games Services
Data, including achievements and scores, from games you play More info

Google Play Movies & TV
Your Google Play Movies & TV preferences, services, watchlist, and ratings.

Google Play Music
A list of the tracks, playlists, radio stations, uploads, and purchases in your Google Play Music library, as well as your playback and search history.

Google Play Store
Data about your app installs, ratings, and orders

Google Shopping
Google Shopping order history, loyalty, addresses and reviews.

Google Translator Toolkit
Documents you have in your Google Translator Toolkit

Google Translator Toolkit
Documents you have in your Google Translator Toolkit

Google products capturing your information (continued)

Google Workspace Marketplace
Metadata which describes an application published in Google Workspace Marketplace.

Groups
Data for your usage of Google Groups and for Google Groups that you own. More info

Hangouts
Your conversation history and attachments from Hangouts.

Home App
Device, room, home and history information from the Home App. More info

Keep
Notes and media attachments stored in Google Keep. More info

Location History
Your Location History data collected while opted-in to Location History.

Mail
Messages and attachments in your Gmail account in MBOX format. User settings from your Gmail account in JSON format. More info

Maps
Your preferences and personal places in Maps

Maps (your places)
Records of your starred places and place reviews. More info

My Activity
Records of your activity data, along with image and audio attachments. More info

My Maps
Maps, layers, features and media stored in your My Maps.

News
Data about the magazines, categories, and sources you are interested in.

Nest
Data from your Nest devices and services including any video history from Nestcams. More info

Pinpoint
Files you have uploaded to Pinpoint

Google products capturing your information (continued)

Posts on Google
Your Posts On Google history data including the collections of account, posts, cameos, metrics data, and all uploaded images and videos on Posts

Profile
Settings and images from your Google profile More info

Purchases & Reservations
Your purchases and reservations made using Search, Maps, and the Assistant. More info

Question Hub
Your activity on Question Hub

Reminders
Reminders that you created with Google. More info

Saved
Collections of saved links (images, places, web pages, etc.) from Google Search and Maps. More info

Search Contributions
Your ratings, reviews, comments and other contributions to Google Search

Shopping Lists
Items you've added to your lists, shopped on Google, or checked off.

Street View
Images and videos you have uploaded to Google Street View

Tasks
Data for your open and completed tasks. More info

Voice
Your saved Google Voice call history, messages and voicemails as well as current linked numbers. More info

YouTube and YouTube Music
Watch and search history, videos, comments and other content you've created on YouTube and YouTube Music More info

Facebook products capturing your information

Posts
Posts you've shared or hidden, and polls you have created

Photos and Videos
Photos and videos you've uploaded and shared

Comments
Comments you've posted on your and other people's posts or your groups

Likes and Reactions
Posts, comments and Pages you've liked or reacted to

Friends
The people you are connected to on Facebook

Stories
Photos and videos you've shared to your story

Following and Followers
People and businesses you chose to see content from, and your followers

Messages
Messages you've exchanged with other people on Messenger

Groups
Groups you belong to or manage, your activity within your groups

Events
Your responses to events and a list of the events you've created

Profile Information
Your contact information, your profile's About section, life events, hobbies, music

Pages
Pages you are the admin of, and pages you've recommended

Marketplace
Your activity on Marketplace

Payment History
A history of payments you've made through Facebook

Saved Items and Collections
A list of the posts you've saved, and your activity within collections

Your Places
A list of places you've created

Apps and Websites
Apps and websites you log into using Facebook and apps you admin

Other Activity
Activity associated with your account, such as Pokes given and received

Facebook products capturing your information (continued)

Facebook Gaming
Your profile for Facebook Gaming

Interactions
Actions you've taken on Facebook

Trash
Items you have moved to trash

Archive
Items you have moved to archive

Short Videos
Your activity with short videos on Facebook

Accounts Center
Accounts you added to Accounts Center

News
Your profile information for Facebook News

Campus
Your campus activity and data

Rewards
Your activity on Rewards

Other Facebook Information about You

Ads and Businesses
Dta collected about you, info you submitted, interactions outside of Facebook

Search History
A history of your searches on Facebook

Location
Information related to your location

About You
Information associated with your Facebook account

Security and Login Information
History of your logins, time, and the devices you used on Facebook.

Your Topics
Topics based on your activity, used for recommendations such as News Feed

Voice Recording and Transcription
A history of your voice recording and transcription on Facebook

Request copies of your personal data

If you want to see what information a company is keeping on you, you can request they provide you with copies of your data. The amount of information you can obtain will depend on the company and their specific policies.

Here are instructions for downloading your data from Google, Facebook, and Twitter. Depending on the website you're contacting, the company behind the site may make it relatively easy or extremely difficult to obtain your data.

Download your Google data

Google Takeout allows users of Google products to download their data. If you use any of the products noted above, you can go to the following address and request your files.

https://takeout.google.com/settings/takeout

Download your Facebook data

If you want to download a copy of your information from Facebook, you can use the Download Your Information tool in Settings.

Select **Settings**, then **Your Facebook Information**.

Click **Download Your Information** and follow instructions.

Download your Twitter data

Twitter restricts you to requesting your data once every 30 days.

Go to **Settings** and then Your **Account**.

Select **Download an archive of your data**.

Be aware of data brokers

In Chapter 18 – *Removing Your Personal Info from the Internet,* we'll discuss steps to remove your information from data brokers, which are another category of company that gathers and then sells your information for profit.

Chapter 8 – Browsing

The topic of safely browsing the internet can take up volumes but (fortunately for you!) we're focusing on the critical, prudent, and practical points to stay protected online. And we'll keep it as brief as possible.

Simply put, there are good websites, questionable websites, and clearly bad websites out there ready and waiting for you to visit. The good sites do what they claim to do – offer news, entertainment, shopping or whatever else you're specifically seeking. The questionable sites offer mostly what you expect, but do so in a way that generates as much revenue to them as possible (including clickbait, where you're urged to keep clicking "next page" or "next slide" to go through Top 10 lists and whatnot). The clearly bad websites may contain phishing schemes or other malicious tactics, which your browser's built-in security should flag for you.

Browsers vs. search engines

A **browser** provides you access to the internet, and a **search engine** lets you search the internet through the browser. Safari, Chrome, Edge, Firefox and Brave are browsers. Google, Bing, and Yahoo are search engines. We'll cover how to make both of these tools work safest for you.

Cut down on tracking cookies

Cookies are pieces of text that websites use to manage your interaction. There are three main types: session cookies, first-party persistent cookies, and third-party persistent cookies. Session cookies are the most basic and temporary, deleted when you close your browser.

Persistent cookies (both first- and third-party) are stored on your device's memory and have an expiration date set by the issuer, which can be whatever timeframe the website dictates. First-party cookies are created by the site you are visiting, and remain on your device after you close your browser. These cookies can make your browsing easier, such as remembering if you've already logged in or what's in your shopping cart.

According to Privacy.net, some of the most common resources that use tracking cookies are advertisements, social media widgets (such as Like and Share buttons and comments), and web analytics.[14]

Third-party cookies, also known as **tracking cookies,** are also stored in your device's memory but they are accessed by sites other than the one you actually visited. This allows third parties to collect your data when you browse. Tracking cookies don't even need you to click anything for your information to be transmitted back to the third party that created them. Your information is shared as soon as whatever web page you visited loads. Tracking cookies are often used for advertising retargeting purposes, which is when your browsing habits are used to customize the ads you see. If you've ever looked at a product on Amazon.com and then have advertisements for that product show up on other websites: congratulations, you've been retargeted.

Social media trackers help companies like Facebook compile exhaustively detailed profiles of your interests (including religious, political, economic, and countless other categories). Social media trackers can make your social media scrolling more enjoyable if you're into, say, videos of baby pandas or baby puppies. However, the detrimental impact of social media tracking on the general public can be vast, and there have been numerous situations where disinformation, propaganda and outright lies have been disseminated to different demographics by interest groups to influence issues ranging from popular trends to social justice to presidential elections. This can occur both in your own neighborhood and around the world.

Also, **tracking pixels** are third-party trackers hidden inside images that appear on your screen and allow data collectors to gather information on your computer and location. Tracking pixels don't require you to do anything for them to activate, which makes them very intrusive. The image they're

---

[14] Dennis Anon, "How Cookies Track You around the Web & How to Stop Them," *Privacy.Net* (blog), February 24, 2018, https://privacy.net/stop-cookies-tracking/.

attached to just has to load on your page or in your email for the third-party to collect information.

How incognito is incognito?

Depending on your browser, this may be called Private, InPrivate, or Incognito mode. These private browsers sessions delete your search and browsing history off of your computer or device when you close the private browser. Private mode prevents anyone else using your computer to know what you've been looking at, but any files you download or bookmarks you make during a private browsing session will remain on your computer.

It's **important** to understand that these private browsers do not make you anonymous to websites or your internet service provider. If you are using your work computer in private mode, your company can still monitor your browsing activity.

Private browsing will not protect you from keystroke loggers or spyware that may already be on your computer. (We'll cover how to remove those bad programs in *Chapter 12 – Block, Remove, Backup, and Restore*.

Use a browser that respects your privacy

Here's the quick answer: Stop using Google Chrome as your browser.

Protecting your privacy from advertisers, social media sites, and other powers that consider you as more of a commodity than a human being is one of the most important steps you can take for your online health. According to the website Statcounter.com, a whopping 70 percent of all desktop users worldwide use Google Chrome for their browsing.[15]

There are a number of easy alternatives to using Google Chrome, which aggressively mines your personal data and allows third parties to track all of your activities. Without going into a long narrative on how invasive Google is, just understand that their original business model was based on

---

[15] "Desktop Browser Market Share Worldwide," StatCounter GlobalStats, https://gs.statcounter.com/browser-market-share/desktop/worldwide.

connecting the dots in individual's online search activities to develop targeted profiles that could be sold to advertisers. The importance and value of online privacy only continues to grow as analytics grow more sophisticated by leaps and bounds. Bottom line, your personal information, browsing activity, and online habits should be your own and not commoditized to be used against you.

Here are some easy replacements for Google Chrome, and you can download the latest version from each publisher's website or from your app store.[16]

More specifically, a browser that protects your privacy should:

1. Block third-party tracking cookies by default
2. Block social media trackers
3. Offer private browsing or Incognito mode
4. Offer a password keeper to encourage you to use long and complicated passwords to secure all of your logins

These four browsers offer all of the above features, which you may have to turn on in the browser's settings:

Apple Safari

Apple Safari uses what it calls Intelligent Tracking Prevention to stop advertisers from tracking your online activity. Safari also prevents advertisers from creating a profile of your device to target you based on characteristics like your browser configuration, and fonts and plug-ins you've installed. To help prevent this, Safari only shares a simplified system profile with websites you visit, making it more difficult for data companies to identify you.

---

[16] "Seven of the Best Browsers in Direct Comparison," Mozilla, https://www.mozilla.org/en-US/firefox/browsers/compare/.

Firefox

Mozilla Firefox

I've become partial to Firefox's free browser because it also offers their Facebook Container free add-on, which prevents Facebook from tracking your activity outside of Facebook. Typically, if you click on a link in Facebook that opens up to an external website, Facebook will continue tracking your activity, even though you might be on Amazon or anywhere else. Facebook Container prevents Facebook from following your outside activity. Facebook will still be able to track everything to watch, read, like, comment, and do on their platform, but Facebook Container gives you back some power over your online privacy from a highly intrusive social media company.

Mozilla, the maker of the popular Firefox browser, is backed by a not-for-profit supporting online privacy and giving users more control of their online lives. Firefox automatically blocks over 2,000 known trackers and its privacy mode also blocks advertising and trackers.

Mozilla also offers a "lighter" mobile browser for iOS and Android called **Firefox Focus**, which automatically strips out ads and simplifies browsing on your smaller-screen mobile devices. By not loading extraneous ads and images, it is a faster mobile browser. You can install both Firefox (for when you want to have a richer browsing experience) and Firefox Focus (for quicker, simpler tasks) on your phone for more flexibility.

Brave Browser

Brave is a browser that automatically blocks trackers, and does not store or collect your browsing data. It also provides secure, encrypted communication by automatically upgrading to HTTPS security. Brave is available for both computers and mobile devices.

 Microsoft Edge

Microsoft Edge[17]

Edge's Tracking Prevention setting lets you choose how strictly you block trackers: Basic, Balanced, and Strict. Basic blocks known harmful trackers but otherwise allows other trackers to monitor you as intended. Strict mode blocks most but not all trackers and may prevent some websites from fully working correctly. If Strict is too restrictive, Balances mode provides a compromise solution.

NOPE, NOT THIS

Sorry, Google. I love your ease of use, but give us some privacy. Google's default settings block nothing by default. You can turn on some privacy features inside Chrome but ensuring the same level of privacy and anonymity as the above browsers takes some work on your part, including adding and enabling privacy extensions (more on this is discussed below).

Google is, however, excellent as a research search engine, and we'll discuss using their browser, Google Maps (and its Street View and Satellite View features), and Google Earth to protect against online harassment in Chapter 14 – *Social Media Discretion* and Chapter *15 – Defend Against Trolls*.

---

[17] S

Extreme browser privacy

Tor Browser

Tor Browser is the gold standard of online privacy. Journalists and human rights advocates working under oppressive governments can use Tor to protect the safety of their sources as well as themselves. Bad people on the Dark Web also use Tor for illegal activities, but (fortunately) sophisticated U.S. law enforcement agencies have been able to identify and successfully arrest online lawbreakers hiding behind Tor. Law enforcement can also identify when someone is using Tor, which may turn a user into a person of interest if there are indications illicit activities are taking place. For the average, honest user, Tor is a heavy-duty privacy tool that will hide your activity from advertisers, ISPs and websites. It may have slower performance than the more popular browsers but that's the tradeoff for anonymity. Tor Browser may still display advertisements, but those ads won't be able to track you.

Tor believes everyone should be able to explore the internet with privacy. It is run by the Tor Project, a 501(c)3 US nonprofit. They state their goal is to advance human rights and defend the public's privacy online through free software and open networks. Tor Browser isolates each website you visit so third-party trackers and ads can't follow you. Any cookies automatically clear when you're done browsing. So will your browsing history. Tor Browser prevents someone watching your connection from knowing what websites you visit. All anyone monitoring your browsing habits can see is that you're using Tor. Tor Browser aims to make all users look the same, making it difficult for you to be fingerprinted based on your browser and device information. Your traffic is relayed and encrypted three times as it passes over the Tor network. The network is composed of thousands of volunteer-run servers known as Tor relays. With Tor Browser, you are also free to access sites your home network may have blocked.

Use a more private search engine

Google and many other search engines make money off of your browsing habits by compiling profiles about you as a targeted consumer using your search history, purchase history and other details (and there are many) it can ascertain from your online activities, which intrudes on your privacy online. Google tracks your searches thanks to tracking cookies it manages on millions of websites. Advertisers can then laser target you, which is why when you search for a product or service, you'll often see advertisements for those exact things when you visit other sites – the advertisers are following you online. And the search engine gets paid for showing the advertising.

DuckDuckGo

DuckDuckGo blocks Google and other third-party trackers, helping to keep your browsing history more private. It is a search engine that makes money from ads, but in a less intrusive manner while protecting your privacy. DuckDuckGo does not collect your personal information, so search ads are based on the search results page you are viewing, and not specifically targeted to your profile. If you were searching for shoes, DuckDuckGo will show you ads about shoes and the advertisers don't know who you are as a detailed profile. They just know someone searched for shoes. DuckDuckGo is a free browser add-on and can be set as your default search engine. DuckDuckGo is also the default search engine for the Tor browser, which speaks well for its ability to protect users' anonymity.

Fix your browser settings for privacy

Go to your browser's settings and check to see that these features are set for your privacy:

Restrict outside permissions

Check to make sure your browser settings require your permission before allowing any website to access:

- Your location
- Your camera
- Your microphone

Disable Pop-ups

Block websites from opening pop-up windows and automatic redirects to other sites.

Turn on Do Not Track

Your browser settings will also have a Do Not Track option that informs third-party cookie creators that you do not want your information collected. Turn it on. Be aware, however, that Do Not Track is a request to the third-parties and there is no enforcement mechanism, so some unscrupulous trackers may (actually, will probably) ignore this.

Clear your existing cookies

In your browser settings, go to your History section and clear your browser history. This will require you to login to your websites the next time you visit, but is a healthy habit to do on a regular basis. The password keeper that you (hopefully) installed will make logging back in quick and painless.

Install an ad blocker for PCs and Androids

Apple devices have built-in ad blockers, much to the dismay of advertising agencies but works to the benefit of its users. PCs and Androids aren't as immune to third-party trackers so I recommend having an ad blocker to improve your privacy.

According to Mozilla, the creator of the Firefox web browser, the average person sees an average of 4,000 ads each day. There is only so much brain space any of us have, and ad blockers help filter the deluge of online noise. Ad blocker extensions block the signal from an advertiser's server so the ad never shows up on your page, and also blocks out sections of a website that could be ads.[18]

Two of the more popular ad blockers / tracker blockers include:

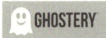

Ghostery

https://www.ghostery.com/

Privacy Badger

https://privacybadger.org/

---

[18] "How to Block Annoying Ads Using an Ad Blocker," Mozilla, accessed October 29, 2020, https://www.mozilla.org/en-US/firefox/features/adblocker/.

To put how invasive websites can be on your privacy in perspective, here are some popular sites, with Ghostery showing how many cookies it is blocking from tracking your information.

The website for the U.S. White House had 4 trackers blocked

The athletic company Nike had 12 trackers blocked

The media and entertainment website Buzzfeed also had a dozen trackers blocked

And the news site CNN had 21 trackers blocked.

It's to your benefit to keep your information private, ad blockers clearly can help.

Know how to read built-in safety features

Web browsers have built-in features for checking security certificates from trusted websites. When you go to any web page, your browser should indicate whether your connection and data are secure or not by showing a symbol next to the URL address.

Look for "https://" (and not "http://" without the "s") and a padlock icon at the beginning of every website URL you visit, which indicates the communication between you and the site is encrypted from prying eyes.

For example, Google's Chrome browser shows this:

Check if a site's connection is secure

To see whether a website is safe to visit, you can check for security info about the site. Chrome will alert you if you can't visit the site safely or privately.

1. In Chrome, open a page.
2. To check a site's security, to the left of the web address, look at the security status:
   - 🔒 Secure
   - ⓘ Info or Not secure
   - ⚠ Not secure or Dangerous
3. To see the site's details and permissions, select the icon. You'll see a summary of how private Chrome thinks the connection is.

Your browser should also warn you before you enter a bad site.

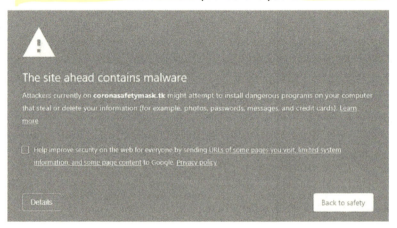

Select individual website privacy options

      Both the safe and somewhat questionable sites aggressively (but legally) collect as much information about you as is permitted by their cookie policies. (We're ignoring the outright fraudulent sites for a moment in this discussion, since they don't have legitimate cookie policies to begin with). More and more, users are able to set their permissions and differentiate between allowing "essential cookies" (which users can't avoid from being installed) to optional cookies that, the sites claim, "enhance your viewing experience".

In practice, the optional cookies help the sites' advertisers target you more specifically based on your browsing habits, device information, and other data for their economic benefit, with negligible benefit to You, the User. Anytime I get onto a new website that discloses its cookie policy (usually a banner message that opens at the bottom of the first page I access) I click it and make sure optional cookies are denied. Otherwise I'm just making myself more exposed to unwanted, intrusive advertising. I recommend you do the same to keep yourself as anonymous as possible.

And here's another version from a different site...

Use caution when downloading

Before downloading programs, files, add-ons or apps from a website, check to see if they are available from reliable sources that review or vet software against harmful features. Sometimes spyware or other malicious apps do sneak onto the below platforms but are eventually caught, whereas those left unmonitored in the wild will likely never be blocked.

Fake apps can artificially inflate their ratings to tout five-star reviews, making them appear, initially at least, legitimate. Before downloading and installing any app that's not coming from a trusted publisher or source, it's wise to spend a few minutes to do your own independent research. Read the reviews, starting with the one-star ratings to see if users are unhappy with the app. Also consider searching for independent reviews, if any exist, before adding an unknown app to your computer. The same goes for your smartphone or tablet.

Apple's App Store. In your System Preferences settings, click Security & Privacy, then click General. It's safest to specify what sources you'll accept downloads from. You can choose from (i) the App Store or (ii) the App Store and identified developers. Option (ii) allows programs from developers registered with Apple and can optionally upload their apps to Apple for a security check.

The Microsoft Store. Microsoft's Store is not as all-encompassing as the App Store but programs and apps are reviewed by Microsoft so considered safe to install.

The Google Play Store. All Android apps undergo security testing before appearing in the Google Play Store. Google reviews every app and developer in Google Play, and suspends those who violate its policies.

Browser extensions

The same diligence applies to enabling browser extensions onto your browsers. Only use those that are available through the browser's own settings tools.

Be mindful of spoof sites

When browsing be aware of spoofed sites that rely on the user accidentally mistyping a legitimate site. A glance at the browser's security icon will help alert you.

When you want to go to Newsweek.com

But accidentally type Newsweel.com, this shows up...

Scan sites or files for known viruses

VirusTotal

https://www.virustotal.com

VirusTotal is a free service that inspects suspicious websites, links and files (that you upload for scanning) with over 70 antivirus scanners and URL/domain blacklisting services, in addition to tools to extract signals from the studied content. Any user can select a file from their computer using their browser and send it to VirusTotal to ensure it's clean before opening it.

Ignore pop-ups claiming you have a virus

If you set your browser settings as recommended above, this scam shouldn't be an issue for you. If you didn't yet, don't trust any pop-up messages that scream you have a virus, urging you to click any buttons or links to solve the crisis. Instead, exit your browser, fix your browser pop-up settings (as recommended above), and reconsider if the web page you were browsing at the time is legitimate.

DO NOT try to close or minimize the pop-up window itself.

The minimize or close buttons are probably fake, and by clicking them you are actually responding to the pop-up.

Chapter 9 – Mobile Device Safety

Locate, lock, or erase your lost devices

If your phone or mobile device goes missing, Apples and Androids have convenient apps that can help you locate, lock down, or delete the contents of your phone to keep your information secure.

Apple Find My app

Apple's iCloud has the Find My app to locate iPhones, iPads, Macs, Apple watches, AirPods, and iPods. The Find my app can even find devices that are offline using the Find My network of connected devices around the world.

To turn on Find My, go to **Settings**, tap **your name**, and then tap **Find My**. Follow the instructions to set up your devices.

To use Find My to locate, lock, or erase your phone, log into https://www.icloud.com/find with your iCloud account information and follow the instructions to locate and, if necessary, lock down or erase your device.

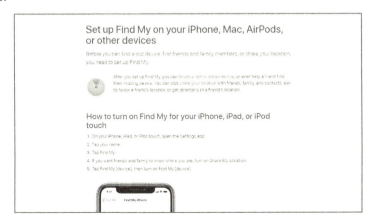

Google Find My Device app

If you lose an Android phone or tablet, you can find, lock, or erase it. If you've added a Google Account to your device, Find My Device is automatically turned on. Google's Find My Device app is conveniently tied to the range of Google services and available in the Google Play Store. To confirm your Android device is set up properly, check the following steps:

Step 1: Check that Find My Device is on. Open your device's **Settings** app. Tap **Security** and then **Find My Device** and check that Find My Device is turned on.

Step 2: Check that Location is on. In the device's Settings app, tap **Location** and confirm location is turned on.

Step 3: Check that Google Play visibility is on. If you hide a device on Google Play, it won't show in Find My Device so you have make it visible. Open https://play.google.com/settings and under **Visibility**, check to ensure your device is visible.

Be alert downloading from Apple Store or Google Play

Apps on either of these platforms are supposed to be reviewed and vetted for security, but be aware that some intentionally bad programs slip through the screening process and do get onto the App Store or Google Play Store. Eventually, hopefully, they are discovered and removed, hopefully again before you've downloaded them. But do be aware that bad apples sometimes exist and are available to unsuspecting downloaders.

Tricking your fingerprints to make purchases

The website Lifehacker.com previously reported on a scam iOS heart rate monitor app that was initially banned from the App Store but then reappeared eight months later. The bogus app claimed to use your fingerprint touch scanner to track your pulse. What it actually did was use your fingerprint as authorization to make a secret $89 in-app purchase using your fingerprint in the background. Other phony apps promise peer-to-peer video chatting, free pornography, sex, but also general quizzes and popular entertainment.[19]

Similar to downloads for your computer, fake mobile apps can artificially inflate their ratings making them appear, initially at least, legitimate. Before downloading and installing any app that's not coming from a trusted publisher or source, it's wise to spend a few minutes to do your own independent research. Read the reviews, starting with the one-star ratings to see if users are unhappy with the app. Also consider searching for independent reviews, if any exist, before adding an unknown app to your phone or tablet.

---

[19] Brendan Hesse, "How to Spot Scam IOS Apps That Sucker You into Making Expensive Purchases," *Lifehacker*, August 8, 2019, https://lifehacker.com/how-to-spot-scam-ios-apps-that-sucker-you-into-making-e-1837053973.

Check your permissions

PermissionDog

Android users can see how intrusive their installed apps are by installing the PermissionDog app, which lists all the applications you have installed and checks out what permissions each app is using. Based on these permissions it scores how dangerous the application can be. PermissionDog also supports real-time protection. Every time you launch an application a notification pops up and shows how many permissions the app is using. Some apps will require meaningful permissions, including Google and banking apps, but some others may be unnecessarily intrusive. You can decide which of your apps are worth giving wide ranging permissions to and which ones aren't worth it.

You can find PermissionDog in the Google Play Store.

Turn off automatic photo backups

Turn off automatic cloud saving. If you have sensitive photos or videos on your phone, lock them away in a photo vault first, delete them from your main photo albums, and then let your phone backup your other photos and videos.

On iPhones

Every photo you take on your iPhone is automatically uploaded to Apple's iCloud. To turn off iCloud sharing, go into Settings > iCloud > scroll down to Photos and slide the option to off. To disable iCloud completely, go to the bottom of the menu and hit "delete account."

On Android phones

Photos can be backed up to the Google Drive service, but this will be off when you first set up a Google account. Double check your settings going to the Photos app > select General Settings > slide Auto-Backup to Off. Check your cloud frequently to know exactly what is stored there.

The same idea applies to other backup services you may use. Check to make sure you know what's stored on your device and in the cloud to ensure you keep your private life tightly controlled.

Keep sensitive photos in a vault

Not the ones of your goldfish, necessarily, but certainly any personal photos that could be used to expose, embarrass or otherwise harm you. Every person has every right to take whatever pictures and videos of themselves they so choose. Unfortunately, there have been an untold number of phone hacks where sleazeballs have stolen people's private, sometimes intimate, images and posted them online. I highly recommend using a photo vault to secure your important albums.

Bear In mind that these apps may not be 100 percent foolproof to sophisticated hackers, but here are some of the more popular secure apps that encrypt both photos and video. There are also many others, but the below apps are known for strong levels or encryption.[20] You can find them on the App Store or Google Play.

---

[20] Xiaolu Zhang, Ibrahim Baggili, and Frank Breitinger, "Breaking into the Vault: Privacy, Security and Forensic Analysis of Android Vault Applications," *Computers & Security* 70 (September 2017): 516–31, https://www.sciencedirect.com/science/article/pii/S0167404817301529.

CoverMe

CoverMe features a photo and video vault and also offers secure text messaging to other CoverMe users.

Keepsafe

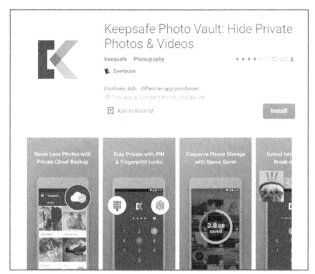

Photo Locker

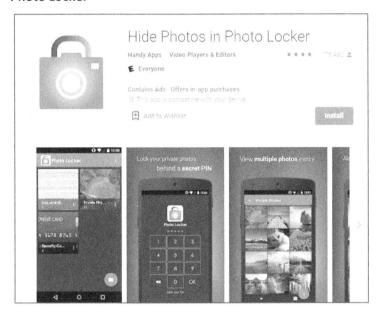

Video Locker

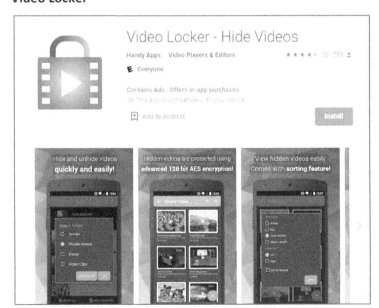

7 signs someone is tracking your cell phone

Is someone tracking or spying on your phone? Here are some red flags to look for. Individually, each clue could be caused by other issues, but if you're seeing a few of these occur it could be an indicator something's not normal. According to a Sept. 24, 2020, Reader's Digest article, here are some clues that your phone might be compromised and tracked:

1. **Your phone gets really hot.** Spyware running in the background can make your phone's components work harder continually, which could cause your device to heat up more than normal.
2. **Your battery runs out faster than usual.** A tracked phone continually sends information from your phone to the bad guys watching, which requires more battery power.
3. **Your phone's using more data than usual.** It's a good practice to check your phone bill monthly. Should you see that your phone is unexplainably using more data than normal it could be a sign your device is covertly sending out data to a hacker.
4. **Your phone reboots unexpectedly.** If malware on your phone is interfering with its normal functioning, your phone might hit a glitch and reboot randomly.
5. **Your phone takes a long time to shut down.** When you shut down your phone normally, it tries to complete any tasks that are still in progress. If there's a process running that's sending information to a hacker(s), that could meaningfully extend the time necessary to shut down.
6. **Your phone has been rooted or jailbroken.** Removing a phone manufacturer's built-in restrictions is known as rooting or jailbreaking, which hackers can do to bypass phone protections. It's a common technique when installing spyware. It's often hard to identify, but might be noticeable if you find strange apps appearing on your home screens. On iPhones, one jailbreaking app is Cydia. On Androids, Superuser is a rooting app to look out for, but there could be others as well. If you didn't install an app that's suddenly on your phone, take caution.

7. **Your phone is slower than normal.** All phones slow down over time, but if your phone is lagging and you're seeing some of these other red flags, it might be a sign your phone is being tracked.

What to do if you think you're being tracked

According to Reader's Digest, the defensive steps to take include:

1. **Reboot your phone.** Many tracking apps rely on uninterrupted connections, so restarting your phone may prevent them from continuing to track your session.
2. **Run a virus scan and a malware removal scan** to see if, in fact, there is spyware at work.
3. **Update your phone** if it hasn't been updated recently to ensure the most recent security patches are in place. And set your device to update its operating system automatically.
4. **Delete any apps** that you didn't install yourself or that you don't recognize.
5. **Turn off your location sharing** when not using it to prevent others from following you.[21]

---

[21] "8 Red Flags Someone's Tracking Your Cell Phone," *Reader's Digest* (blog), September 26, 2020, https://www.rd.com/article/red-flags-someones-tracking-your-cell-phone/.

Encrypt your chats and texts

Just because an app claims to offer encrypted messaging, don't assume it fully protects your communication. For some apps, encryption needs to be turned on for it to work, and some apps may not encrypt in all situations. The most secure messaging apps offer end-to-end, default (meaning encryption is always on when you use it), and open source code. Open source code allows the outside world to see the inner workings of an app and bring attention to any vulnerabilities in the code, which the developer can then address and tighten up.

The most secure messaging apps you can use

Here are secure apps to consider using to protect your privacy.

Signal

Considered the gold standard of secure messaging, Signal automatically encrypts all its messages between people using its app so only the sender and receiver can read them. The company that publishes Signal, Open Whisper Systems, cannot even read the messages sent through its app, and messages can self-destruct after a set period of time. Signal offers encrypted text messaging, voice calls, group messages and video calls. You can set messages to disappear after a certain amount of time elapses and can also lock the app with a password. Signal is available for both iPhones and Androids.

Wickr

Wickr offers both a personal version (Wickr Me, which is free) and business version (Wickr Pro, which is a paid service). Similar to Signal, Wickr is considered top of its class for end-to-end encryption. Wickr will alert the sender if a recipient tries to take a screenshot of any messaging. Wicker is available for both iPhones and Androids.

Dust

Dust deletes messages within 24 hours or as soon as they're read, whichever comes first. Dust is available for both iPhones and Androids.

The most popular apps have some privacy weaknesses

The most common apps are good but not great for privacy, and should be used cautiously if you are concerned about extreme privacy.

Apple iMessage

iMessage offers end-to-end encryption only between iPhone users, and unencrypted text messages when sent to Android users. iMessages backed up to iCloud are encrypted by Apple, not by you. If your iCloud is hacked (or if Apple is subpoenaed by a court), your messages could be revealed.

Facebook Messenger

Messenger's encryption features must be turned on, they are not set by default, which can be confusing for some users. Facebook's corporate actions and attitude toward privacy raises concerns on how aggressively it may handle (or collect) its users' data, such as with the Cambridge Analytica scandal (If you haven't read about this event, I highly recommend you look it up. It's chilling and disconcerting.). Simply put, it's difficult to know how much Facebook respects or doesn't respect its users' privacy.

 **WhatsApp**

WhatsApp

I love WhatsApp, it's easy and quick with simple controls, but it's owned by Facebook, so the same concerns about Facebook's data collection stance should be considered here. Also, WhatsApp messages backed up on Google Drive are not encrypted, and could be exposed (to prevent this you can disable WhatsApp backups on Google Drive).

Your state's cell phone location tracking laws

Smartphone location records can reveal an enormous amount of information about a person. According to the American Civil Liberties Union (ACLU), privacy laws haven't kept up with advances in technology, and law enforcement has previously claimed the authority to access this information from cell phone companies without warrants. While Congress and the Supreme Court haven't yet weighed in on whether a warrant should be required for location information, little by little, state legislatures and lower courts are expanding privacy protections for more and more Americans. In practical terms, the status of your privacy protections depends on where you are. For example, your location information is protected in Montana, but not in Georgia. In Illinois, police need a warrant to know where you are right now, but not where you were last week. In California, your location information is protected against warrantless search by state and local police, but not by federal authorities. In Florida, state and federal courts are at odds on the matter.

The ACLU has an interactive map on their website that details the status of cell phone location tracking laws by state.

https://www.aclu.org/issues/privacy-technology/location-tracking/cell-phone-location-tracking-laws-state

Extreme privacy

Sometimes a person just needs to keep to themselves.

In some severe circumstances, you may encounter an oppressive government or other actor trying to steal or coerce your phone data from you. This might be performed overtly, for example if you are arrested and your belongings are confiscated and inspected, or covertly, for example if an oppressive government screens your phone as you pass through international customs. The possibilities are endless, and much of the technology needed for copying or cloning a phone's information can be easily purchased on the open market.

In addition to the important safety steps discussed above, there are some additional steps you can take – in advance of something really bad happening – to protect your privacy including:

- Locking your SIM card,
- Disabling fingerprint login and facial recognition, and
- Being prepared to factory reset your phone

Lock your SIM card

Every cellphone uses a SIM card (short for Subscriber Identity Module), which is a tiny memory chip that stores a 17-digit code that identifies the SIM card's country code of origin, phone carrier (such as Verizon or T-Mobile), and a unique user ID. The user ID is how your phone company identifies your phone and charges you accordingly. SIM cards are designed to be easy to install and remove, and can be transferred from one phone to another.

But...

If someone copies your SIM card, they can create a duplicate phone to yours and monitor your voice calls and text messages going forward.

Modern SIM cards often come with a default PIN code. If someone wants to copy your SIM card they would need the default code but, guess what, default PIN codes are easily searchable online. Often the phone carriers will post them on their websites.

To make it harder for an unauthorized person to copy your SIM card, you can change your SIM PIN code. You'll have to enter your PIN code each time you restart your phone or remove your SIM card. You can also switch the PIN code requirement on and off, so once you are out of potential danger, you can turn off the PIN if desired.

Be aware, entering the wrong PIN code too many times will lock your phone, so pay attention when changing your code. If you don't know what your default SIM card PIN code is, do not try to guess it. Check your carrier's customer service page or the documents that came with your wireless plan. Or you can contact your carrier.

For illustrative purposes, here is how you change a SIM card PIN code on a Verizon Android phone

1. From a web browser, sign in to your account on Verizon's website
2. Click on Account, go to My devices, then click Device overview
3. Select your phone and click Manage Device
4. Select PIN and Personal Unblocking Key
5. The default PIN and Unblocking Key (PUK) key are displayed once link is clicked. The PUK is another recovery key you can enter if you ever lock your SIM card by too many incorrect PIN codes.

For Apple devices, including iPads that use SIM cards

1. If you have an iPhone, go to Settings, then Cellular, and then SIM PIN. If you have an iPad, go to Settings > Mobile Data > SIM PIN
2. Turn on your SIM PIN code
3. If you've never used a SIM code, enter the default SIM PIN from your carrier
4. Tap Done

Disable fingerprint and facial recognition

In some severe circumstances, such as having oppressive government, law enforcement or other actors trying to coerce or force you to unlock your phone, having fingerprint login or facial recognition may leave you vulnerable to forced entry of your device. Either by physically compelling you to place your finger or face in position, holding your phone up to your face, or tricking you to do so, biometric logins can be exploited to work against you.

From a civil rights standpoint, it is more difficult for a government agency to force you to disclose your passcode or PIN to unlock your phone, and you can go on the record as stating you refuse to disclose your password, depending on the particular circumstances you might encounter.

Alternatively, if you are going to be traveling to or returning from places outside of your country, turn off fingerprint and other biometric logins. If you are going to, say, a peaceful protest or any other situation where there might be civil "friction", do the same. In both scenarios, you can re-enable your biometric logins after you're back home safely.

The Fifth Amendment to the U.S. Constitution prevents the government (forbids it, actually) from forcing a person to give evidence against themselves. When someone "takes the Fifth," this is the Constitutional right they are referring to. The Fifth Amendment also means you don't have to talk to the police if arrested, as when they inform you "you have the right to remain silent."

There is some confusion on whether law enforcement can or cannot force a person to unlock their phone using their biometric features. In the past, U.S. courts have allowed law enforcement to do so, but a judge in the District Court for the Northern District of California has ruled the opposite.[22] To best protect yourself, it's smart to turn off biometric logins if you may be placed in sensitive situations.

---

[22] Ryan Whitman, "Judge: Police Can't Force You to Unlock Phone With Fingerprint or Face ID - ExtremeTech," *ExtremeTech* (blog), January 15, 2019, https://www.extremetech.com/mobile/283795-judge-police-cant-force-you-to-unlock-phone-with-fingerprint-or-face-id.

On an iPhone

Go to Settings > Face ID & Passcode (or Touch ID and Passcode on older devices). Toggle off facial recognition or fingerprint scanning for unlocking your phone. Next, scroll down to Change Passcode if you need to create a stronger PIN.

On an Android Phone

Go to Settings > Security > Face unlock. Under "Use face unlock for," turn off "Unlocking your phone." From your security settings page, you can also disable fingerprint scanning or delete saved fingerprints, depending on what kind of phone you're using.[23]

Be prepared to factory reset your phone

There may be situations where the safest action for you to take (especially if time is of the essence to avoid having your phone confiscated, cloned or inspected) is to factory reset your device, then get through your sticky situation, and then restore your settings and data once you are in a safe place.

As an example, there have been times I have travelled overseas where it was unclear how welcoming my reception at customs might be as a foreigner. Depending on the threat, I have been prepared to factory reset my phone before entering customs areas if there was reason to believe mobile devices might be inspected. If there is a possibility that my phone might be out of my possession for even one minute, I would wipe my phone and then let them inspect my device with zero information. Afterwards, once safely situated, I would restore my information from its cloud backup.

We discuss how to backup your phone's data and settings in Chapter 12 – *Block, Remove, Backup, and Restore.* To give yourself the readily available

---

[23] Thomas Germain, "How to Protect Phone Privacy and Security During a Protest," *Consumer Reports*, June 3, 2020, https://www.consumerreports.org/privacy/protect-phone-privacy-security-during-a-protest/.

option of factory resetting your phone, ensure you've set up automatic backups first.

      To factory reset your phone, go to your phone's Settings menu. Look for the reset options available for your device. Remember how to find the Factory Reset option before you go anywhere or possibly do anything that may put you in a compromised situation.

Chapter 10 – Tried-and-True Phone Scams

As phones get smarter and offer newer features, it's inevitable that new scams will be invented to exploit the latest release of, well, everything. It's important to remember, however, that scammers and thieves still employ old fashioned scams (very successfully I would add) using actual phone calls to separate marks from their money. Here are some ways you can protect yourself and those around you.

Know thy caller

Phone numbers can be spoofed just like emails and websites, so be aware when receiving calls from unknown numbers, and know that Caller ID will display the information that it's been provided by the caller, who may or may not be legitimate.

Some of the most common phone scams include:

- Imposter scams from a government agency, IRS, family member, or computer tech repair,
- Debt relief and credit repair scams,
- Business and investment scams,
- Charity scams,
- Extended car warranties,
- Free trials,
- Loan scams,
- Prize and lottery scams,
- Travel scams and timeshare scams, and
- Fake kidnapping calls demanding ransom for return of a family member

Phone Scams

According to the U.S. Federal Trade Commission, remember these common-sense rules to avoid being scammed:

There is no prize. If you have to pay a fee, delivery charge or taxes to get a prize, it's not a prize.

You won't be arrested. Law enforcement, the IRS, or federal agencies don't give courtesy calls to say you can pay your fines to avoid arrest. So, don't.

There's no rush. Legitimate businesses will give you time to decide before making a purchase. Do not let yourself get pressured into making a decision on the spot.

Never pay in cash, gift cards or money transfer apps. Anyone who asks you to pay that way is a scammer.

Government agencies don't call to verify your sensitive information. Ever.

The Do Not Call List

The FTC's national Do Not Call list began over 17 years ago to stop unwanted sales calls. It is free to register and companies seeking to make sales calls are supposed to abide by it. So, at best, legitimate companies will follow it. The Do Not Call list, however, does not apply to:

- political calls,
- charitable calls,
- debt collection calls,
- purely informational calls, and
- surveys

The above calls are not supposed to include a sales pitch. Scammers, spammers and robocallers ignore the Do Not Call list, but it will help block off a sliver of the annoying dialers out there wanting to solicit you.

The Do Not Call Registry accepts registrations from both cell phones and landlines. To register by telephone, call 1-888-382-1222. You must call from the phone number that you want to register. To register online at https://www.donotcall.gov, you will have to respond to a confirmation email. If you have registered a mobile or other telephone number already, you don't need to re-register. Once registered, a telephone number stays on the Do Not Call Registry until the registration is canceled or service for the number is discontinued.

Can you hear me? NO!

According to a March 24, 2017, Los Angeles Times article, scammers are tricking victims into giving verbal authorization over the phone, then using the victim's words – actually just one word – against them.

As the scam plays out, a robocaller will contact you and after you pick up the phone, the robocaller will pretend the connection is giving them trouble and ask "Can you hear me?"

Do not say Yes.

According to the Los Angeles Times, police departments nationwide have warned that offering an affirmative response can be edited to make it seem you've given permission for a purchase or some other transaction. A recorded "Yes" could also be used to deny refunds to any unwitting customer who later complains.

"If someone calls and asks, 'Can you hear me?', do not answer yes," advised the Better Business Bureau. "Just hang up. Scammers change their tactics as the public catches on, so be alert for other questions designed to solicit a simple yes answer."[24]

---

[24] "Whatever You Do, Don't Say Yes When This Chatbot Asks, 'Can You Hear Me?,'" Los Angeles Times, March 24, 2017, https://www.latimes.com/business/lazarus/la-fi-lazarus-chatbot-phone-scam-20170324-story.html.

One ring to rule them all

Some phone spammer bots are designed to call a target's phone number and ring just once or twice, hoping that the target's curiosity will get the better of them and they'll call back to see who was trying to reach them. Don't call single ring callbacks, even if the number looks familiar. First, it tells the robot that there's a real person at that number. Second, it also lets the spammer know the target is the type of person who would call back an unknown number, a prime candidate for further targeting. What's more, the number you're calling back could be charging you an exorbitant rate, such as 900 numbers or other prefixes that charge their callers.

Let it go into voicemail and then you can delete it.

The story of Jolene

Or

Chinese con men pose as police and DHL to empty victim's investment portfolios

Note: This is a longer read than other case studies in this guide, and it provides insight into a lot of the psychology con men manipulate for their scams.

Recently, a Chinese friend of mine working here in the U.S. received a phone call from someone claiming to be with the Washington, DC administrative office of DHL, the international shipping company. DHL is similar to FedEx or UPS and active overseas, including Asia. The "agent" told my friend, "Jolene" that Shanghai customs officials confiscated a package filled with passports and credit cards sent under Jolene's name.

[I changed my friend's name to protect her identity (and to send some appreciation to Dolly Parton). This article is pretty long, but that's because this was a pretty long con. Stay with me to see the play-by-play that fell two days short of robbing Jolene of her life savings.]

119

Jolene told the DHL agent she did not send any package. The person on the phone suggested it might be identity theft and Jolene should contact the Shanghai police to obtain the equivalent of an affidavit claiming she's a victim of identity theft and provide it back to DHL. The (fake) DHL agent transferred Jolene to the police station in the ChangNing District, the region where the package was addressed. The local police would have jurisdiction over this identity theft.

A man who identified himself as "Officer Li" answered the phone. Jolene explained (frantically) what happened, and [this is very, very clever] Li told Jolene to look up the phone number for the ChangNing police station (where she believed the DHL agent connected her to) and he would call her back in a few minutes from that same listed number so she can confirm his identity as law enforcement. The fake officer hung up.

Jolene Googled the police station in China and saw their real phone number (+86-21-6290-6290). Meanwhile, Li spoofed the same phone number so it would look legitimate on Jolene's caller ID, and called her back. Spoofing a phone – pretending to be calling from a different number – is incredibly easy to do and is widely used by scammers as well as telemarketers. Naturally, at that point in her state of fear and possibly panic, Jolene believed she was speaking with the real authorities.

Officer Li/Awful Sir Li (see what I did there) asked Jolene to provide her Chinese National Identity number so he could pull the relevant information from their headquarters. Li said, according to their records, Jolene was a major suspect in the highly-publicized Chinese Zheng Shaodong international money laundering case, which involved around 7,000 suspects and millions of dollars. A decade earlier, Zheng Shaodong was a high-ranking public security official responsible for investigating economic crimes and (ironically) convicted for taking over $1 million in bribes. In 2010, the Chinese courts gave him a suspended death sentence, which they reduced to life in prison.

According to written notes Jolene provided for this article, Li said Zheng confessed and identified Jolene as an accomplice who used her personal accounts to help him launder money. Zheng claimed Jolene collected about $14,000 (98,000 Chinese Yuan) in fees. What's more, Li said, the victims in China confirmed they transferred money into accounts that are under Jolene's name and were jointly filing a lawsuit against her.

Jolene Panic Mode: 1,000 percent.

Li asked Jolene how many financial accounts she has in total, and the amount of assets in each account. (You can be sure he took good notes at this point in the call.)

"I was lost and desperately trying to defend myself," Jolene said.

Their phone conversation got interrupted when Li's superior, "Officer Zhang," joined the call. Zhang said that, due to the severity of the case, he would be taking over the case directly.

If what just happened took place in the business development group of a typical company, Officer Li would be a low-level sales associate screening a prospect (just another name on a cold call list) to determine the likelihood they might become a potential customer. After getting the details on the amount of money in Jolene's accounts (her entire life savings, so a material number), Li elevated her up the food chain to a more experienced salesperson who would be able to reel her in.

Before leaving the call, Li asked for Jolene's Skype account so the department could contact her more easily (and probably cheaper too).

And here's one of the thieves' many clever, cruel manipulations: The officers advised Jolene not to discuss this situation with anyone, including her family, because it would "interfere" with the investigation.

End of Day 1 of Jolene's Terrible Horrible No Good Day.

The next afternoon, Officer Zhang contacted her on Skype voice. He said he needed to go to another city to execute an arrest and would be handing her case over to Officer Xia, and introduced them together on the call.

Officer Xia asked Jolene to recount previous scenarios where she might have used her identity card. He claimed he wanted to find clues to help her clear her name (what a helpful bastard). He also said the leadership team knew about her situation and should reach a final decision soon.

The next day (Day 3), Xia forwarded Jolene a warrant for her arrest, showing her name and personal information filled in. It also showed her photograph from her National Identification card. Jolene insisted that the warrant was unreasonable(!). Xia said he could try to help her discuss it with his superior directly and maybe they can prioritize her investigation. Apparently, Xia told her, because of the scale of that larger crime with so many victims, the investigation was backed up.

"Thanks to his help, I was able to Skype via video with Qian Sun (the prosecutor)", Jolene said, in her written statement. (Note her word choice here, that she felt appreciation toward the fake officer for connecting her to the fake prosecutor.) On the video call were two Asian men wearing police uniforms sitting behind an office desk in an empty, nondescript room. The drab background setting was so unimpressive that it looked like an authentic government office.

Every step of the way so far, the fake cops were making Jolene more and more dependent on them for help. She needed to speak with them, she's desperately waiting to hear from the only people who might make this nightmare go away.

The prosecutor Qian Sun (and also the 4th or 5th person in this scam, depending on whether or not one of them also played the fake DHL representative) agreed to apply for "priority investigation" provided that (drumroll please... here it comes...) Jolene liquidates all her investments and transfers the funds into her checking account. According to Sun, the Chinese government only has the ability to inquire and investigate bank accounts in its system, not investment accounts.

Even living on American soil, Jolene feared the Chinese government would somehow abduct her, throw a black bag over her head, throw her into an unmarked van, fly her back to China, and throw her in jail. (There was a lot of throwing in her mind as her fear-fueled imagination ran wild). Keep in mind, Zheng Shaodong, the bribe-taking official, got life in prison, so Jolene's terror at being pursued relentlessly by Chinese authorities is understandable, considering all the manipulation she had been subjected to.

Speaking in a telephone interview, Jolene said, "The fear ... was so overwhelming ... because I mean my whole life is here (in the U.S.). The consequences, getting arrested and losing everything pretty much, and the impact on my family, it's just beyond imagination. I think that basically [they] deprived me of all the ability to think logically. They really got a grasp on how to get you emotionally."

So… Jolene liquidated ALL her investment accounts, put the proceeds into her checking account, and waited anxiously for further instructions.

Jolene's Performance Review So Far…

According to "What You Should Know About the Stages of Grief," an article in Healthline.com, the five stages of grief are: denial, anger, bargaining, depression, and finally acceptance.

"Not everyone will experience all five stages, and you may not go through them in this order," the article states. "Grief is different for every person, so you may begin coping with loss in the bargaining stage and find yourself in anger or denial next. You may remain for months in one of the five stages but skip others entirely."

Jolene went through denial (100 percent correct thing to do). It would have been good if she could have stayed in adamant, violent denial, but the con didn't allow her to stay there. The con was too well-packaged, too tight to not fall prey to (initially, at least).

Anger? Of course. Someone decided to steal her identity (supposedly) and ruin her life. Who wouldn't be angry?

Jolene tried bargaining with the nice policemen who were investigating her, trying to rationalize with them to understand and accept her innocence, but to no avail.

Depression? Without question. Alone, warned not to confide in anyone, fearing she would be arrested and thrown into prison in China while awaiting trial, mistakenly connected to a corrupt ex-official serving life in prison.

Acceptance. Jolene liquidated all her assets as directed by the police, hoping they would continue their investigation, prove her righteous innocence, and someday put the nightmare behind her. Jolene's acceptance would be her downfall.

But then…

That night Jolene spoke with her female friend, "Sam", and let it all out. Jolene genuinely feared she would be abducted and nobody would know what happened to her. She gave Sam copies of her house keys and car keys, her parents' contact information and all the information related to her case.

After getting over her own initial shock, Sam went home and spoke to her husband, "Diego", immediately after. Looking at it objectively, their instinct told them the identity theft story made sense but Jolene being told to liquidate her assets made no sense.

Working backwards, they Googled the information Jolene provided and found one of the phone numbers flagged on a crowdsourced fraud website as being a scam number. Not surprisingly, discovering that this was all a malicious fairytale provided Jolene immediate relief.

If Jolene hadn't confided in her friends, what likely would have happened next would be the police telling Jolene a global law firm had been engaged to hold accounts in escrow while the investigations were ongoing. They likely would have provided authentic-looking PDF documents of authorization letters or other official looking legal documents on falsified letterhead of the major law firm, attesting that they have been engaged by the Chinese government as fiduciary for holding the assets of victims like Jolene safe during the investigation period. The paperwork would have the law firm's real China address, and probably (fake) signed using the name of one of the firm's actual partners. With wiring instructions, of course, for where Jolene should deposit her money, including Jolene-specific reference numbers so she can feel comfortable that they won't lose track of her funds.

Thank goodness the Chinese authorities are being so helpful and understanding, Jolene would be led to think. *This nightmare will be over eventually...*

As soon as Jolene wired her life savings into the designated account, the thieves would wire the money out to another and it would disappear. Thank you very much, Jolene. What's more, for a long while Jolene might not even realize her life savings had been stolen, she would just call the "authorities" for updates and given the runaround.

To push the con even further, the thieves, if they were brazen enough, could try to continue scamming her by coming back and saying, say, she needs to pay escrow fees to the lawyers otherwise she'll get put to the back of the investigation pile or some other persuasive fiction.

Or they could just cut and run, significantly richer than when they started, have a laugh at Jolene's expense, and move on to the next victim(s).

Had they succeeded, for just a few day's work, from the thieves' perspective, this would have been time very well spent.

"I skyped them to let them know that I was aware of the trap and then blacklisted their contact in my Skype account," Jolene said.

The Play-by-Play Breakdown

In her eye-opening book, *The Confidence Game: Why We Fall For It... Every Time*[25], journalist and professional poker player Maria Konnikova breaks down the key steps in a well-crafted con. Jolene's antagonists played their scheme accordingly. Here's what played out in 10 stages:

1. The Put-Up. The Put-Up is all about the confidence man (known as the Grifter) selecting us as a victim (known as the Mark): learning what makes us who we are, what we hold dear, what moves us, and what leaves us cold.

Jolene was a Chinese national working in the U.S. in a big company with a good title and with good credentials (all of which can be discovered by browsing her Linkedin or other social media profiles). The grifters could easily find her home address, if her neighborhood is affluent or not, and even figure out if she rents or owns. At first glance, even if they were screening thousands of candidates a day, Jolene would make the cut as a person of interest.

2. The Play. The Play is the moment a grifter first hooks us and begins to gain our trust. And that is accomplished, first and foremost, through emotion. Once our emotions have been captured, once the con artist has cased us closely enough to identify what we want, feeling takes over from thinking, at least for the moment.

Jolene didn't want to go to jail, simple as that.

---

[25] Maria Konnikova, *The Confidence Game: Why We Fall for It . . . Every Time* (Penguin Books, 2017).

3. The Rope. The Rope is the alpha and omega of the confidence game: after targeting us as a mark and lowering our defenses through a "bit of fancy emotional footwork," Konnikova writes, it's time for the actual persuasive pitch. An alpha proposal, increasing the appeal of something, is the more frequent con. The omega proposal decreases resistance from another angle. In the alpha, the grifter does what he or she can to make their proposition, whatever it may be, more attractive. They rev up the fictitious opportunity's backstory – why something is such a wonderful opportunity, why you (the mark) are the perfect person to do it, how much everyone will gain, and the like. In the omega, you (yes, You, not the grifter) make a request or offer seem so easy as to be a no-brainer – why wouldn't I do this? What do I have to lose? This juxtaposition is called the approach-avoidance model of persuasion: you can convince me of something by making me want to approach it and decreasing any reasons I might have to avoid it.

In Jolene's situation, the "nice" policemen on the phone were willing to help investigate her claims of innocence in the massive fraud case about to ruin her life. Of course, she was innocent, 100 percent innocent in fact, Jolene would insist. How can she make these people believe her?

4. The Tale. When the Tale is told – that is, we're told how we, personally, will benefit – it's no longer really being told to us. We are the ones who are now doing the telling. A good confidence man has been working his way up to this very moment, the moment when "Too good to be true" turns into "Actually, it makes perfect sense": He convinces the mark to believe "I am exceptional, and I deserve it. It's not too good to be true; it is exactly what I had coming to me. The changes may be less than 1%, but then again, I'm a less than 1% kind of person."

Jolene knew she was innocent, she just had to wait for others to see so too.

5. The Convincer. The Convincer makes it seem like you're winning and everything is going according to plan. You're getting money on your investment. Your wrinkles are disappearing and your weight is dropping. The horse you bet on, both literal and figurative, is coming in a winner. The Tale made us fully aware of our own exceptional nature, and precisely what now seems to transpire: we are indeed justified in putting our initial trust in the game. No self-respecting con artist is complete fluff. There needs to be something real to anchor the whole thing. Just for a moment, the grifter needs his mark to feel as if he is holding a winning ticket.

Jolene, fortunately, stopped herself before reaching this point by discussing the situation with her friends, who helped recalibrate reality. If she hadn't, the con would likely have continued as follows:

6. The Breakdown. From the con man's perspective, this is the ideal moment to make a killing: pull the plug just when your mark is at his most convinced. The mark has already tasted victory and lauded himself on his discernment and prowess. He is already hooked. If the grifter lets him keep winning, it doesn't do him any additional good. Everything that goes to the mark, after all, is less for the con man. Instead, what if the grifter now makes the mark lose? At least a bit? In other words, what do we do when reality suddenly doesn't match the expectancy we've built?

The fake cops might tell Jolene that the prosecutor doesn't believe her innocence and is now investigating her even harder. Whatever the breakdown, Jolene would receive some bad news to make her panic and fear increase dramatically, making her even more desperate to resolve this nightmare.

7. The Send. This is the part of the con where the victim is recommitted, asked to invest increasingly greater money, time and resources into the con artist's scheme.

In Jolene's case, the con men/fake police might have come back to Jolene and claimed they discovered she had other money she's "hiding" from them, forcing her to sell other assets and adding the proceeds into her checking account. Or maybe she'll have to pony up, say, $20,000 for advance legal fees.

8. The Touch. The con finally comes to its fruition and the mark is completely, irrevocably fleeced. The mark has been taken for all she has. The grifter has gotten all that he is after and is ready to disappear from our lives.

Had Jolene wired her life savings into the fake escrow account, the grifters would have won.

9. The Blow-Off. According to Konnikova, once the con man grabs the prize, the mark has to be gotten out of the way as quickly as possible.

The Blow-Off is often the final step of the con, the grifter's smooth disappearance after the game has been played out.

Jolene would suddenly find herself unable to contact the fake police, the Skype number no longer picks up, her increasingly frantic messages are not returned. If she then decided to call the police station's listed phone number, she would be told by the real police that there's no Inspectors Li, Zhang or Xia, or prosecutor Sun who work there. (Or maybe people with those names actually do work there but they're not the imposters Jolene had been speaking to, their own identities had been stolen by the scammers).

10. The Fix. If the mark is not complacent, there's one more step the con man may take: the Fix, when the grifters put off the involvement of law enforcement to prevent marks from making their complaints official.

If the grifters decide not to blow off Jolene, they could easily drag their conversations out for months, maybe years, because investigations take time. Lots of time, they could credibly claim. But don't worry, Jolene, they're working on it and it's looking promising, just be patient...

What to Do if This Happens to You (Yes, YOU!)

If this were a movie, the kickoff to this con would probably be given an overly-dramatic name. Shock and Awe. The 180 (turn the mark upside down). Maybe the Gut Punch. Whatever it would be called, the goal is to throw the target into such a panic that they do, in fact, stop thinking logically. The mark becomes 100 percent reactive, trying to make sense of a situation that simply doesn't make sense. Here are some important steps that can save you from becoming a Blown-Off Mark.

Don't solve your problems alone. There's strength in numbers. Too many con men, con women, and con persons are well-trained in emotional and psychological manipulation. They don't even have to be cyber-scammers. Think about that one relative you know who sponges off all your other family members, all the time. Moving from one person to the next and then, after exhausting the patience, money or kindness of every family member (which may take months or even years to squeeze everyone), the manipulative family member goes full circle and mooches off the first person again with a new story about turning a new leaf, if only he or she could catch a little break or bit of help. In Jolene's situation, the absurdity of the story only made sense to an outsider, in this case Sam and Diego.

Google everything, then Google it again. Malcolm Gladwell, the prolific writer and researcher, noted that choking is about thinking too much, panic is about thinking too little. Jolene, like most anyone would do, let emotion lead the way.

In his insightful book, *Deep Survival, Who Lives Who Dies & Why / True Stories of Miraculous Endurance & Sudden Death*[26], Laurence Gonzales says that turning fear into focus in the first act of a survivor. At least 75 percent of people caught in a catastrophe either freeze or simply wander in a daze, according to some psychologists. They can't think, they can't act correctly. When the United State attacked Hiroshima and Nagasaki with atomic bombs, the Japanese noticed the same phenomenon among their survivors. They named it burabura, which means "do-nothing sickness."

According to Gonzales, the French author, journalist and aviator Antoine de Saint-Exupéry (who also wrote the classic children's book *The Little Prince*) observed that, in the heat of a crisis, the only thought you can allow yourself concerns your next correct action.

A simple online search by her more objective friends found the clarity that Jolene missed and could see how things simply didn't make logical sense. Police don't tell people to liquidate their assets.

Call a lawyer. If Jolene's identity had truly been stolen to send passports to China and if someone opened bank accounts in her name to defraud others, legal representation would be incredibly important. Any half-decent attorney would have or should have seen through the con in the first consultation. Certainly, a lawyer should have stopped her from wiring her money to an "escrow" account if the con got that far.

Even if a person's first lawyer contact isn't knowledgeable in the subject in question, lawyers refer clients to other lawyers all the time. The

---

[26] Laurence Gonzales, *Deep Survival: Who Lives, Who Dies, and Why* (W. W. Norton & Company, 2017).

first legal contact should be able to direct the potential victim to another lawyer or law firm that can help. If someone doesn't know any people in the legal profession to ask, they can contact a local firm they find on Google and request an initial phone consultation.

Jolene was warned by the Chinese officials not to discuss her case with anyone but without going into excessive detail, Jolene would have been able to provide a general idea of the problem, then determine if the lawyer she found might be suitable to advise her.

Granted, hiring a lawyer costs money. It might even cost thousands for the initial conversations, but in Jolene's case that cost would have been a fraction of what she was about to be robbed of, a relatively small cost compared to losing her life savings. And even if she wasn't going to be swindled by the grifters, if this were real you bet she'd want a lawyer on call if the Chinese authorities actually were investigating her.

The Aftermath

Jolene said, "I mean, I honestly think that if this happened to me [again], I probably would have fallen into this trap again. Like, I don't know at what juncture would I have chosen to take a different action rather than maybe contacting [my friends] earlier?"

She contacted the real authorities in China, including the ChangNing police to let them know criminals were impersonating them. The police aren't likely to catch these grifters (let alone even know who they are) but it is worthwhile and important to report these crimes so authorities are aware of the severity, extent, and new variations of cybercrime. And it probably gave her a very small amount of comfort knowing she reported the scammers to real law enforcement authorities.

Jolene, not surprisingly, is more wary of her online activity. She did wonder if there were support groups for people who had experiences like hers, and searched a bit, but then moved on.

Jolene ultimately emerged lucky. Although she managed not to be robbed of all her savings, Jolene liquidated her portfolios in a down stock market and incurred tax implications as well. "Only" selling at a loss and owing the IRS is a perverse silver lining in Jolene's storm cloud, but she'll take it. An expensive lesson learned but fortunately not a devastating one.

Jolene wanted to share her story to make the public better informed, in the hope that her expensive lesson learned will be valuable in protecting others.

Chapter 11 – Encrypt Your Devices

Encrypting your devices and communications will keep your information private from prying eyes, whether they be run-of-the-mill hackers to more organized actors including law enforcement.

What encrypting your devices won't do

If you have spyware already running on your computer or phone and it's stolen, the spyware hacker (who could be different from the person who stole your computer) might already be watching your activities and stealing your information. Encryption doesn't stop them because they're not trying to read your drive outside of your computer system, they're already in it. Nevertheless, encrypting your devices, if it's not already set up by default, provides important peace of mind should your devices ever go missing.

Here's how you can check:

Computers and laptops

Apple MacBooks

Apple's more recent MacBooks (sold after 2018) with the Apple T2 Security Chip have built-in encryption so, provided your computer requires a startup password, you're all set.

Older MacBooks rely on FileVault to encrypt data. You can check if your computer is secured by going into System Preferences, click Security & Privacy, click the FileVault tab, and then click Turn On FileVault.

Microsoft Windows

Windows uses BitLocker to secure a computer's hard drives. In Settings, search for "Encryption" or "BitLocker" and follow the instructions. BitLocker's setup will provide you with an encryption key (a long string of characters) and give you the option to save a copy of that information. Save copies in both digital and printed format. I have three secure locations where I store my confirmation codes both physically on paper (filed away neatly in my personal cyber security binder), on a USB thumb drive for that sole purpose, and on a cloud backup. I am assuming that when I do actually need to use that, it will likely be in a moment of high stress so I want to have this critical information available to me without having to remember too hard where I stored it.

Phones and tablets

Encryption on a phone works the same way. An average attacker (that is, a non-government intelligence agency) won't (usually) be able to plug in to access the data without the encryption key. More often than not, phone thieves might be interested in factory-resetting or wiping your phone and selling the device, but it makes sense to protect your information.

Also, if you haven't yet set up a **passcode or PIN** to unlock your phone, this is the time to do so. In the Settings menu, look at your Security or Display/Screen Lock settings (the wording may be different depending on your device) and set a reasonably challenging passcode or PIN. You should set your phone to require a passcode or PIN at startup, as well as when waking the phone from sleep or after a brief period of inactivity. I set my phone to require a PIN after 10 minutes of inactivity. Without a passcode or PIN to protect your phone, a thief would be able to have full access to your data anyway so encryption would be useless.

iPhones and iPads

Apple's iPhones by default encrypt their data when their screens are locked, provided the iPhone requires a passcode or Touch ID to unlock. If you don't have a passcode or Touch ID set on your phone, it's important to add one (or both) to ensure your data is protected against theft should someone acquire your device.

Android phones

To see if your phone is encrypted, go into the phone's Settings and search for the word "Encrypted." Here you'll see that this phone is already encrypted. If yours is not, turn on Encryption and follow the prompts to secure your device. And make sure your phone requires a passcode or PIN to unlock.

Chapter 12 – Block, Remove, Backup, and Restore

Things to avoid getting on your devices:

Viruses, malware, spyware, ransomware

Ways to avoid being infected with the above:

Install an antivirus program and a malware removal tool

Ways to protect your data in case you do get infected

Backup your files constantly

Empty your trash

To start with, let's quickly review some terms to be clear:

A **virus** spreads from computer to computer, installing code that will affect how your device operates with potential to cause serious damage such as corrupting important data or destroying files. **Malware** disrupts, damages or permits access to a device or an entire system (such as a network). **Spyware** monitors your activity and collects your information such as bank account details, or usernames and passwords. **Ransomware** blocks access to a computer or device until money is paid for its release, with the risk that ransom gets paid but no release is made in return.

In summary, these are really annoying things that exist to make a victim's life miserable.

Computer systems have basic levels of protection built in, but the real world has shown that persistent hackers, scammers and miscreants still frequently find ways to infiltrate computers, devices and entire systems. They can become nuisances or wreak full-on havoc. The time and sometimes minor dollar cost to practice thoughtful habits more than make up for the risk, frustration and potential loss of valuable work and data from disruptions, data corruption or targeted attacks against you.

The quick and easier solution

Install a comprehensive protection package such as Norton 360 Deluxe.

Norton 360 Deluxe

For comprehensive protection for your online activities, the short answer is to purchase and install Norton 360 Deluxe. Norton 360 Deluxe provides protection for up to five PCs, Macs, smartphones or tablets. It features a wide suite of protections, 100GB of cloud backup, password manager and other useful bells and whistles.

I think this is one of the most robust solutions out there when installed. I personally use Norton 360 Deluxe for my personal and professional lives, as well as my family's online protection. The price for the software subscription is about $40 annually to protect five computers or mobile devices.

Alternatively, if you are willing to put the time and effort into assembling your own defenses, at a minimum you should install an antivirus scanner and malware removal tool. The below publishers offer free and premium versions.

Add an antivirus scanner

Antivirus programs are real-time scanners to detect quickly the presence of malicious files trying to infect your device, or finding baddies already on your device. A good antivirus program also helps protect against ransomware from infecting your computer and phishing attempts from going through. Antivirus programs find and block bad problems but don't remove them.

BitDefender Antivirus and malware removal

https://www.bitdefender.com/solutions/free.html

Bitdefender's Antivirus free version also includes malware removal so this is a good 2-for-1 solution.

AVG Antivirus

https://www.avg.com/x

AVG free version blocks viruses and malware, but doesn't remove existing malware.

Avast Antivirus

https://www.avast.com/

Avast like the above offers real-time virus protection.

Add a malware removal program

Malware removal can quarantine, isolate and remove spyware, ransomware and other malware. Windows and Apple have anti-virus and antispyware security built into their platforms but there's always a possibility malware can slip through onto your computer. Fortunately, there are numerous free and paid solutions that can scan your devices for programs that mean to do you harm. The paid upgrades will allow you to schedule automated scans of your device. Here are some of the most popular:

BitDefender Antivirus and malware removal

https://www.bitdefender.com/solutions/free.html

As mentioned above, BitDefender can remove malware as well as block viruses from infecting your computer.

Malwarebytes Anti-Malware

https://www.malwarebytes.com/

SuperAntiSpyware

https://www.superantispyware.com/

Microsoft Safety Scanner

https://docs.microsoft.com/en-us/windows/security/threat-protection/intelligence/safety-scanner-download

Set up automatic backups

The best way to protect yourself from ransomware, should it slip past your antivirus and malware removal protections, is to have your device and important files backed up continually as changes are made to files. This can be done automatically in the background so you don't even have to pay attention to it once it's been set up properly. You can backup your valuable info (as well as cat memes or anything else that gives you pleasure) onto a hard disk that is separate from your computer or in the cloud. I do both, and suggest you do the same.

Backing your files onto a **separate hard drive** is convenient, in that the spare drive is usually in your physical possession. If you need to retrieve files quickly, this is convenient albeit not a foolproof solution. Physical drives can get lost, stolen, corrupted or destroyed depending on how bad of a day you might be having. But when they work, they're nice to have on hand.

Cloud storage can take many different forms. Your device likely offers some free storage, and can likely be upgraded affordably for more capacity.

Backblaze

This is my primary backup service, which has worked seamlessly to protect my files for years. I regularly check the status and it consistently remains up to date, having backed up my most recent files just minutes earlier. 1TB of storage costs $6 monthly as if this publication date, and files are backed up continuously. Retrieving files from Backblaze is also convenient.

Apple iCloud

Apple's iCloud works on both Apple devices (iPads, iPhones, Macs, etc.) and PCs. Apple provides 5GB of free storage, and can be increased to 50GB ($1 monthly), 200GB ($3 monthly) or 2TB ($10 monthly)

Microsoft OneDrive

You can back up a maximum of 5GB of files in OneDrive for free, or up to 1 TB with a Microsoft 365 subscription. The price for a one-user Microsoft 365 license is about $70 annually, or a family subscription for up to six people is $100 annually, both of which include Microsoft Office programs.

Google Drive

Google provides 15GB of free space to use across Google Drive, Gmail, and Google Photos. For more storage, you can upgrade to Google One, which offers 100GB (currently $20 annually), 200GB ($30 annually) all the way up to 10TB of storage ($600 annually, but that's a lot of storage to use). Both Android and iOS users can use Google Drive's free 15GB of storage for Google Photos, Google Calendar and Google Contacts.

Long-term storage with Amazon Glacier.

Amazon S3 Glacier and S3 Glacier Deep Archive are secure, durable, and lower-cost Amazon storage for data archiving and long-term backup. Their interface takes some learning, but it is quite a failsafe backup to archive your important files.

What to do if your Windows or MacOS fails

Sometimes either a virus or other issue can cause your computer to fail on startup. To protect yourself, it's a very good idea to know how to restore your operating system.

Create a Windows recovery drive

A recovery drive helps reinstall the Windows operating system in case of hardware failure and is different from a regular file backup. It's a good idea to create a recovery drive. That way, if your PC ever experiences a major issue such as hardware failure, you'll be able to use the recovery drive to reinstall Windows. Windows updates itself to improve security and PC performance periodically so it is recommended to recreate the recovery drive annually. Personal files and any applications that did not come with your PC will not be backed up. You can find instructions in Windows settings and will need a USB thumb drive with at least 16 gigabytes of memory.

Apple's macOS Recovery reinstalls Mac operating systems

The utilities in macOS Recovery help you restore your Mac from a Time Machine, reinstall macOS, get help online, repair or erase a hard disk. macOS Recovery is part of the built-in recovery system of your Mac. You can start up from macOS Recovery and use its utilities to recover from certain software issues or take other actions on your Mac. If you have hardware issues requiring you to start up from macOS Recovery, turn on your Mac and immediately press and hold these two keys: Command (⌘) and R. In Recovery mode you can still use Safari to browse the web and find help for your Mac. Links to Apple's support website are included.

Sanitize your trash

When you delete a file on your PC or Mac, the file is placed in the recycle bin or trash folder. When you empty the recycling or trash, the file disappears from the folder but in reality still remains on your computer. It's hidden from sight and will remain until another file needs the disk space where it resides and overwrites it. Until it is overwritten, deleted files can be recovered should someone want to know what's really on your computer. To completely remove your deleted files, they will have to be overwritten with the 0s and 1s of a new file.

Disk cleaning programs can remove deleted files completely. They also clean up junk and temporary files that may be taking up disk space and slowing your computer. The free versions typically require you to run the cleaning manually, and paid versions offer regularly scheduled cleanups for convenience.

Ccleaner for Windows

https://www.ccleaner.com/

 CleanMyMac

CleanMyMac for Macs

https://cleanmymac.com/

Chapter 13 – On the Road

In addition to securing your physical assets as discussed in *Chapter 1 – Secure Your Assets*, when you're traveling or working on the road there are several simple but highly practical steps you can take to secure both your privacy and your possessions.

Use your phone's hotspot whenever possible

Granted, don't stream all eight seasons of Game of Thrones unless you have a really good data plan, but using your phone's hotspot is a better route than using public WiFi whenever possible. It's important to have a robust, hard-to-crack hotspot password just like you (now) do on your home WiFi so nearby hackers (who intentionally hang around public gathering places) can't gain access.

And name your hotspot something that can't be used to identify you personally.

Know whom you're connecting to

It's not unusual for hackers to offer their own public WiFi to unsuspecting users, with official-sounding names such as Terminal 4 WiFi or even simply Free WiFi. People who connect will have their information monitored and stolen. If in doubt when seeking public WiFi, look for printed signs or ask the customer service personnel for the name of the facility's official WiFi.

Virtual Private Networks (VPNs) explained in 30 seconds

To explain what a virtual private network (or VPN) is, let's start by explaining what not having a VPN is like. Imagine browsing the internet (along with everyone else) is like cars on a public highway, going from Point A (your computer) to Point B (whatever website you're looking for). Anyone else on that road, if they're paying close enough attention, can follow your car and monitor your activity – what you look like, your license plate number, where you go, what you do. They can stalk you and make your life difficult, or they can steal your vehicle when you're not looking. You and your activity on the public highway (or public WiFi) are exposed to those who are looking to track you.

A VPN is like your own private, underground tunnel from your garage that connects directly to your destination, hidden from prying eyes. A VPN helps you get from Point A (your computer) to Point B (whatever website you're looking for) and back without other people being able to see where you're going or monitoring your activity.

If you're using a public WiFi network, say at a coffee shop or airport or anywhere in between, hackers can stalk your browsing, capture your passwords, see your credit card information if you're shopping, and any other number of your secrets. VPNs are not foolproof, especially if you're trying to stay under the radar to prevent your government or law enforcement monitoring your activity. But a good VPN service is pretty good against non-state-sponsored hackers.

Fortunately, there are a number of easy-to-use VPN services (all of which require a subscription) that make using a VPN in your day-to-day activity almost seamless. They can turn on automatically and run silently in the background. I use my VPN every day, whether I'm at home or outside, both on my laptop and mobile phone. Since I subscribed to my service, I like having the additional layer of protection and anonymity at all times.

Some reasons to use a VPN

- Hides your browsing history from prying eyes,
- Hides your IP address and location,
- Protects your data (such as personal information, credit cards and logins) from being stolen, and
  - Bypass government censorship in oppressive regimes

Downsides of using a VPN

- Good VPNs charge a fee,
- May result in marginally slower internet speed, and
- Can't always connect to all websites. Some sites will not allow access from foreign countries, for instance, online banking or entertainment streaming services may not allow access if it appears you're located somewhere they're not operating.

Do not use free VPN services

Oftentimes they include advertising on their app, which defeats the purpose of staying anonymous.

Here are some VPN service providers to consider. Each charge anywhere from around $5 to $13 per month, some may offer coverage for multiple devices, and some will have cheaper annual plans. Usually you can try a trial version to see if you like their platform.

PureVPN

https://www.purevpn.com/

Private Internet Access

https://www.privateinternetaccess.com/

NordVPN

https://nordvpn.com/

Norton Secure VPN

https://us.norton.com/products/norton-secure-vpn

I **travel overseas** fairly regularly and I've found it helps to have multiple VPN services available to me. Some can be used on a month-by-month subscription so I'll pre-pay for a backup VPN in advance of my travel in case my primary VPN runs into issues in a foreign country. To get access to, say, my Gmail account when I'm in some Asian countries, I need to use a VPN to get past that country's blockers (that's happened to me in China). For about $4 a month during my travels, having a backup piece of mind is well worth it for me.

Extend your reach

Don't leave devices unattended in public, including when you leave them to recharge, as they could be stolen or tampered with. Either use a really long charge cord (such as a 10-foot USB cord) that can reach from the public outlet to where you are sitting, or a lightweight extension cord so you can always be close to electricity. Having an extension cord also gives you some more outlets if people are vying for the precious two wall outlets available. You can always share your outlets if you feel so inclined.

Track your bags

I put a Tile tracking device in my briefcase and a second one in my smaller computer case that I sometimes use. I also put a Tile credit card-sized tracker in my wallet for good measure. These devices are extremely small and easily concealed in the folds or pockets of your bags. Tile sells their devices in multi-packs that are reasonably inexpensive, and the Tile app is easy to set up and use.

Each Tile needs to be within the standard Bluetooth range of a device that has location services to communicate its location to the app. This means

Tile cannot track objects as they move in real-time, unless there is a device within range moving with it, which is where Tile's crowdsourced network can be valuable. Whenever a person who is running the Tile app on their phone passes within range of your Tile, their device will automatically and anonymously update your app with your Tile's most recent location. You'll then receive a notification of your Tile's last known location so you can journey back there to try to find and retrieve it.

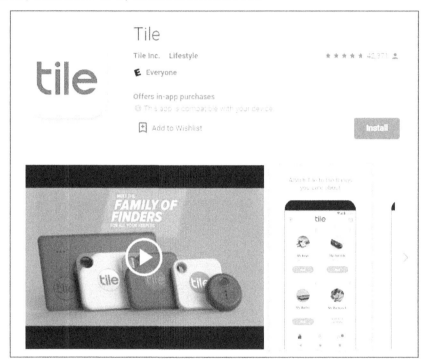

Tether your bags

Traveling is stressful, particularly when using public transportation – airports, trains, even ferries. First there's the often-lengthy waiting periods before boarding, then the ride itself, then going through hectic arrival processes. When I travel, I am always technology-heavy with computers and often high-end camera equipment that, even though I have insurance, losing my gear in transit would probably crush my ability to work on whatever project I'm traveling for. I also tend to travel with multiple bags in hand (in addition to whatever I had to check underneath if flying) so being ever-vigilant can get tiring. I try to set up checks and balances against my tendency to not pay attention all the time.

If I'm parking myself at a table or seat waiting for my departure, I'll often string an inexpensive luggage cable through the handles of my bags to keep them together. (If you don't already have one, these can be easily purchased at the newsstands or shops of whatever terminal you are in). I like how lightweight and convenient these cable locks can be, and all I'm trying to do is make it hard if someone tries to walk off with one of my bags. By being linked together, pulling on one bag will cause enough of a scene that – even if I had fallen asleep in my chair – I would be woken up by the disruption.

If I'm parking myself at a coffee shop to work for an hour, I'll do the same. If I don't have a luggage cable with me I'll make sure to step my leg through the shoulder strap of my bag. Or I may unclip one end of the shoulder strap, put it through an opening in my chair, and clip it secure. I'll unlink it when I'm ready to leave. Either method is discrete and allows me to focus on my work.

Section III – Online Self-Defense

Section Table of Contents

Topic	Page
Chapter 14 – Social Media Discretion	155
Separate work from pleasure	155
TMI - Too much information	156
A selfie is worth a million words	*157*
Case studies in photo privacy	158
Be healthy and stealthy	171
Metadata = Metadangerous	172
Watch for social media phishing	174
Use a burner phone number	175
Specific social media privacy settings	177
Chapter 15 – Defend Against Trolls	179
Immediate steps to take	180
Collaborate	182
Spread the word	182
Document the full situation	182
Contact local law enforcement	183
Do not be intimidated	184
Defining Online Abuse by PEN America	185
Glossary of Terms	186
Report harassment to social media platforms	202
Search engines might not remove harassment	225
Set up Google Alerts	226
Use social media for good. Your good.	226
Research your troll's images	230
Reverse image lookups	230
Document the information you uncover	235

Chapter 16 – Non-Consensual Pornography / Revenge Porn 239
    Half a million people have seen me naked 239
  Steps to try to delete your leaked photos 242
  Speak with trained professionals 243
  Report threats to law enforcement 245
  Remove your content from the internet 247
  Contact the website owner 247
  Remove your images from search engines 248
  Keep sensitive photos in a vault..................................254
    Perspective from an advocate 257

Chapter 17 – Protecting Teens and Children........................259
    Sextortion leads to crushing real-life consequences........259
  Don't be afraid to call for help 262
  Sextortion: What parents need to know.....................262
    Sextortion: Ask your kids to read this 266
  Social media awareness 269
  Consider doing these 6 steps now 270
  The National Sex Offender Public Website 274
  Age-appropriate education for younger children 275

Chapter 18 – Removing Your Personal Info from the Internet 277
  Have Google blur your home from Street View Maps...............277
  Remove your info from data brokers manually 280
  Consider using a paid removal service to get the job done........282

Chapter 19 – Identity Theft 285
  It is far from a victimless crime 285
  So, what to do? 287
  Identity theft recovery steps.......................................289

This section covers important safeguards about

- Social media discretion
- Defending against trolls
- Non-consensual pornography / revenge porn
- Protecting teens and children
- Removing your personal Info from the internet
- Identity theft

These are serious issues that are important for internet users to be aware of, and there can be severe, sometimes fatal, repercussions from suffering online abuse. The goal here is to help readers understand the potential magnitude and damage these online threats can inflict on you, your loved ones, or your acquaintances.

Importantly, these chapters include actionable steps that you can take to defend against online attacks, both in advance of any unpleasant situation as well as in real time should you be faced with online harassment.

The best online offense is a good online defense. These next chapters provide concrete steps to protect yourself.

Chapter 14 – Social Media Discretion

Thanks for sharing

It's so lovely that you posted your vacation photos from today on social media. You look fabulous. And now I know that, I can go rob your home since you are thousands of miles away and possibly not returning for days.

Honestly, no matter how good a time you are having on vacation or at that conference, there's negligible value (in the bigger picture) to be gained by broadcasting your whereabouts to the general public. #ComeStealMyStuff

Announcing you're attending a family wedding is even better, because that signals most or all of your relatives are away too.

What's more, if someone is posting fabulous photos of their luxury (or at least expensive) getaway, odds are they probably have some equally expensive items in their home that can be stolen while they're away. If you want proof, search #vacation on Facebook, Twitter, Instagram, or TikTok and see for yourself who isn't home right now. Trolls and thieves can easily follow thousands of people within driving distance of their home base, waiting to make trouble when opportunity presents (or posts) itself.

Sharing is great, it keeps us connected to others, but it would be wise to wait until you return home to post your vacation photos. There may not be the immediate endorphin rush of your contacts replying with nice comments, but they will still come eventually.

Separate work from pleasure

Consider having two separate social media accounts on your platforms that separate your personal life from your work life, keeping both sets of contacts apart. If an attacker gains access to one of your accounts, the other side of your life can be better shielded from exploitation.

TMI - Too much information

Simply put, don't ever post anything that can be used against you. Have an opinion you are really emotional about? Take a long pause and choose your words thoughtfully before hitting send. Want to share a tweet to voice your displeasure at someone or something? Honestly, the world would probably be a slightly happier place if we took a deep breath and a pause.

And once you put it out there, it really is there probably forever.

Don't believe me? Go to **AllMyTweets.net** and grab the last 3,200 tweets (that's three thousand two hundred!) from any user account. Journalists may use this site when an individual becomes a person of interest for whatever reason, whether for a good reason or naught reason. Sites like this can capture a person's lengthy online history much faster than that person in question might be able to delete their posts. Better to not create the tenuous situation to begin with by being reserved in words and actions online.

https://www.allmytweets.net/connect/

Consider deleting old social media posts or using a service that will delete past tweets. Abusers will often resurface old posts you have made as a way to discredit you.

A selfie is worth a million words

In 2019, Japanese pop star Ena Matsuoka was attacked and assaulted outside her home by a crazed fan. The man was able to identify her home address by analyzing a selfie the victim posted. More specifically, the singer took what appeared to be a simple selfie photo outdoors, with no blatantly obvious indications of her location. The stalker zoomed in on the reflection in her eyes, where he was able to find reflections of buildings and a street sign. The man went to the location and waited for Matsuoka. The assailant attacked her, dragged her into a secluded area, and assaulted her. Fortunately, she eventually escaped. The Tokyo Metropolitan Police eventually arrested the man.[27]

---

[27] K Thor Jensen, "Stalker Finds Japanese Idol's Home from Reflections in Her Pupils.," *Newsweek*, October 10, 2019, https://www.newsweek.com/stalker-finds-idol-reflection-pupils-1464373.

Case studies in photo privacy

To illustrate how much subtle information photographs can reveal, here are some examples of what can be found in images people might post. Of course, there are a myriad of variations on what may be in a person's collection of photos across different social media accounts. Looking at a single photo may reveal elements of a person's information. A hacker, stalker, or troll would likely compile a range of clues from a target's accounts to compose a comprehensive profile of that person's habits, interests, and activities.

For all the following examples, I used publicly available stock photos which are intended for commercial use. The individuals in the photos gave their respective photographers permission to use their images for publication. There is no intention to reveal personal information on any individuals in these photographs.

An online stalker could easily magnify photos to search for details. In the following examples you will be asked to inspect the photos for clues to their location or other details. In the answers, I will provide details on what closer inspection can reveal in each photo.

While Google is not great for protecting your personal privacy, their search tools otherwise are top notch. Google Maps, including their Street View and Satellite View features, and Google Earth are extremely powerful tools to do reconnaissance, as you'll see in these examples.

The purpose of these next exercises are not to scare you into never posting photos, but to make you well aware of how images can be manipulated to work against your best and safest interests.

Study #1

Where was this photograph of these two women taken?

(Photo by Gabriella Clare Marino on Unsplash)

Answers on next page.

Study #1 Answers

Zooming in on the top center of the photograph reveals the street behind them is named Della Posta Vecchia.

Initially, it was unclear exactly what the street name was as the letters were blurry. When I was searching for that name using Google, Google conveniently auto-completed the proper spelling after I entered the first two words. Having Google's suggested spelling, I was then able to confirm that was the street name in the photo.

Searching Google Maps for Della Posta Vecchia provided a handful of cities with that street name. Using Google Maps Street View I was able to locate the specific city.

Study #2

What can you determine about where this photo was taken?

(Photo by Henry Ivany on lifeofpix.com)

Answers on next page.

Study #2 Answers

Zooming in on the reflection on the roof and windshield, you can see more details of the building and sky above. This photo appears to be taken on the roof deck of a parking structure, next to the building in the reflection.

The building façade itself appears to be a lighter color on the lower portion, and darker on the upper portion. Or they are two buildings, one is short and lighter in color, the other is taller with more windows. You can also see the patterns, relative sizes, and patterns of different parts of the building or buildings.

If you knew which city or town this photo might have been taken in (for example, if you knew what city the person in the photo lived in), you could use the process of elimination to try to pinpoint this location. Searching for "parking garage" on Google Maps, then looking at locations using Street View and Google Earth to find the building(s) in the reflection would help narrow down possibilities.

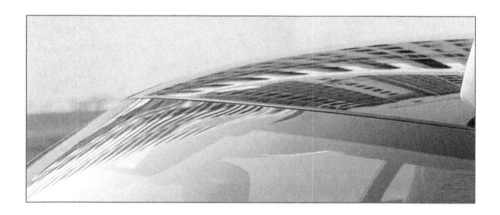

Study #3

What details can you deduce from this photo?

(Photo by Chloe Kal on Pexels)

Answers on next page.

Study #3 Answers

Zooming in on the reflection on his sunglasses is revealing.

You can see that a woman with shoulder-length hair, who appears to be wearing a short-sleeved shirt and a skirt, is taking his photo. She is using what appears to be a digital camera based on how she is holding the device in both hands and the position of her arms. (Someone taking a photo with their smartphone would not hold it that way.)

Directly behind the man is a building or buildings directly and an adjoining wall. In the sunglasses reflection there appears to be a light-colored, stepped wall and an in-ground pool. There are large trees on the other side of the wall.

If you knew the general location where the man lived, a search using Google Maps in Satellite View (to give a bird's eye view of the area) might help locate the buildings and enclosed pool area bordered by trees on the other side of the wall. Google Maps Street View could show you the front of the location as well as the street address.

Study #4

What can you determine about where this man is located?

(Photo by Sina Khansari on Unsplash)

Answers on next page.

Study #4 Answers

The building he is in is painted a dark exterior color, and from the exterior wall it appears to have wood siding.

The balcony has a short wall, approximately, three feet high, and a metal safety railing above it.

The door and window to the balcony appear to have relatively large panes of glass, giving them a distinctive pattern that may be easy to identify from the street.

There appear to be tall trees in front of the balcony.

Not too far away, roughly 500 to 1000 feet away, is a tall building that appears to be at least 10 stories tall, likely taller. It is very wide with a sloped roof. From the look of it, it might be a hotel or possibly an apartment building.

Searching online based on the above information and other breadcrumbs collected on a target from other photos and sources could yield very accurate location information.

Study #5

What time of day was this photo taken?

What else can you determine about this location?

(Photo by Andrea Piacquadio on Pexels)

Answers on next two pages.

Study #5 Answers

Notice the angle of the sunlight on the stone blocks above the woman's head. That there is no sunlight at ground level would imply this photo was taken at dusk as the sun was beginning to set. The lower light would be blocked by the trees across the street. You might argue that this could also have been taken at sunrise, when the sun is also low. That's possible, but looking at the photo's context, including the woman's demeanor, it seems more likely that this would have been taken during the day rather than very early in the morning. It's an assumption to make, but not an unreasonable one.

Assuming this is, in fact, at dusk, then the sunlight on the wall would sugggest this side of the building faces west, the direction the sun sets. So if someone were looking for this location they would know which side of the street to look on, significantly reducing the number of places to search.

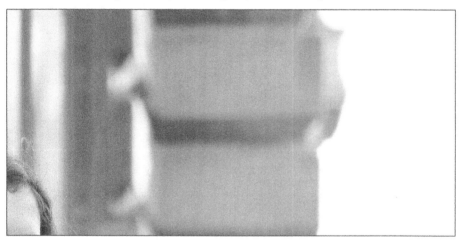

Answers continued on next page.

Study #5 Answers (continued)

Zooming in on the reflection on the glass window behind the woman's head reveals what appears to be a streetlamp, which may have a distinctive style. It appears to be an old-fashioned black streetlamp with glass panes.

If it's not a streetlamp, it is still likely distinctive enough that appearing in a search next to the building would confirm the location of the photograph.

Additionally...

You can easily make out the building's details including the architectural style and light-colored stone as well as the large plate glass windows at street level.

Across the street you can see the thin, tall trees lining the sidewalk. The street signs on the pole further down the street would help confirm the location if someone were looking for it.

Study #6

Where is this?

(Photo by Yogendra Singh on Pexels)

This photo was taken in India. If someone were broadly familiar with the region, there are some clues that might help identify this specific location.

The wide pathway is flat and well-maintained, clearly intended for people to walk on. The local trees and foliage can be researched if helpful. Also, the steep rock formations indicate this path was cut into the side of a hill or mountain.

Make note of what clues you can gather on the people in the photo. The adult, who appears likely to be male, is using a hiking stick. It appears to be a hiking stick rather than a walking cane because of the height of the stick. A walking cane would be shorter. Use of a hiking stick implies this is a long trail to walk on.

So, how did you do on these exercises?

Be healthy and stealthy

Consider taking these steps to reduce the amount of your personal information that's put out into the world.

Make your profile photo impersonal

On your social media accounts, consider using different images for each account that doesn't include your face so you're not immediately findable. If possible, use a non-personal screen name as well. You'll still be able to find your friends, but the general public may have an incrementally harder time tracking you down.

Disable location sharing

If someone truly needs to know where you are, they'll ask you. Otherwise you're giving unnecessary amounts of detail that provide little benefit and can show patterns should anyone desire to monitor your activity.

Don't check in

Think twice about posting your location consistently via checking in to restaurants or other locations. Avoid using "nearby friends" apps that consistently track your location.

Don't post your children

This recommendation will be controversial to some readers, but given the way social media can quickly turn toxic, I recommend not posting photos, stories, or other information on your children until they are older, at least older teenagers. Certainly, there's a natural tendency for parents to want to showcase their children's wonderful accomplishments to the world but the internet can be a fickle and sometimes unhealthy place.

Metadata = Metadangerous

Metadata means "data about data," and provides background details about an electronic file, including photos and videos. **Photo metadata is** information attached to an image file that may include the location where the photo was taken, date, time, and other information such as the names of people, companies, or products in the image. Also, captions, keywords, and headlines may be added to provide more detail on what the image shows. Photo metadata is also known as **Exchangeable Image File Format (or EXIF) data**.

Smartphones and digital cameras can automatically record location and date information, so be aware that a photo you share online may reveal much more about your activities than meets the eye.

Facebook, Instagram, Twitter scrub metadata

When people upload photos to Facebook, Instagram, or Twitter, the metadata is automatically removed before publishing, which is helpful.

Do be aware, however that the human factor can provide much more information than metadata may otherwise have provided. For example, friends tagging you in their photos, checking in to the location where the photo was taken, and commenting on the activity can be enormously revealing. What's more, reverse image searching may reveal similar photos taken in your location, and a determined stalker can connect the dots to your location.

Delete your photo's metadata before sharing

Photo editing programs such as **Adobe Photoshop** have tools for deleting an image's metadata if you are sharing images online on a platform that doesn't automatically scrub out metadata.

Signal

You can strip out metadata automatically by sending an image in Signal, and then saving the sent image under a new filename.

On Windows

Right click on the photo, open the **Properties**, go into **Details**, and click **Remove Properties and Personal Information**, and **Save** the image as a new copy.

On Macs

Open the photo using **Preview**, go to **Tools**, select **Show Inspector**, click the **Exif** tab and remove the data.

On Androids

Photo Exif Editor for Android devices allows you to view, modify and remove the EXIF data of your pictures. You can also change the location of the picture to anywhere you choose.

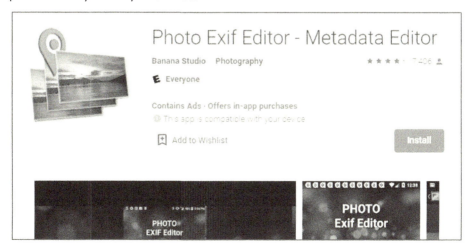

On iPhones

Photo Investigator for iOS devices lets you edit or remove location data, dates, and other information.

Watch for social media phishing

Facebook, Instagram, TikTok, and other social media platforms are easy avenues for distributing scams, malware, and phishing campaigns. Threats like these will always exist so be vigilant before clicking random links. Make sure they're coming from trustworthy sources, whether that be contacts, groups, or companies.

Use a burner phone number

With our incredible reliance on our cell phones, having one private number for family and key relationships and a different public number for the rest of the world – work, play, account contact information, shopping, bills, dating – can provide a buffer for your privacy. Rather than purchasing a second phone, burner phone apps can do the same job more affordably, sometimes requiring a monthly or annual fee but not requiring you to own a second device. Burner apps let you make and receive calls like a regular phone, send texts and other features.

Here are some of the most popular burner phone apps:

Google Voice

Google Voice will provide you with a free phone number through its app.

Burner App

https://www.burnerapp.com/

Hushed App

https://hushed.com/

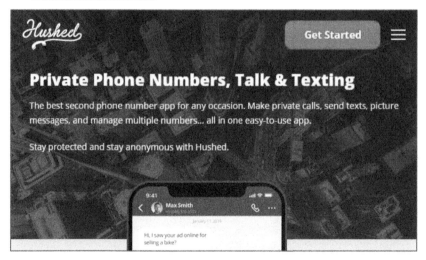

Specific social media privacy settings

Below are instructions on how to change the privacy settings of several social media sites. Other sites not included below likely have similar steps to change your settings. In general, it's best to allow only your friends, and friends of friends if you choose, to see your personal pages.

Note: Different site and apps may use either ••• or ⋮ or ≡ or some other symbol for the More Options menu. For purposes of simplicity in this guide, we'll be using ••• (called an ellipsis) as the general symbol for selecting the More Options menu, but it may vary with the above symbols depending on your computer or mobile device.

Facebook privacy settings

1. Only allow Friends of Friends to connect with you, not Everyone.
2. Set your privacy to reduce how people can look you up, by email or phone.
3. Restrict search engines from finding your timeline.
4. Turn off the option for people to review your past posts.
5. Check the setting requiring your permission before friends tag you in photos.
6. Block people who are not beneficial to your wellbeing.

Instagram privacy settings

1. Personal Instagram accounts can be set to either Public or Private. When someone wants to follow a Private account, they have to send a request to the account owner, who can either approve or deny their access.
2. Keep in mind that a Private account sharing on other social media, such as Twitter, may make their Instagram-private post visible on a public Twitter account.

3. If someone was already following you before you set your Instagram posts to Private and you don't want them to see your posts, you can block them.
4. People can still send a photo or video directly to you even if they're not following you.

Snapchat privacy settings

1. On the Camera screen, tap your profile icon at the top
2. Tap ⚙ to open **Settings**
3. Scroll down to the **Who Can...** section and tap **Contact Me**
4. Choose **My Friends** to make it so only your friends will be able to Snap and Chat you
5. Tap the **Back** button to update your privacy settings.

TikTok privacy settings

To make your TikTok private, tap the ••• in the upper right portion of the screen, and then navigate to **Privacy and Safety** and change your settings.

Twitter privacy settings

To make your tweets private, go to **Privacy and safety settings** and check **Protect my Tweets**.

Chapter 15 – Defend Against Trolls

"Isn't online harassment the price you pay for engaging with the internet?

"No, absolutely not. Everyone has the right to live a life free from any form of abuse and harassment and this concept does not suddenly fail to apply in the online world. Being online doesn't make a threat less real or a racist comment less hurtful and they should be held to the same standards as those of offline harassment. It is not your responsibility to accept harassment for using the internet; it is the responsibility of harassers not to harass you.

"Who experiences online harassment?

"According to a Pew Research Center survey, 40% of people have been harassed online and 73% of people witnessed someone else being harassed online. We know that folks from all walks of life experience and even perpetuate online harassment. However, when it comes to threats, women, people of color, and LGBTQ folks are disproportionately impacted. Of those who have experienced online harassment, 66% said their most recent incident occurred on a social networking site or app."

The above two questions were thoughtfully answered on the website HeartMob.com, which provides support to people being harassed online. [28]

People can fall victim to online abuse and trolling for any reason, and often for no reason. It's critical to be able to protect yourself as best as possible if strangers try to abuse, harass, and harm you online.

---

[28] "Join the Movement to End Online Harassment," HeartMob, https://www.iheartmob.org.

Journalists, due to their role in reporting on challenging and sometimes controversial issues, are particularly vulnerable to both real-world and online harassment. Abuse and threats from online trolls can often be extreme, with threats of real-world violence being an all-too-frequent reality for journalists around the world. Let's look at their playbook on defending from trolls, which can also be applied to many other situations.

Immediate steps to take

The Committee to Protect Journalists is an independent, nonprofit organization that promotes press freedom worldwide and defends the right of journalists to report the news safely and without fear of reprisal. The organization has issued guidelines to protect journalists, which are also highly applicable to victims generally. In summary:

1. **Consider your mental health.** It's common to struggle when trying to deal with a serious incident. Seeking support from peers or counselling early on can help. A personal support network is also extremely valuable to help with the feelings of isolation and being overwhelmed that situations like this cause.

2. **Don't read the trolls' comments.** That's what they want you to do, intentionally trying to upset, scare, and hurt you emotionally, psychologically, and even physically. Instead, have a trusted friend or colleague read them for you, and have them make you aware of what you need to know. Your friend can be a more objective filter, and buffer you from the emotional turmoil and fear the trolls hope to inflict upon you.

3. **Document everything**, keeping screenshots and records of any online harassment. Report the abuse to the social media company the threats are being made on. Documentation is important if you decide to contact law enforcement or press charges in the future.

4. **Block or mute abusers.** An abuser who is blocked will be informed they've been blocked, which may cause them to become more vitriolic, and open another account(s). An abuser will not know they've been muted and will continue directing their abuse, but into the endless void and not onto your screen. Block emails as well, or send them to a separate folder.

5. Make your family and/or close friends **aware of the situation**, and ask them to be cautious about the information they share online about themselves as well as you. Trolls often target family members.

6. **Inform your employer** if necessary, if you are concerned the person may contact you or your co-workers at your workplace.

7. If you are continuing to post online, make future posts **viewable only by friends (not the public)**. Disable replies in your posts. Be aware of the photos of you that exist online and how they may be able to be manipulated against you. Decide if you want to **delete or suspend** your social media accounts until the dust settles. Trolls will eventually move onto other targets, although it may take months or years.

8. Trolls will try to hack your accounts, make sure your social media and email **logins are secure**.

9. **Turn notifications off at night** so that you can have a mental break from being connected all the time. Keep your phone out of your bedroom at night.

10. Be aware that **paid trolls may be hired** to direct abuse toward a victim. Although it is difficult to separate from the emotional turmoil, recognize that the vitriol being aimed at you may not be personal.

11. **Set up Google Alerts** for your name, and spelling variations of your name, to keep apprised of any public posts that may involve you. Also consider setting up alerts for your family members. If being alerted may cause you undue stress, you can have a trusted person set up the alerts to be sent to their email instead. (Instructions are provided later in this chapter.)[29, 30]

---

[29] "Digital Safety: Protecting against Targeted Online Attacks," *Committee to Protect Journalists* (blog), September 28, 2020, https://cpj.org/2020/05/digital-safety-protecting-against-targeted-online-attacks/.

[30] "Psychological Safety: Online Harassment and How to Protect Your Mental Health," *Committee to Protect Journalists* (blog), September 4, 2019,

Collaborate

Even Batman had Alfred, his butler, and sometimes Robin to use as a sounding board. If you're going to go down this road of at least protecting yourself (which, obviously, I'm supportive of) and standing your ground (which I am also supportive of) make sure you do so in a rational manner. Cheap revenge doesn't get you far, but pursuing justice will.

Spread the word

If you have successfully identified the troll – with complete confirmation that individual is, without doubt, the antagonist – what do you do next? First consider filing a police report if the level of threat warrants it (and, in my opinion, your internal threshold to report a harasser should be set very, very low. You don't have to suffer abuse by anyone. It is your inalienable right to protect yourself at all costs.) Filing a police report also can be important documentation should the situation escalate further. After discussing it with your trusted, objective collaborator, consider whether it's appropriate to inform those with influence over the troll, such as their employer or school or even their parents.

Document the full situation

PEN America, a literature and human rights advocacy group, advises that when documenting instances of harassment, "ensure that you're saving all relevant evidence and not just the evidence that paints you in a favorable light. For example, if you contributed offensive dialogue or heated language to an online exchange that you're planning to document, be sure to include those aspects of the exchange, too. Though you may regret having said certain things, a failure to document all aspects of your harassment could end

---

https://cpj.org/2019/09/psychological-safety-online-harassment-emotional-health-journalists/.

up harming you if you ever end up in court. You don't have to prove you've reacted perfectly at every step to pursue your harasser."[31]

I recommend documenting information in multiple formats to ensure redundancy in your recordkeeping to prevent losing valuable evidence:

1. Take screenshots of web pages (instructions provided further in this chapter) and organize them into a computer folder (and subfolders as necessary to stay organized),
2. Save web pages as PDF files and organize documents in the folder(s) noted above, and
3. Print to physical paper and organize the pages in an evidence binder

Contact local law enforcement

If you feel that you are in immediate danger, consider calling 911.

Some victims may hesitate out of concern they might be "bothering" law enforcement or other authorities, but that is not the case. These are by no means the only reasons you might wish to turn to law enforcement for help. In these situations, I always recommend trusting your instincts, with an overabundance of caution. Even if reporting online harassment to your local precinct doesn't result in immediate action, it will establish a paper trail that might be needed later on.

In more general situations, the police are more likely to be able to help in some way with the following forms of online harassment. According to PEN America, you may want to consider contacting law enforcement when:

- You've received or been named in direct threats of violence (threats that suggest a time, place, or location are more likely to be taken seriously by law enforcement),
- An online abuser has published non-consensual, sexually-explicit images of you (more information on this type of

---

[31] "Documenting Online Harassment," PEN America, Online Harassment Field Manual, https://onlineharassmentfieldmanual.pen.org/documenting-online-harassment/.

harassment is provided in Chapter 16 – *Non-Consensual Pornography / Revenge Porn)*,

- You've been stalked via electronic communication, or
- You know your online harasser and wish to seek a restraining order. [32]

Do not be intimidated

This suggestion is situation-dependent, and should be considered on a case-by-case basis depending on each troll's level of aggressiveness, or to everyone trolling you. Discuss the situation with a trusted, objective supporter. Consider sending a message to the harasser warning that any further contact will result in a police report being filed. Some communication may stop there. Reply only once per troll, and document your communication.

---

[32] "Reporting to Law Enforcement," PEN America, Online Harassment Field Manual, https://onlineharassmentfieldmanual.pen.org/reporting-to-law-enforcement/.

Defining Online Abuse by PEN America

PEN America has put out a well-written Online Harassment Field Manual providing insight on the different forms online harassment can take. They have graciously given permission to share important definitions in this book. Because it is important to understand the myriad of ways online abuse may be perpetrated, we are including PEN America's comprehensive listing, which can help you protect not only yourself but those that you care about.

"Online abuse" – also known as "cyber harassment," "cyber abuse," and "online harassment" – includes, but is not limited to, the behaviors described below, carried out in an online setting. Online settings include email, social media platforms (such as Twitter, Facebook, and Instagram), messaging apps (such as Facebook Messenger and WhatsApp), blogging platforms (such as Medium, Tumblr, and WordPress), and comments sections (such as those found on digital news platforms, personal blogs, YouTube pages, and Amazon book reviews). This glossary is intended for two audiences:

Targets of online abuse. This glossary will help you identify the particular form of online harassment you're experiencing and offer tips and resources for addressing that particular abuse. Each "What to Do" section offers a brief and immediate course of action for that particular form of harassment.

Witnesses, allies, loved ones, and employers. This glossary will help educate groups and individuals who intersect with victims about the specific kinds of online harassment out there. Raising collective awareness around online harassment and fighting back requires possessing a vocabulary for describing and addressing the abuse.

Sources and references for further information are noted throughout this glossary, and additional information is also available on PEN America's website at https://www.pen.org.[33]

---

[33] "Defining 'Online Abuse': A Glossary of Terms," PEN America, Online Harassment Field Manual, https://onlineharassmentfieldmanual.pen.org/defining-online-harassment-a-glossary-of-terms/.

Glossary of Terms

Astroturfing
Definition: Astroturfing is the dissemination or amplification of content (including abuse) that appears to arise organically at the grassroots level and spread, but is actually coordinated (often using multiple fake accounts) by an individual, interest group, political party, or organization.

> Example: In 2012, Russian youth group Nashi was accused of paying people to criticize negative articles and dislike negative YouTube videos about Vladimir Putin.[34]
>
> **What to do:** Astroturfing is effective because harassers go to great lengths to make fake accounts seem real. Nevertheless, it's a good idea to check for signs that an account might be fake (see the guidance on fake accounts below). You can try deploying a supportive community to help you report accounts, block and mute, and document the abuse. If you're considering investigating the astroturfing campaign to expose and discredit it, PEN American provides guidelines for practicing counterspeech on their website.[35]

Concern Trolling
Definition: Abusers pose as fans or supporters of a target's work and make harmful and demeaning messages comments masked as constructive feedback.

---

[34] Miriam Elder, "Hacked Emails Allege Russian Youth Group Nashi Paying Bloggers," *The Guardian*, February 7, 2012, sec. World news, http://www.theguardian.com/world/2012/feb/07/hacked-emails-nashi-putin-bloggers.

[35] "Fight Back/Write Back," PEN America, Online Harassment Field Manual, https://onlineharassmentfieldmanual.pen.org/fight-back-write-back/.

Sealioning is the "confrontational practice of leaping into an online discussion with endless demands for answers and evidence" according to the Oxford Dictionary of Social Media.[36]

Example: According to Anita Sarkeesian's Guide to Internetting While Female, "when targeting women, [concern trolling] is most often done through 'helpful' suggestions on how to improve one's appearance... The concern troll's disingenuous comments are actually designed to undercut or demean you."[37]

Cross platform harassment
Definition: Cross-platform harassment is coordinated and deliberately deployed across multiple social media and communications platforms, taking advantage of the fact that most platforms only moderate content on their own sites.[38]

Example: After publishing a satirical feminist article, a writer found herself in the midst of a Twitter storm, which rapidly spread to her professional Facebook Page, the website of a professional membership organization she belonged to, and beyond; abusive trolls coordinated these attacks on platforms like 4Chan and Reddit.[39]

---

[36] Daniel Chandler and Rod Munday, "Sealioning," in *A Dictionary of Social Media*, 2016th ed. (Oxford University Press, 2016), https://www.oxfordreference.com/view/10.1093/acref/9780191803093.001.0001/acref-9780191803093-e-1257.

[37] Anita Sarkeesian, "Anita Sarkeesian's Guide to Internetting While Female," *Marie Claire*, February 20, 2015, https://www.marieclaire.com/culture/news/a13403/online-harassment-terms-fight-back/.

[38] "Online Abuse 101," Women's Media Center, https://womensmediacenter.com/speech-project/online-abuse-101.

[39] Anonymous, "How a Group of Online Misogynists Tried to Ruin My Professional Life," *Women's Media Center* (blog), March 31, 2016, https://womensmediacenter.com/speech-project/how-a-group-of-online-misogynists-tried-to-ruin-my-professional-life.

What to do: There is no easy way to deal with coordinated cross-platform harassment. It's critically important to tighten your cyber security to protect yourself from hacking and doxing. To cope with the volume and reach of the attacks, it helps to rally a supportive cyber community to share the burden of documenting, reporting, blocking and muting the abuse.

Cyberbullying

Definition: An umbrella term, cyberbullying encompasses many harassing behaviors, but boils down to "willful and repeated harm inflicted through the use of computers, cell phones, and other electronic devices." The term is primarily used in relation to children and young adults.[40]

Example: In a tragic and now infamous episode of cyberbullying, a twelve-year-old girl took her own life in New Jersey.[41]

What to do: Visit https://www.cyberbullying.org for the best resources and information related to cyberbullying.

Cyber-Mob Attacks (aka Dogpiling)

Definition: When a large group of abusers collectively attacks a target through a barrage of threats, slurs, insults, and other abusive tactics.

Outrage/Shame Mobs

A form of mob justice focused on publicly exposing, humiliating, and punishing a target, often for expressing opinions on politically charged topics or ideas the outrage mob disagrees with and/or has taken out of context to promote a particular agenda.

---

[40] "What Is Cyberbullying?," *Cyberbullying Research Center* (blog), December 23, 2014, https://cyberbullying.org/what-is-cyberbullying.

[41] Kalhan Rosenblatt, "New Jersey Family to Sue School District after 12-Year-Old Daughter's Suicide," *NBC News*, August 1, 2017, https://www.nbcnews.com/news/us-news/new-jersey-family-sue-school-district-after-12-year-old-n788506.

Example: Ricochet editor and politically-conservative columnist Bethany Mandel experienced a surge of anti-Semitic trolling from self-identified white nationalists via Facebook and Twitter after publicly declaring her opposition to Donald Trump.[42]

What to do: Trying to navigate cyber-mob attacks can feel like an exhausting game of whack-a-mole. If reporting the abuse isn't getting you anywhere, consider asking a member of your support community to monitor and report the abuse on your behalf while you take a break. Other options include: launching a counterspeech campaign to reestablish a narrative or reclaim a hashtag associated with your username; making a statement on social media alerting your social network to the negative activity; and consider temporarily taking a break from or going private on your social media accounts until the worst of the harassment has passed.[43]

Cyberstalking

Definition: In a legal context, "cyberstalking" is the prolonged and repeated use of abusive behaviors online (a "course of conduct") intended "to kill, injure, harass, intimidate, or place under surveillance with intent to kill, injure, harass, or intimidate" a target.[44]

Example: Over a 15-year period, a freelance journalist at Scientific American was the target of cyberstalking from a man who would go on to steal her identity and threaten her career.[45]

What to do: Cyberstalking is a federal offense, and many states have cyberstalking laws on the books. If you're comfortable contacting law

---

[42] "Jewish Reporters Harassed By Trump's Anti-Semitic Supporters," NPR.org, July 6, 2016, https://www.npr.org/2016/07/06/484987245/jewish-reporters-harassed-by-trumps-anti-semitic-supporters.

[43] "Fight Back/Write Back."

[44] "18 U.S. Code § 2261A - Stalking," Legal Information Institute, n.d., https://www.law.cornell.edu/uscode/text/18/2261A.

[45] Roni Jacobson, "I've Had a Cyberstalker Since I Was 12," WIRED, February 29, 2016, https://www.wired.com/2016/02/ive-had-a-cyberstalker-since-i-was-12/.

enforcement or seeking the advice of a lawyer, you might wish to take legal action against a cyberstalker. Other strategies include blocking your stalker on social media, documenting every harassing incident that occurs in relation to cyberstalking, making sure your online accounts are protected if you anticipate identity fraud, and enlisting your support community.

Deepfake

Definition: The use of "a form of artificial intelligence called deep learning" to make manufactured images, audio, and/or video that appear real.[46] These images, audio, and/or video are mimicking speech or facial expressions so as to make it appear that someone has said or done something they haven't.[47].

> Example: A deepfake porn video created using the image of investigative journalist Rana Ayyub was shared more than 40,000 times in an attempt to humiliate and silence her. She was brave enough to share her story in a 2018 Huffington Post article.[48]

Denial of Access

Definition: Leveraging the features of a technology or platform to harm the target, usually by preventing access to essential digital tools or platforms.

> ### Mass Report (aka False Reporting)
> Abusers coordinate to falsely report a target's account as abusive or otherwise harmful to try to get it suspended or shut down.

---

[46] Ian Sample, "What Are Deepfakes – and How Can You Spot Them?," *The Guardian*, January 13, 2020, sec. News, https://www.theguardian.com/technology/2020/jan/13/what-are-deepfakes-and-how-can-you-spot-them.

[47] Pakinam Amer, "Deepfakes Are Getting Better. Should We Be Worried?," *Boston Globe*, December 13, 2019, https://www.bostonglobe.com/2019/12/13/opinion/deepfakes-are-coming-what-do-we-do/.

[48] Rana Ayyub, "I Was The Victim Of A Deepfake Porn Plot Intended To Silence Me," Huffington Post UK, November 21, 2018, https://www.huffingtonpost.co.uk/entry/deepfake-porn_uk_5bf2c126e4b0f32bd58ba316.

Message Bombing (aka Flooding)
Abusers flood an individual or institution's phone or email accounts with unwanted messages meant to limit or block the target's ability to use that platform.

Example: In 2017, a flood of emails sent by bot accounts shut down the servers at ProPublica.com in a retaliatory attack against ProPublica journalists who had written a controversial article about the relationship between tech companies and extremist websites. The attack prevented the company's employees from accessing important emails and interfered enormously with the news outlet's day-to-day operations.[49]

What to do: Immediately report the incident to the social media platform, phone provider, internet company, or email provider where the harassment is taking place. If necessary, create a new and/or temporary email address or username to inform your colleagues, family, and friends that you have been message bombed and no longer have access to your usual accounts.[50]

Denial of Service (DoS) Attacks
Definition: A cyberattack that temporarily or indefinitely causes a website or network to crash or become inoperable by overwhelming a system with data. DoS attacks can prevent you from accessing your own devices and data, and they can compromise sensitive information stored on your devices.

Distributed Denial of Service (DDoS)
When an attacker takes control of multiple users' computers to attack a different user's computer. This can force the hijacked computers to

---

[49] Julia Angwin, "How Journalists Fought Back Against Crippling Email and Subscription Bombs," *WIRED*, November 9, 2017, https://www.wired.com/story/how-journalists-fought-back-against-crippling-email-bombs/.

[50] "Reporting to Platforms," PEN America, Online Harassment Field Manual, https://onlineharassmentfieldmanual.pen.org/reporting-online-harassment-to-platforms/.

send large amounts of data to a particular website or send spam to targeted email addresses.

Example: In 2016, the British Broadcasting Company suffered a targeted DDoS attack in its U.S. offices, which also caused limited access to Reddit, Twitter, Etsy, GitHub, , and Spotify.[51]

What to do: Because DoS attacks target email addresses, websites, and online accounts, it's essential that you contact the necessary providers to report the abuse.[52]

Dog Whistling
Definition: Using words or symbols with a double (or coded) meaning that is abusive or harmful, sometimes to signal a group of online abusers to attack a specific target.[53]

Example: In 2016, white supremacists on Twitter began using triple parentheses—an (((echo)))—around an individual's name to identify them as Jewish and instigate a coordinated campaign of abuse.[54] Jewish writers and journalists banded together to reclaim the symbol, proactively adding triple parentheses to their own Twitter handles.[55]

---

[51] "Cyber Attacks Briefly Knock out Top Sites," *BBC News* (blog), October 21, 2016, https://www.bbc.com/news/technology-37728015.

[52] Lenny Zeltser, "Network DDoS Incident Response Cheat Sheet," *Lenny Zeltser* (blog), September 23, 2016, https://zeltser.com/ddos-incident-cheat-sheet/.

[53] "Totem Project," Totem Project, https://learn.totem-project.org/.

[54] Cooper Fleishman and Anthony Smith, "'Coincidence Detector': The Google Chrome Extension White Supremacists Use to Track Jews," *Mic*, June 2, 2016, https://www.mic.com/articles/145105/coincidence-detector-the-google-extension-white-supremacists-use-to-track-jews.

[55] "Punctuation Protest against Far Right Trolls on Twitter," *BBC News*, June 8, 2016, sec. Trending, https://www.bbc.com/news/blogs-trending-36470879.

Doxing (aka Doxxing)
Definition: The publishing of sensitive personal information online—including home address, email, phone number, social security number, photos, etc.—to harass, intimidate, extort, stalk, or steal the identity of a target. Short for "dropping docs," doxing was a revenge tactic among '90s computer hackers, according to HTML.com.[56]

> Example: After reporting on the police officer involved in the shooting of Michael Brown in Ferguson, Missouri, two reporters for The New York Times were forced to flee their homes when their personal addresses were posted online in retaliation for their coverage.[57]
>
> **What to do:** If you've already been subjected to doxing, immediately report the dox to the platform on which it appears, and do your best to assess the threat level to your safety.[58] If you believe that the doxed information could fall into the hands of someone intent on harming you, consider involving your local law enforcement immediately.[59]

Online Sexual Harassment (aka, Cybersexual Abuse, Gender-Based Harassment)
Online sexual harassment encompasses a wide range of sexual misconduct on digital platforms. Those who identify as women and/or LGBTQIA+ are disproportionately targeted.

---

[56] "What Is Doxing? (And Why Is It So Scary?): An Infographic," *HTML.Com* (blog), https://html.com/blog/doxing/.

[57] Sarah Kessler, "Why Online Harassment Is Still Ruining Lives–And How We Can Stop It," *Fast Company*, June 3, 2015, https://www.fastcompany.com/3046772/why-online-harassment-is-still-ruining-lives-and-how-we-can-stop-it.

[58] "Protecting from Doxing," PEN America, Online Harassment Field Manual, https://onlineharassmentfieldmanual.pen.org/protecting-information-from-doxing/.

[59] "Reporting to Law Enforcement."

Deadnaming

Revealing a target's former name against their wishes to do them harm, a technique "most commonly used to out members of the LGTBQIA+ community who may have changed their birth names for any variety of reasons, including to avoid professional discrimination and physical danger."[60]

Lollipopping

"Anything meant to infantilize a [woman], from calling her "hon" or "sweetie" to telling her she'll get it when she gets older. Named after the candy that doctors and merchants handed out to young children, to placate them."[61]

Non-Consensual Intimate Images (see below)

Sextortion

A form of blackmail in which an abuser threatens "to expose a nude or sexually explicit image in order to get a person to do something."[62]

Unsolicited Pornography

Sending sexually explicit or violent images and videos to a target.[63]

Unwanted Sexualization

Sending "unwelcome sexual requests, comments and content" to a target.[64]

---

[60] "Online Abuse 101."

[61] Sarah Seltzer, "Beyond Mansplaining: A New Lexicon of Misogynist Trolling Behaviors," *Flavorwire*, March 24, 2015, https://www.flavorwire.com/511063/beyond-mansplaining-a-new-lexicon-of-misogynist-trolling-behaviors.

[62] "Definitions," Cyber Civil Rights Initiative, https://www.cybercivilrights.org/definitions/.

[63] "Online Abuse 101."

[64] Childnet, "About Project DeSHAME," Childnet International, http://www.childnet.com/our-projects/project-deshame/about-project-deshame.

Example: When author, attorney, and feminist blogger Jill Filipovic was a student at New York University's School of Law, she discovered hundreds of threads on an anonymous message board that were filled with rape threats – many of them graphic – directed at her. The online threats transitioned into offline contexts when harassers began appearing at Filipovic's law school and later on at her law firm. Filipovic writes that her confidence and safety were compromised as a result of the online sexual harassment she faced.[65]

What to do: An important place to start is reporting the harassment to the platform on which it was received[66] and documenting the abuse[67]. Online sexual harassment can be extremely traumatic for a target, and may require legal intervention. (There are currently 46 states with non-consensual pornography laws on the books—check to see if yours is one of them.)[68] If you do wish to seek help from law enforcement or a lawyer, visit the Legal Considerations section of PEN America's Online Harassment Field Manual.[69]

If you are a target of online sexual harassment, it is extremely important to keep in mind that you are not alone. Reaching out to others for support can go a long way in taking care of your mental health. Take a look at the PEN America's Guidelines for Talking to Friends and Loved Ones section of their online Field Manual for more

---

[65] Jill Filipovic, "Let's Be Real: Online Harassment Isn't 'Virtual' For Women," Talking Points Memo, January 10, 2014, https://talkingpointsmemo.com/cafe/let-s-be-real-online-harassment-isn-t-virtual-for-women.

[66] "Reporting to Platforms."

[67] "Documenting Online Harassment."

[68] "46 States + DC + One Territory NOW Have Revenge Porn Laws," Cyber Civil Rights Initiative, n.d., https://www.cybercivilrights.org/revenge-porn-laws/.

[69] "Legal Considerations," PEN America, Online Harassment Field Manual, https://onlineharassmentfieldmanual.pen.org/legal-considerations/.

tips on how to discuss sensitive topics, including online sexual harassment, with those around you.[70]

Hacking
Definition: The unauthorized intrusion into a device or network, hacking is often carried out with the intention to attack, harm, or incriminate another individual by stealing their data, violating their privacy, or infecting their devices with viruses. When hacking is used to perform illegal activities or intimidate a target, it is a cybercrime.[71]

Example: Fancy Bear, a Russian hacking unit, has targeted hundreds of journalists, including independent Russian reporters, at least 50 New York Times journalists, and several reporters at The Daily Beast, among other journalists who report on intelligence, national security, and Russian troll farms.[72]

What to do: Practicing rigorous cyber security is critical to protecting yourself from hacking.[73]

Hateful speech
Definition: Expression that attacks a specific aspect of a person's identity, such as their race, ethnicity, gender identity, religion, sexual orientation, disability, etc. Hateful speech online often takes the form of *ad hominem* attacks, which invoke prejudicial feelings over intellectual arguments to avoid discussion of the topic at hand by attacking a person's character or attributes.

---

[70] "Guidelines for Talking to Friends and Allies," PEN America, Online Harassment Field Manual, https://onlineharassmentfieldmanual.pen.org/guidelines-for-talking-to-friends-and-loved-ones/.

[71] "Cyber Crime," Federal Bureau of Investigation, https://www.fbi.gov/investigate/cyber.

[72] Raphael Satter, Jeff Donn, and Nataliya Vasilyeva, "Russian Hackers Fancy Bear Targeted Hundreds of Journalists," Associated Press, December 22, 2017, https://apnews.com/article/c3b26c647e794073b7626befa146caad.

[73] "Protecting from Hacking and Impersonation," PEN America, Online Harassment Field Manual, https://onlineharassmentfieldmanual.pen.org/protecting-from-hacking-impersonation/.

Example: In 2016, comedian Leslie Jones was the target of a widespread trolling campaign built on racist, misogynist messaging, which culminated in her being subjected to revenge porn, doxing, and hacking. (The incident also resulted in notorious troll Milo Yiannopoulos being kicked off Twitter for his targeted, publicly racist abuse—thanks in part to a #LoveforLeslieJ Twitter campaign launched by her supporters.)[74]

What to do: Depending on the level of threat and intimidation couched in these attacks, you may wish to block or mute a user, engage in counterspeech, or, in some cases, even consider directly confronting your troll. If you don't feel safe responding to or blocking a user, turn to your support community and make sure you're practicing self-care. If you've been named in a threat of violence or sexual intimidation and are afraid for your safety, please consider contacting law enforcement.[75]

Non-Consensual Intimate Images (aka Revenge Porn)
Definition: Non-Consensual pornography is "the distribution of private, sexually-explicit images [or videos] of individuals without their consent."[76]

Example: Countless women and high-profile celebrities have been the targets of non-consensual pornography. Leading revenge-porn expert Carrie Goldberg, a Cyber Civil Rights Initiative board member and lawyer who has dedicated her career to taking on cases around sexual

---

[74] Katie Rogers, "Leslie Jones, Star of 'Ghostbusters,' Becomes a Target of Online Trolls," *The New York Times*, July 19, 2016, sec. Movies, https://www.nytimes.com/2016/07/20/movies/leslie-jones-star-of-ghostbusters-becomes-a-target-of-online-trolls.html.

[75] "Reporting to Law Enforcement."

[76] "Definitions."

privacy and internet abuse, was herself a former victim of non-consensual intimate images by an ex-boyfriend.[77]

What to do: Undergoing an attack of non-consensual pornography can be extremely traumatic and may require legal intervention. (There are currently 46 states with non-consensual pornography laws on the books—check to see if yours is one of them.)[78] If an explicit image has been posted to a social media platform or chat forum, flag it for removal and, if possible, contact the platform's administrators.[79] Be sure to lean on your support community for help during this time as well.

Online Impersonation

Definition: Creation of a hoax social media account, often using the target's name and/or photo, to post offensive or inflammatory statements to defame, discredit, or instigate further abuse. A harasser can also impersonate someone the target knows to cause harm.

Example: Writer Lindy West was subject to a particularly cruel episode of impersonation trolling when an online troll posed as her deceased father. Her story has an unusual ending, however: the abusive troll ended up apologizing.[80]

What to do: Immediately report the impersonation to the platform on which it appears.[81] You may want to consider making a statement on

---

[77] Margaret Talbot, "The Attorney Fighting Revenge Porn," *The New Yorker*, November 28, 2016, https://www.newyorker.com/magazine/2016/12/05/the-attorney-fighting-revenge-porn.

[78] "46 States + DC + One Territory NOW Have Revenge Porn Laws."

[79] "Reporting to Platforms."

[80] Lindy West, "What Happened When I Confronted My Cruellest Troll," *The Guardian*, February 2, 2015, sec. Society, http://www.theguardian.com/society/2015/feb/02/what-happened-confronted-cruellest-troll-lindy-west.

[81] "Reporting to Platforms."

your real social media accounts alerting your online communities to the imposter. (If the harassment is taking place on Twitter, you can "pin" a tweet to the top of your profile for a period of time, so it's visible whenever someone visits your real Twitter profile.) In some cases, it may be appropriate to inform your employer[82] or your loved ones[83] of the abuse, especially in cases in which they're implicated in the impersonator's comments.

Phishing

Definition: An online scam that starts with some form of communication—an email, a text, a WhatsApp message—designed to look like it comes from a trusted source. The aim is to trick you into doing something—usually clicking on a link or opening an attachment, which may automatically download a virus onto your device or lead you to enter private information, like login details, which could then be used to gain control over your online accounts, impersonate you, or sell your info to others.[84]

Threats

Definition: "A statement of an intention to inflict pain, injury, damage, or other hostile action" against a target.[85] This includes death threats, threats of physical violence, and, for women, often threats of sexual violence.

> Example: Writer Jessica Valenti has been the target of rampant misogyny, toxic (and irrelevant) character attacks, and rape and death threats throughout her 14-year career as an online writer.[86] In 2016,

---

[82] "Guidelines for Talking to Employers about Abuse," PEN America, Online Harassment Field Manual, https://onlineharassmentfieldmanual.pen.org/guidelines-for-talking-to-employers-and-professional-contacts/.

[83] "Guidelines for Talking to Friends and Allies."

[84] "Totem Project."

[85] "Threat | Definition of Threat by Oxford Dictionary on Lexico.Com Also Meaning of Threat," Lexico Dictionaries | English, https://www.lexico.com/en/definition/threat.

[86] Jessica Valenti, "Insults and Rape Threats. Writers Shouldn't Have to Deal with This | Jessica Valenti," *The Guardian*, April 14, 2016, sec. Technology,

she temporarily quit social media after online rape and death threats were directed at her 5-year-old daughter.[87]

Swatting
Definition: Placing a hoax call to law enforcement detailing a completely false threatening event taking place at a target's home or business, with the intention of sending a fully armed police unit (SWAT team) to the target's address. Swatting is rare, but extremely dangerous, and a clear example of how online harassment has the potential to cause harm in offline life.

> Example: In 2013, an online security journalist was swatted at his home in Virginia, where 10 to 12 police officers surrounded his driveway with their guns drawn.[88]

> **What to do:** Swatting is illegal. It is often the result of a doxing incident, in which a person's home or business address has been posted online. You can take measures to proactively protect your information from doxing.[89] If you believe you could be the target of swatting in future, consider informing your local law enforcement to prepare them for this possibility.[90] If you've been the target of swatting, you may want to pursue legal action.[91]

---

https://www.theguardian.com/commentisfree/2016/apr/14/insults-rape-threats-writers-online-harassment.

[87] David Z. Morris, "Bestselling Feminist Author Jessica Valenti Quits Social Media After Rape and Death Threats Directed at Daughter," *Fortune*, July 31, 2016, https://fortune.com/2016/07/31/bestselling-feminist-author-jessica-valenti-quits-social-media-after-rape-and-death-threats-directed-at-daughter/.

[88] Adrianne Jeffries, "Meet 'swatting,' the Dangerous Prank That Could Get Someone Killed," *The Verge*, April 23, 2013, https://www.theverge.com/2013/4/23/4253014/swatting-911-prank-wont-stop-hackers-celebrities.

[89] "Protecting from Doxing."

[90] "Reporting to Law Enforcement."

[91] "Legal Resources for Writers & Journalists," PEN America, Online Harassment Field Manual, https://onlineharassmentfieldmanual.pen.org/legal-resources-for-writers-and-journalists/.

Zoombombing

Definition: "The act of hijacking a virtual meeting and disrupting communication through the sharing of text, video, or audio... commonly referred to as "raiding" or "bombing" ... Sometimes these raids are... [for] targeted reasons, including disruption of business activities and identity-based attacks on marginalized groups."[92]

> Example: Journalists Kara Swisher and Jessica Lessin were forced to shut down a Zoom event focused on the challenges faced by women in tech when abusive trolls bombed the session with pornography.[93]
>
> **What to do:** Specific recommendations to avoid being zoombombed are provided in *Chapter 22 – Online Meetings*. Also be sure to regularly update Zoom and any other videoconferencing software because they are constantly releasing new security features.

The primary source for the above definitions, examples and action steps is: PEN America, Online Harassment Field Manual
https://onlineharassmentfieldmanual.pen.org/

---

[92] Brian Friedberg, Gabrielle Lim, and Joan Donovan, "Space Invaders: The Networked Terrain of Zoom Bombing" (Technology and Social Change Research Project, June 9, 2020), https://doi.org/10.37016/TASC-2020-02.

[93] Taylor Lorenz, "'Zoombombing': When Video Conferences Go Wrong," *The New York Times*, March 20, 2020, sec. Style, https://www.nytimes.com/2020/03/20/style/zoombombing-zoom-trolling.html.

Report harassment to social media platforms

If you are being abused on social media, you should report the harassment to the platform on which it occurs.

Below are instructions for reporting harassment on the major social media and photo sharing platforms. Screenshots of the actual reporting process are included so you have a clearer picture of what to expect. The intention is to make the reporting process more transparent, more efficient, and less intimidating during what would likely be a stressful time if image removal is ever required. Several of the screenshots show how to report non-consensual pornography (otherwise known as revenge porn), which we will discuss in next in Chapter 16 – *Non-Consensual Pornography / Revenge Porn*, but harassment of any kind can (and should) be reported.

The social media sites included are (in alphabetical order):

Facebook

Imgur

Instagram

Reddit

Snapchat

Tumblr

Twitter

YouTube

Other sites not included in this book likely have similar methods of reporting harassment. Usernames and other identifying information have been redacted in the following examples.

Different site and apps may use either ●●● or ⋮ or ☰ or some other symbol for the More Options menu. For purposes of simplicity in this guide, we'll be using ●●● as the general symbol for selecting **More Options**.

Report harassment to Facebook

Tap ••• above the post for More Options.

Select **Find support or report post.** Report the post for harassment against you or a friend. Here you can also block or unfollow the harasser's account.

Report harassment to Imgur

Click the ••• on the post you want to report.

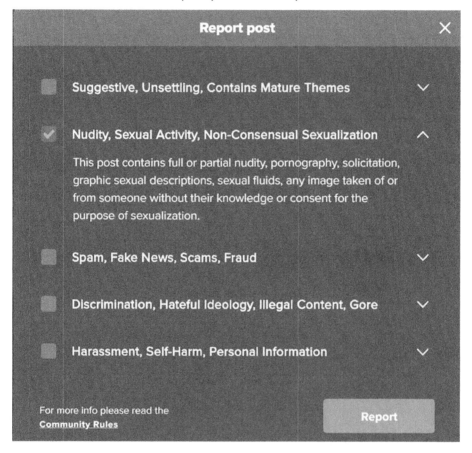

You can also go to the below address to request removal of specific images:

https://imgur.com/removalrequest

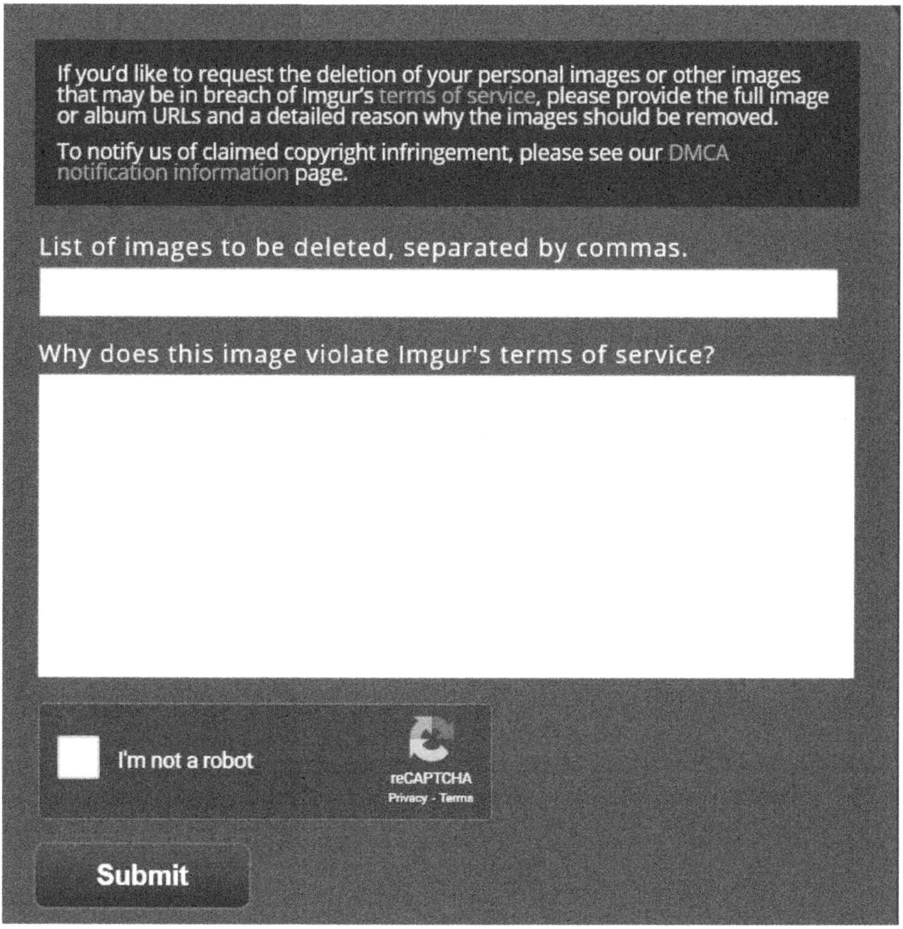
If you'd like to request the deletion of your personal images or other images that may be in breach of Imgur's terms of service, please provide the full image or album URLs and a detailed reason why the images should be removed.
To notify us of claimed copyright infringement, please see our DMCA notification information page.
List of images to be deleted, separated by commas.
Why does this image violate Imgur's terms of service?
I'm not a robot
reCAPTCHA
Privacy - Terms
Submit

Report harassment to Instagram

If you have an Instagram account, you can report abuse, spam or anything else that doesn't follow their Community Guidelines from within the app. According to Instagram, your report is anonymous, except if you're reporting an intellectual property infringement. The account you reported won't see who reported them.

How to report a post or a profile

Tap ••• above the post for More Options. Select **Report**.

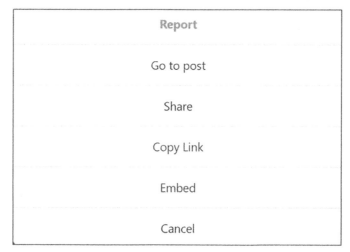

Report the post as inappropriate.

If you have an Instagram account, more information on reporting a post or profile for abuse or spam are at this address:

https://help.instagram.com/192435014247952

> ### How do I report a post or profile for abuse or spam on Instagram?
>
> If you don't have an Instagram account, you can report abuse, spam or anything else that doesn't follow our Community Guidelines using this form.
>
> If you have an Instagram account, you can report abuse, spam or anything else that doesn't follow our Community Guidelines from within the app.
>
> - How to report a post
> - How to report a profile
> - How to report something when using Instagram on the web
>
> Learn how to report a comment.
>
> Keep in mind that your report is anonymous, except if you're reporting an intellectual property infringement. The account you reported won't see who reported them.

If you don't have an Instagram account, you can report abuse, spam or anything else that doesn't follow their Community Guidelines at this address

https://help.instagram.com/contact/383679321740945

Report Violations of Our Community Guidelines

Please use this form to report content (ex. photos, videos) on Instagram that violates our Community Guidelines. When you report something, your information isn't shared with the person whose post or profile you're reporting.

Do you have an Instagram account?

- Yes
- No

Where does the violation you're reporting appear?

- Photo or video
- Comment
- An entire profile

How is this photo or video violating our guidelines?

- Nudity or pornography
- Violence or drug abuse
- Self harm or suicide

Click here if you wish to report harassment or bullying

Your Instagram username (if applicable):

To find your username, we suggest using the web browser version of our site (instagram.com/[username])

Your email address:

Username of the person who posted the content you are reporting:

Full name of the person who posted the content as listed on their account (optional):

Link(s) to the specific photo(s), violating profile(s), stories or comment(s) you're reporting:

Do you know this person in real life? If so, please provide as much contact information for this person as possible.

Additional information:

[Send]

Report harassment to Reddit

At the bottom of the post select the **report** option

164 comments   share   save   hide   give award   report   crosspost

Provide information on the Report an Issue popup that opens up.

The first screen:

○ This is spam
○ This is misinformation
○ This is abusive or harassing
○ It breaks r/█████████ rules
○ Other issues
Read the Reddit Content Policy and r/█████████ rules.   CANCEL   NEXT

The second screen:

● It's targeted harassment
○ It threatens violence or physical harm
○ It's promoting hate based on identity or vulnerability
○ It's rude, vulgar or offensive
○ It's abusing the report button
Read the Reddit Content Policy and r/█████████ rules.   BACK   NEXT

And the third screen:

You can also send the URL of the comments page to

contact@reddit.com

with the subject "Nonconsensual Pornography Report" or another appropriate, clear description of the harassment.

Report harassment to Snapchat

To report a Snapchat account, go to their profile and click ●●● for More Options and select the appropriate information.

You can report their account, block them and remove them as a friend.

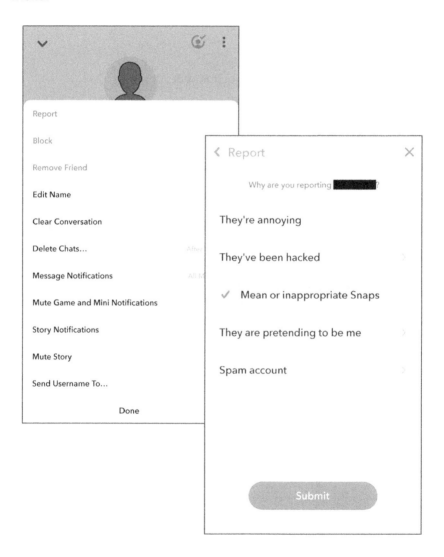

To report a Snapchatter's Story, go to the Snap you want to report and click ●●● for More Options and select the appropriate information.

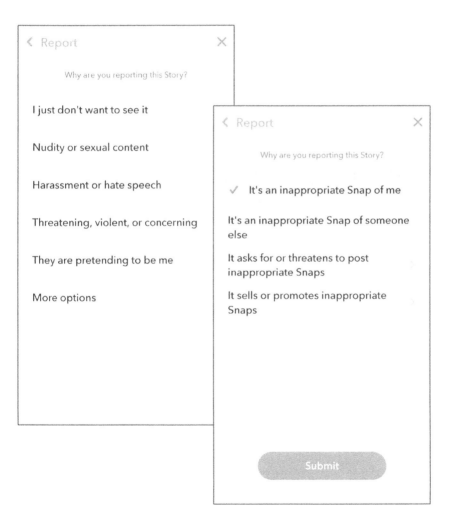

Report harassment to Tumblr

Tap ●●● above the post. Provide information on the "Report an issue" popup that opens up.

This allows you to flag and block the content. Additional steps are below.

To provide additional details about harassment to Tumblr, go to the below address. Provide information on the "Report an issue" page that opens up.

https://www.tumblr.com/abuse/harassment

The first screen:

Harassment

If anyone is sending you unwanted messages or reblogging your posts in an abusive way, we encourage you to be proactive and block the hell out of them. And if someone blocks you, don't attempt to circumvent the block feature or otherwise try to communicate with them. Bear in mind that many victims of online harassment are younger; being a teenager is complicated enough without the anxiety, sadness and isolation caused by bullying.

Are you the person being harassed?

Yes

No

The second screen:

> ## Harassment
>
> If anyone is sending you unwanted messages or reblogging your posts in an abusive way, we encourage you to be proactive and block the hell out of them. And if someone blocks you, don't attempt to circumvent the block feature or otherwise try to communicate with them. Bear in mind that many victims of online harassment are younger; being a teenager is complicated enough without the anxiety, sadness and isolation caused by bullying.
>
> **What kind of harassment is taking place?**
>
> My privacy is being violated (e.g. explicit private photos or personal contact information).
>
> I'm being threatened with specific bodily harm, theft, property damage, or financial harm.
>
> Someone posted content sexualizing me against my wishes.
>
> I'm being targeted and harassed.

The third screen:

> ## Privacy violation
>
> Don't post content that violates anyone's privacy, especially personally identifying or confidential information like credit card numbers, social security numbers, or unlisted contact information. Absolutely do not post non-consensual pornography —that is, private photos or videos taken or posted without the subject's consent.
>
> **What kind of content are you reporting**
>
> My name
>
> My IP address
>
> Unwanted sexualization
>
> My personal contact information
>
> My explicit private images

And the submit screen:

Privacy violation

Don't post content that violates anyone's privacy, especially personally identifying or confidential information like credit card numbers, social security numbers, or unlisted contact information. Absolutely do not post non-consensual pornography —that is, private photos or videos taken or posted without the subject's consent.

Need help finding a permalink? Click here.

Content you're reporting — URL of the post

A little about yourself — Name — Optional

[ ] I'm not a robot   reCAPTCHA
Privacy - Terms

Go back

Submit

Report harassment to Twitter

How to report a tweet or user

Tap ●●● above the post for More Options.

Provide information on the "Report an issue" popup that opens up.

The first screen:

← **Report an issue**

Help us understand the problem. What is going on with this Tweet?

I'm not interested in this Tweet

It's suspicious or spam

It's abusive or harmful

It expresses intentions of self-harm or suicide

Learn more about reporting violations of our rules

The second screen:

> ← **Report an issue**
>
> How is this Tweet abusive or harmful?
>
> It's disrespectful or offensive
>
> Includes private information
>
> Includes targeted harassment
>
> It directs hate against a protected category (e.g., race, religion, gender, orientation, disability)
>
> Threatening violence or physical harm
>
> They're encouraging self-harm or suicide

And the third screen before submitting the report:

> ← **Report an issue**
>
> Who is @█████████ targeting?
>
> Me
>
> Someone else

Report harassment to YouTube

You can submit a privacy complaint at this address:

https://support.google.com/youtube/contact/privacy2/

or you can report a video on the site. Below the player for the video you want to report, click ••• for More Options. In the drop-down menu, choose **Report**.

You'll have to go through several screens to report a complaint:

```
Report video
○  Sexual content  ⓘ
○  Violent or repulsive content  ⓘ
○  Hateful or abusive content  ⓘ
○  Harmful or dangerous acts  ⓘ
○  Child abuse  ⓘ
○  Promotes terrorism  ⓘ
○  Spam or misleading  ⓘ
●  Infringes my rights  ⓘ
     Privacy issue                          ▼
○  Captions issue  ⓘ

Flagged videos and users are reviewed by YouTube staff 24 hours a day, 7
days a week to determine whether they violate Community Guidelines.
Accounts are penalized for Community Guidelines violations, and serious or
repeated violations can lead to account termination. Report channel

                                      CANCEL    NEXT
```

The Privacy Complaint Process has six preliminary steps before providing information:

Privacy Complaint Process

Every day, people come to YouTube to share videos and engage with each other. We want you to feel safe when you're on YouTube, which is why we encourage you to let us know if videos or comments on the site violate your privacy or sense of safety, including if you have been recorded without your knowledge in private or sensitive circumstances.

We understand that you may not feel comfortable with all content that features you on YouTube, so we've created this process to help you submit a privacy complaint. Please ensure that you are uniquely identifiable within the content you seek to report before proceeding with the Privacy Complaint Process.

If someone copies a video that you created or content that you own, you may wish to file a copyright complaint. If you believe the content violates YouTube Community Guidelines, we encourage you to learn how to report inappropriate content.

Contact your local authorities for further assistance if you feel you are in physical danger.

[Continue]

Privacy Complaint Process: 2 of 6

Are you being harassed?

Having your privacy violated can often feel harassing by nature.

If someone is maliciously posting a video of you or directing insults at you, this may be considered harassment.

[I would like to learn more about Harassment]
[I still wish to submit a privacy complaint]

Privacy Complaint Process: 3 of 6

Contact the Uploader

If you think that a video posted to YouTube violates your privacy, begin by contacting the uploader to let them know. It's possible that the uploader isn't aware that someone feels uncomfortable with a video or comment that they've posted. Some creators list ways they can be contacted in their channel. Learn more about how to get in touch with others here.

Please contact the uploader before you decide to file a complaint.

[Continue]

Privacy Complaint Process: 4 of 6

Flag the video

Does this video or comment violate your privacy or is there something else about it that you find objectionable? If you've found material that violates YouTube's Community Guidelines, please use the flagging feature to bring it to our attention. You may learn more about this feature on our Flagging Content article.

I have reviewed the Community Guidelines

I have not reviewed the Community Guidelines

Privacy Complaint Process: 5 of 6

Abusing the privacy process may result in account suspension

If you're using this contact form to harass other people on the site or to create false privacy reports, your YouTube account may be suspended.

I understand that I may lose my account if I submit a false privacy claim.

Continue

Privacy Complaint Process: 6 of 6

What personal information is being revealed?

Your image or full name

(Image or full name refers to still images, audio and video footage or text that uniquely identifies you.)

Other personal information

(Personal information refers to an individual's contact information (e.g., home address, email address), identification information (e.g., social security number or national identification number), financial information (e.g., credit card number), or other personal identification information.)

You then provide detailed information on the following screen.

Submit a Privacy Complaint

To notify the uploader of the privacy complaint and provide them an opportunity to remove or edit their content, we ask that you fill in the information below. Your privacy is respected in this process. At no point will your name or contact information be released to the uploader without your consent.

The uploader may have 48 hours to take action on the complaint. You will be notified if the uploader removes the content or if YouTube has taken action on the content. Our communications to you about this process will be sent to your email address. Add support@youtube.com to your spam filter to ensure you receive these messages.

* Required field

Please complete the following required information

Your legal first name *

[   ]

Your legal last name *

[   ]

Country *

[▼]

Email address *

[   ]

Please include the URL of the channel that is revealing your personal information *

[   ]

Please include the URL(s) of the video(s) in question *

[   ]

Please include all URLs within one report separated by spaces.

If another user has copied your video, please submit a Copyright Infringement Notification

Please indicate the information you wish to report. Select all that apply *

☐ My image is shown

☐ My full legal name is shown

☐ My voice is being broadcast

☐ My child is shown

☐ Other

[   ]

The YouTube Privacy Complaint form continued...

Please identify where the questionable content appears within the video *

○ Within the title or video description

○ Within the video

○ Within the channel background

Where in the video does the questionable content appear? (example: 2:14) If your image or information appears for a duration of the video please indicate that (example: 3:00-3:10). *

[   ]

Add additional

If you have selected multiple video URLs to report, please click "Add an additional field" to identify where you are located within each URL. If you have not properly identified yourself within the content, we may not be able to review your issue.

Has this content been copied from your own channel or video? *

○ Yes

○ No

☐ I am the legal guardian of a child or dependent in the video.

Please provide additional information regarding your appearance or actions that differentiate you from others in the content reported. This information will not be forwarded to the uploader, and will only be reviewed by YouTube. *

[   ]

Please note: If you do not clearly identify yourself within the video, we will not take action to remove the reported content.

Agree to the following statements *

☐ "I have a good faith belief that this content violates my privacy."

☐ "I represent that the information in this notification is true and correct."

[Submit]

Some account and system information will be sent to Google, and support calls and chats may be recorded. We will use this information to improve support quality and training, to help address technical issues, and to improve our products and services, subject to our Privacy Policy and Terms of Service.

Search engines might not remove harassment

Google, Bing, and Yahoo have more rigid guidelines on the types of harassment they will assist in removing from their search engines. Search engines will typically not remove the broad range of online harassment that can occur.

Google, for example, states they will assist in removing:

- Non-consensual explicit or intimate personal images,
- Involuntary fake pornography,
- Content about you on sites with exploitative removal practices,
- Select financial, medical and national ID information, and
- doxing content exposing contact information with an intent to harm

Specific instructions for removing harassment that falls into the above categories are provided in the next chapter, Chapter 16 – *Non-Consensual Pornography / Revenge Porn*.

Set up Google Alerts

Google Alerts

https://www.google.com/alerts

Go to the above site and enter your name, as well as variations on your name with possible spelling errors, and set the frequency you would like to receive alerts if Google finds your name in new articles or posts online.

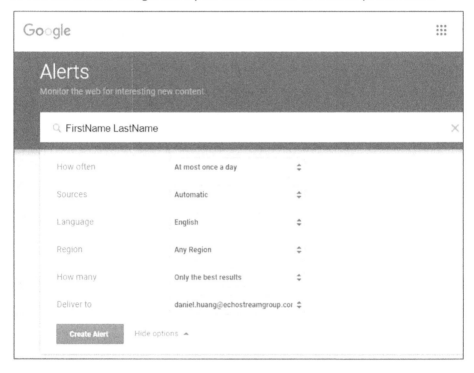

Use social media for good. Your good.

Similar to the way trolls might target a victim, you can reverse-engineer social media to gather information on harassers, with the goal of developing enough information to assess the threat level directed at you so you can determine the best course of action to protect yourself.

Work with a trusted friend to try to assess objectively the level of threat being directed at you so you can protect yourself accordingly. Does the harassment you are receiving appear to be a coordinated effort against you or is the attention being directed at you more individual and random?

As you investigate, make sure to save to PDF or screenshot the information you uncover, and keep it organized in your files should you need to present evidence to authorities, which may be law enforcement or even the troll's family, school, or employer depending on the situation. It's best to capture any information you come across the first time you see it. Don't expect to retrace your steps in the future. Retracing steps can be time consuming, and trolls may also delete their information.

If trolls are contacting you through social media, see what breadcrumbs you can gather to develop a sense of:

1. who they are (individually, professionally, academically),
2. their network of friends, supporters, and cronies,
3. who or what they follow (friends, groups, websites, interests, even sports teams to narrow down geographic location),
4. what they love (political, local, social),
5. what they hate,
6. their location (country, state, city, or actual home or work address),
7. their other trolling activities (and other victims they have previously or are currently targeting),
8. save images they post by right clicking them and downloading the image file (hopefully these might contain useful metadata). Don't just save screenshots of images, which will not save original metadata, and
9. any timeline of their activity that may be relevant to connecting the dots further.

Twitter-specific searching

Forget their password

Using your VPN, and incognito mode for good measure, try logging into their Twitter account. You're not actually trying to gain access into their account, rather click on **"forgot password"**. Twitter will show you some masked information, such as some of the letters of their email address or digits of their phone number. Make note of the breadcrumbs you find so you can cross-reference them against other information you accumulate on the troll.

Check their followers

Not surprisingly, trolls will often use nondescript names to hide in the shadows. You can try to get a sense of the troll's support network and affiliations by looking at their Twitter followers. More specifically, scroll down to the beginning of their follower list and see who their early followers are and inspect their activity. Are they also troll-ish? Are they identifiable individuals?

Also, you can inspect who the troll in question is following. The early connections may provide insight into the harasser's main circle of associations.

AllMyTweets

https://www.allmytweets.net/connect/

Use AllMyTweets.net to capture the troll's last 3,200 tweets. Have they tweeted about obscure people or issues? State or local politicians that would indicate they are a constituent, which can narrow down location? Or sports teams?

Check their Follower / Following Timelines

Who are their circle of friends? Scroll and search through their list of people they follow, and who also follow them. Twitter lists connections in chronological order, so the troll's first connections are at the bottom of the list. Look to see which individuals or groups they first associated with, and see what information and insight you can gather from those leads. Cross reference these accounts against the other social media to develop a broader picture of the troll's support system.

LinkedIn-specific searching

ContactOut

ContactOut is a Chrome extension that will reveal the email address of LinkedIn accounts and also has a search feature to look for a person's work email.

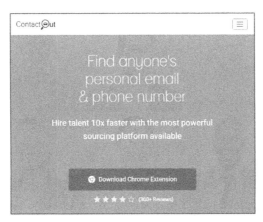

Research your troll's images

Let's be clear here, I am not encouraging vigilante justice. Victims should be armed with the same tools as their attackers, in case their trolls need to be identified. If you are able to obtain images of your trolls, here are some ways you can reverse-engineer their images to gather more intel on them. If anything, knowing where their general location may help you determine if they are merely distant nuisances or potential threats. The more solid information you have on genuine harassers, the better you can assist law enforcement or other authorities (such as their employers or parents) if necessary.

Reverse image lookups

Reverse image lookups can provide clues to other social media sites the troll uses, which can provide additional details on the troll's identity, contacts, affiliations, and activities. Are they serial trollers? Is there a pattern to their harassment, such as targeting specific groups of women, ethnicities, professions?

Search Google for Image

Using a Google Chrome browser, you can right click on an image and Google's **Search Google for Image** pops up as an option. Reverse image searching will display other images that appear like the one you're searching for. Google's feature is helpful and quick, but doesn't always deliver solid results. It's a good start, however.

Microsoft Bing

Bing has an image icon in its search bar where you select an image or URL to search.

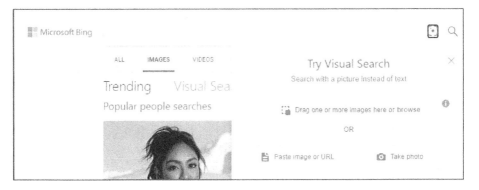

Yandex

https://yandex.com/

The Russian site Yandex provides a more robust image search tool, with strong capabilities to recognize faces, landscapes, and objects. It draws heavily on user-generated content and social networks to find similar photos taken from different angles. It's strongest for European or Eastern European content. North America and other continents are not as richly populated in their searches but still a good resource to use in your research.

TinEye

https://tineye.com/

TinEye looks for exact matches of images, including those that have been cropped, resized, or edited. It does not typically find similar, varied images.

Look for visual clues

In Chapter 14 – *Social Media Discretion*, several examples were provided of the visual clues you can discern from photos.

If you find images posted by the trolls, what can you discern from what you see? Are they wearing clothing that would indicate any affiliation, sports team, or activity? You'd be surprised what you can discern from a background. If there's an outdoor setting, are there any buildings or landmarks visible or any geographic markers (such as rivers, roads, signage).

Working in isolation, staring at a photo, searching for real information all by yourself can feel hopeless. It's a good idea to work with a trusted, insightful friend or colleague who could help you evaluate the elements of an image, piece by piece. And then cross reference your hunches on the internet, using basic tools such as Google Street View or photos of businesses or other public places.

Investigate their metadata

Turning the tables, search for what you can inside images posted by trolls. GPS location, date taken, name of the person who took the photo, even the equipment it was taken on can be helpful in compiling a comprehensive profile.

Using the internet

There are numerous free EXIF reader websites that will display information in images, if any exists. They typically allow you to either provide the URL where the image appears or you can upload the image. Search for "EXIF reader" in your browser. These sites tend to be fairly simple, since they don't need to be fancy to display the file information in an image.

Print or take screenshots of the information displayed for your documentation.

Locally on your computer

Using your computer's file manager, create a separate folder somewhere on your computer, where you can organize your information on the trolls and download the image in question. Right click on the file and open up the Properties. See if there is any information shown in the Details view and make note of anything useful.

Adobe Photoshop

You can also look at the photo's file information in Adobe Photoshop and other editing programs. In Photoshop, go to **File** and then **File Info** to see available details.

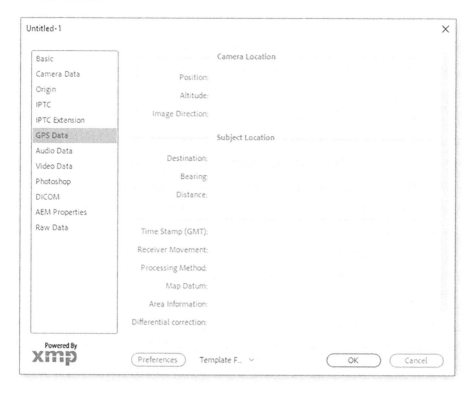

Document the information you uncover

How to capture screenshots

There are several ways to capture your screen for documentation and evidence purposes. Make sure to capture the URL, data information and other identifying details to help validate the information being captured.

Here's how to screenshot your computers and smartphones:

On Macs

Press [Shift]+[Command]+[4] keys at the same time. The screenshot should save to your desktop.

On Windows PCs

Press the [Windows]+[PrintScreen] button at the same time. The file will be default saved to the Pictures>Screenshots folder.

On iPhones

For iPhones with FaceID, press the [Side Button] and [Volume Up] buttons at the same time.

For iPhones with TouchID and Side Button, press the Side button. Press the [Side Button] and [Home] button at the same time.

On Android devices

Press [Power] and {Volume Down] at the same time for a few seconds. If that doesn't work, try holding [Power] down for a few seconds.

How to capture an entire web page

Archive Today

https://archive.is/

Archive Today is a time capsule for web pages. It takes a 'snapshot' of a web page that will always be online even if the original page disappears. It saves a text and a graphical copy of the page for better accuracy and provides a short and reliable link to an unalterable record of any web page. This can be useful if you want to take a 'snapshot' of a page that could be changed or deleted soon. Saved pages will have no active elements and no scripts, so they keep you safe as they cannot have any popups or malware.

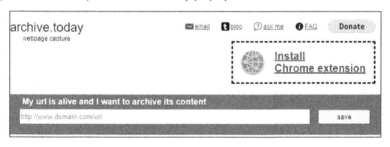

Snagit

https://www.techsmith.com/screen-capture.html

Snagit is a paid service (currently a one-time cost of $50) that has more features, including capturing your entire desktop, a window, or a scrolling screen.

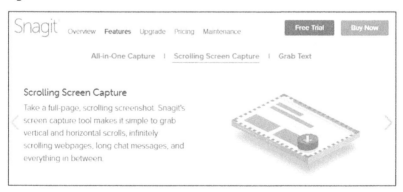

How to save to a PDF

Adobe PDF
https://helpx.adobe.com/acrobat/using/print-to-pdf.html

You can select Adobe PDF in almost any Windows or macOS application while printing. Print to PDF creates an electronic copy of your file that you can save to disk. **Adobe Acrobat** needs to be installed on your computer, otherwise, the Adobe PDF printer or the Save As Adobe PDF option won't appear.

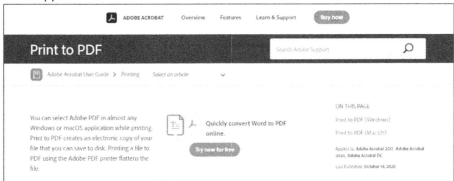

Chapter 16 – Non-Consensual Pornography / Revenge Porn

Non-consensual pornography is "the distribution of private, sexually-explicit images [or videos] of individuals without their consent."[94]

> ### *Half a million people have seen me naked*
>
> In 2018, Cher Scarlett wrote the article "Half a million people have seen me naked" for Medium.com. Cher discussed the years of harassment she suffered after an ex-boyfriend posted her private photos to the Twitch online gaming community where she was an active member.
>
> Cher Scarlett has graciously permitted sharing her experience for this book to raise awareness of the severe harm non-consensual pornography can cause. Best shared in her own words, the following are excerpts from her article (a link to the full article is included at the end).
>
> Cher discussed how her photos were first posted without her consent in 2011.
>
> *"I had been involved with someone online and he was the person who originally set out to humiliate me by leaking naked photographs of me to our entire server. He had written some kind of program that automatically re-uploaded the photos whenever I managed to get them deleted, and was sharing them with everyone we knew. It sucked. It was*

---

[94] "Definitions."

my first time being humiliated by someone I used to care about in that way, and I had to talk to the police about how to get him to stop.

After getting some very intimidating verbiage to use from the cops, I talked with this person and he agreed to stop, and delete them from his computer. I don't know if he felt guilty, or scared, but in my mind it was over. This person has since apologized to me for his behavior and made amends."

But it didn't stop.

In July 2012, Cher discovered someone else had saved those photos, and was angry at her for being involved with another member of their World of Warcraft gaming community that wasn't him. The harasser was repeatedly reposting the photos to Imgur, a popular photo sharing site, and also to Twitch chats that Cher frequented. Cher hoped that by staying silent the interest would die down. Her boyfriend at the time and her friends reported the image to Imgur as abuse posted without consent. If anyone asked, Cher, her boyfriend and her friends denied those were her photos.

Eventually people stopped talking about them after Imgur deleted the last photo in August 2012.

Until two months later...

"In the third week of October of 2012, I started receiving dozens and dozens of messages on Twitch about the photos.

Everyone seemed quite certain at this point they were me, and the volume of messages I was getting was outrageous. Everyone was talking about them. Critiquing them. A streamer said that my veins looked like an atlas, and I was ridiculed as 'The World Map tits'. I couldn't really understand why all of the sudden this had started up again when it seemed to have died down nearly two months before. ...

Someone finally linked me the album, and my heart was in my stomach. It had over 300,000 views. Unlike the other albums, this one wasn't uploaded anonymously. It belonged to an Imgur user named Uncleswagg, who was apparently known for hoarding and distributing nudes from women on Twitch and World of Warcraft. He had dozens of albums of nude photographs, the most complete collection in all of the Twitch community. When he received the small collection of my photographs from a source, he learned there was someone I had been involved with in the past who may have more and contacted him to get more photos for his album.

The worst part of it was that Uncleswagg was proud of it. No number of emails to Twitch and Imgur staff seemed to result in the deletion of the albums, and he prided himself on his ability to keep the links permanent. He had gained the notoriety he so desperately wanted by harassing women with revenge porn, and being the central hub for 'exposing' the women of the gaming industry with illegal nudes. ...

The harassment was ongoing, and I couldn't enter a Twitch channel without hearing some commentary about my breasts, or being called a whore. I deleted my Twitch account, and made a new one. A fresh start, sans the sexual abuse via messages and chat comments. ...

... but then in May of 2013, the harassing messages started again on my new account. ...

I, and others, are still harassed over these photographs, even five years later."

Her harassers faced little or no consequence for their abuse and actions.

"I am absolutely tired of seeing women's online lives be destroyed by revenge porn, and it's something that ran absolutely rampant on Twitch because of a single individual, Uncleswagg. Uncleswagg, who has never faced any consequences for his actions that have never stopped affecting the women he harassed, and is now being rewarded for his dedication to Blizzard [the company behind World of Warcraft] and Overwatch [another Blizzard game] as some impeccable Twitch moderator. Please.

> *The single most demeaning part of his rise to becoming a moderator in competitive esports is that he didn't even feel the need to change his username. Must be nice."*[95]
>
> More of Cher's story is continued at the end of this chapter. If you would like to read her full article, you can find it on Medium.com at this address:
>
> https://medium.com/@cherp/half-a-million-people-have-seen-me-naked-e70e8b89269c

Steps to try to delete your leaked photos

Unfortunately, be forewarned there is no guarantee that you will be able to completely remove your personal images once they are put out into the internet but you can take meaningful steps to try and recover your privacy. If your photos or videos are put online without your consent, here are major steps you can take to try to have the material removed:

1. Talk with trained professionals,
2. Report threats to law enforcement, and
3. Request removal of your content from search engines and social media platforms

Detailed instructions for each of these steps are in the following pages.

---

[95] Cher Scarlett, "Half a Million People Have Seen Me Naked," *Medium*, October 2, 2018, https://medium.com/@cherp/half-a-million-people-have-seen-me-naked-e70e8b89269c.

Speak with trained professionals

If you or your family are in physical danger, please call law enforcement at 911 immediately.

Cyber Civil Rights Initiative

https://www.cybercivilrights.org/

If you are a victim of non-consensual pornography ("NCP", also known as "revenge porn"), recorded sexual assault (RSA), or sextortion and you reside in the United States, you can call the **Cyber Civil Rights Initiative (CCRI) Crisis Helpline at 844-878-CCRI (2274)**. Trained representatives can provide information, support, referrals, and non-legal advice. The toll-free CCRI Crisis Helpline is available 24 hours a day and seven days a week, and interpretation is available in most languages.

The CCRI Crisis Helpline is able to provide assistance to victims calling from the U.S. Their website also provides some information for victims residing in Australia, Brazil, Israel and Palestine, Pakistan, South Korea, Taiwan, and the United Kingdom.

CopyByte

https://copybyte.com/stop-revenge-pornography/

For victims of non-consensual pornography, CopyByte offers a free service to help secure the removal of private images, videos and other content. This service is provided through a partnership with the Cyber Civil Rights Initiative. If you are in need of this service, contact the CCRI directly (information is above) as they can help determine if CopyByte is the correct solution and also provide additional guidance.

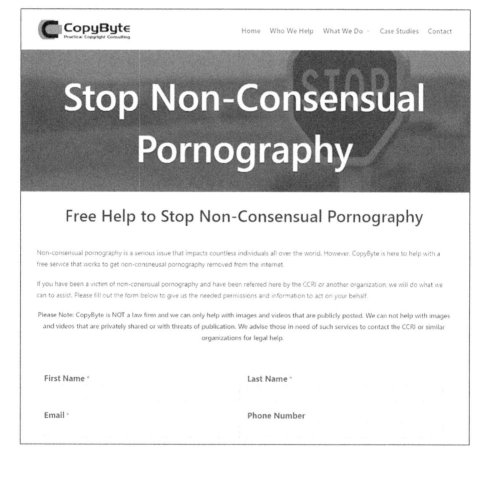

Report threats to law enforcement

You may wish to report threats of violence to law enforcement. While there have been some cases where harassers have faced legal consequences, this is unfortunately rare. Getting law enforcement to do things like subpoenaing for IP addresses is extremely difficult. This is where record-keeping becomes extremely important – both of the harassment and of the interactions you have with the police. Having records of harassment can be helpful if things escalate.

Bring a friend with you for interactions with the authorities

This is important both for moral support and for having a second person there to witness the interactions. If you're calling the police, put them on a speakerphone or if possible record the call.

Keep detailed records

The organization Without My Consent (now part of the Cyber Civil Rights Initiative) recommends documenting evidence of harassment in an organized format, such as this table:[96]

Date	What Happened	Evidence It Happened	Who You Think Did It	Evidence They Did It	Evidence Still Needed & Who Has It

An example of the level of detail that would be helpful to document, if possible, is provided below:

---

[96] "Without My Consent," Without My Consent, https://withoutmyconsent.org/.

Date	What Happened	Evidence It Happened	Who You Think Did It	Evidence They Did It	Evidence Still Needed & Who Has It
May 1, 2020	Ex-husband called 4 times, becoming increasingly verbally abusive toward me.	Screenshot of phone log showing date and times. Screenshot saved to my computer and printed to binder (Exhibit A).	Ex-husband	Phone log displays caller ID by name and number.	Ex-husband's phone log may have saved call history showing calls were placed.
May 2, 2020	Ex-husband sent 6 text messages that included calling me sexually abusive names.	Screenshots of text messages captured, saved to my computer and printed in binder (Exhibit B).	Ex-husband	Screenshots show the sender name and phone number the text messages were coming from.	Texts may also be on ex-husband's phone if not deleted.
May 4, 2020	Sexually explicit photos of me were posted on [website name] without my consent. The posts were made at 9:14PM on May 4, 2020. [Insert website URLs and other relevant information.]	Screenshots of the posts and PDF copies of web pages are saved to my computer and printed in binder (Exhibit C).	Ex-husband	Ex-husband took those photos. He was the only person I ever allowed to have the photos. In the post comments, the poster said he was previously in a relationship with me but did not provide details.	Husband should have photos on his phone, possibly downloaded elsewhere.
May 6, 2020	My sister did a reverse image search and found more photos on [insert URL addresses]	Screenshots of the posts and PDF copies of web pages are saved to my computer and printed in binder (Exhibit D).	Ex-husband	Ex-husband took those photos. He was the only person I ever gave the photos to.	Sister also saved screenshots and PDF copies of posts and web pages.

Remove your content from the internet

In Chapter 15 – *Defend Against Trolls,* detailed instructions are provided to report harassment on social media platforms. Victims on non-consensual pornography should also file reports with the social media platforms where abuse is occurring using those instructions.

If your information is shared on other websites, you can consider contacting the website owner if you think they may be willing to help. If you don't want to contact the website owner or if they are unwilling to help, you can request Google, Bing, and Yahoo remove your images from their search results.

Instructions for both approaches are detailed below.

Contact the website owner

According to Google's policy, the best way to remove information about yourself from showing up in Google's search results is to contact the website owner who published the information or images. According to Google, if the website owner has removed the information, it will eventually be removed from Google Search as part of Google's regular updating process. To speed up the process of removing it from Google Search, use Google's Outdated Content Removal tool (which you can search for online).

There are different ways to reach the website owner:

"Contact us" link

Use the site's "Contact us" link or an email address for the site owner, often found at the bottom of the site's homepage.

Use Whois.net

http://www.whois.net

The website Whois.net will give you the registration information for different sites. Often the site you want to reach may have contact information listed there.

Contact the site's hosting company

The Whois.net search result usually includes information about who hosts the website. If you're unable to reach the website owner, try contacting the site's hosting company.

Remove your images from search engines

You can contact Google, Microsoft, and Yahoo, the three largest search engines, to request they remove your non-consensual images from their search results.

Report non-consensual material to Google

If the website owner won't remove your information or if you don't want to contact the website owner directly, Google will remove certain types of sensitive personal information that creates significant risks of identity theft, financial fraud, or other specific harms from Google searches, including:

- Non-consensual explicit or intimate personal images,
- Involuntary fake pornography,
- Content about you on sites with exploitative removal practices,
- Select financial, medical and national ID information, and
- doxing content exposing contact information with an intent to harm

To request removal by Google for information in these areas, search online for "**Remove your personal information from Google**" or type in the below address:

https://support.google.com/websearch/troubleshooter/9685456?hl=en

Click on Google's official page and follow the instructions.

Request to remove your personal information on Google

Use the options below, to contact Google about a personal information removal.

What do you want to do? Remove information you see in Google Search

Let us know where you saw the information you want to have removed.

The information I want removed is: In Google's search results and on a website

Have you contacted the site's website owner?

No, I prefer not to.

I want to remove Nude or sexually explicit items, or names on porn sites

A nude, sexual or intimate picture or video

Are you (or someone you are authorized to represent) in the images or videos and are you nude or are they otherwise sexually explicit? Yes

Have you ever consented to the distribution of the images or videos? No

We recognize that the non-consensual posting of nude and sexually explicit images and videos is distressing for victims. We may remove such content from Google search results upon request. Note that this policy does not apply to images or videos where you have consented to distribution. To submit a copyright or other legal removal request, click here.

Please use this form to report a nude or sexually explicit image of you appearing in search results. To fill out this form on behalf of someone else, you must have the authority to act on their behalf.

It is important to remember that even if we delete a specific URL from Google search, the webpage hosting the content may still exist. You must request removal from the webmaster in order to remove the content from the hosting site. [Learn more .]

* Required field

Personal Information

The full name of the person appearing in the image(s) or video(s): *

You can file a second report with Google specific to non-consensual pornography. Search for "Remove non-consensual explicit or intimate personal images from Google" or type in the below address:

https://support.google.com/websearch/answer/6302812?hl=en

Look for Google's official page that will provide instructions on how to request removal of images.

Remove non-consensual explicit or intimate personal images from Google

We recognize that the non-consensual sharing of intimate or explicit images and videos (sometimes referred to as "revenge porn") is distressing. This article is intended to support you through the process for removal requests of such images and videos from Google search results. To request that this content be removed from Google search results, please use this form. You may also have an authorized representative complete the form on your behalf.

So we can help you, please make sure the content removal request meets **both** of these requirements:

1. The imagery shows you (or the individual you're representing) nude, in a sexual act or an intimate state and
2. You (or the individual you're representing) didn't consent to the imagery or the act and it was made publicly available
   OR
   You intended the content to be private and the imagery was made publicly available without your consent, like "revenge porn"

We take public interest and newsworthiness into account when determining if content will be removed. In the vast majority of cases, these types of images and the content that accompanies them have no public interest value. In very rare cases, we may not remove reported content based on a strong public interest need to make it available to users. In other cases, there may be information provided alongside an image that is in the public interest to remain available in our results, but instances of the image itself without context may be removed.

While we can prevent a page from appearing in our search results, we are not able to remove content from websites that host it, so we recommend reaching out to the website owner to request removal first. Get more details on that process ☑ .

Request to remove your personal information on Google

Use the options below, to contact Google about a personal information removal.

What do you want to do? Remove information you see in Google Search

Let us know where you saw the information you want to have removed.

The information I want removed is: In Google's search results and on a website

Have you contacted the site's website owner?

○ No, how do I do that?
○ No, I prefer not to.
○ Yes

Report non-consensual material to Microsoft

Similar to the Google process, go to the below link and follow Microsoft's instructions:

https://www.microsoft.com/en-us/concern/revengeporn

Non-consensual pornography reporting form

Use this form to ask us to remove a nude or sexually explicit image or video of you that has been shared without your consent. Helpful video.

Know that the information you submit may be shared with others, including the publisher of any webpage we agree to block.

Please note we can only remove content from Microsoft services. You need to work with other companies, including the owners of any website pages you listed on this form, in order to remove pages from their services. Otherwise, the images will still be accessible on the Internet.

Do not use this form to upload pictures of suspected non-consensual pornography or child sexual abuse material.

* Indicates required fields

Your name*

Your email address

We will use this to contact you if needed

Where did you find the content? *

Please select an option

Report non-consensual material to Yahoo

Go to the below link and follow Yahoo's instructions to request removal from Yahoo Search, Yahoo Answers, and other Yahoo sites.

https://help.yahoo.com/kb/posts-intimate-content-permission-sln26123.html#/

> **Get help if someone posts intimate content of you without your permission**
>
> Finding out that someone put your private images or videos online without your consent can be devastating. Here are some resources to help you take action and get the support you might need.
>
> As always, if you feel as though your physical safety or the safety of another person may be in jeopardy, we suggest that you contact your local law enforcement agency immediately.
>
> **Report it**
>
> If this happened on Yahoo, let us know so we can investigate and remove the content. Click a Yahoo site below for instructions on how to submit a report.
>
> ⊕ Yahoo Answers
> ⊕ Yahoo Search
> ⊕ Other Yahoo site

Non-consensual material on DuckDuckGo

While DuckDuckGo is a good browser for protecting your anonymity, it does not offer support to help block information, including non-consensual pornography, from its search results. DuckDuckGo claims to gather data from over 400 sources[97], similar to how the other search engines work. Unfortunately, the publisher does not provide specific instructions or offer guidance on how to request image removal from its search results.

Non-consensual material on Apple Safari searches

---

[97] "DuckDuckGo Help Pages: Results, Sources," DuckDuckGo Help Pages, https://help.duckduckgo.com/duckduckgo-help-pages/results/sources/.

Apple Safari uses Google as its default search engine. Users can change their search engine to Bing, Yahoo, or DuckDuckGo in the Safari tab of the Settings menu. If images are removed from a search engine, those images will likewise be removed when using Safari with that same search engine. You will have to request removal of non-consensual images directly from Google, Bing, and Yahoo.

Keep sensitive photos in a vault

As mentioned in *Chapter 9 – Mobile Device Safety*, and it is worth repeating here, any personal photos and videos that could be used to expose, embarrass, or otherwise harm you should be stored in an encrypted app. Unfortunately, there have been an untold number of phone hacks where sleazeballs have stolen people's private, sometimes intimate, images and posted them online. I highly recommend using a photo vault to secure your important albums.

Bear In mind that these apps may not be 100 percent foolproof to sophisticated hackers but here are some of the more popular secure apps that encrypt both photos and video. There are also many others, but the below apps are known for strong level or encryption.[98] You can find them on the App Store or Google Play.

---

[98] Zhang, Baggili, and Breitinger, "Breaking into the Vault."

CoverMe

CoverMe features a photo and video vault and also offers secure text messaging to other CoverMe users.

Keepsafe

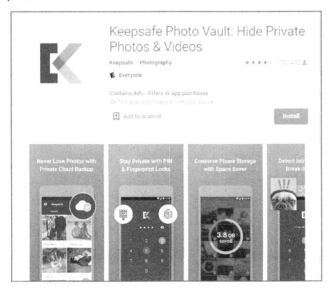

Photo Locker

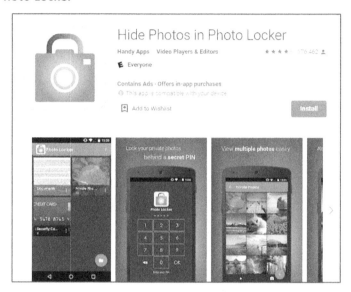

Video Locker

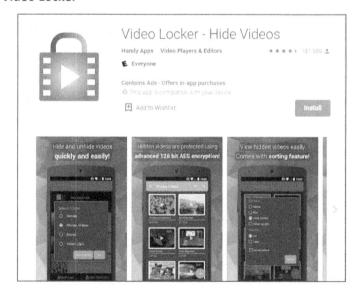

Perspective from an advocate

Cher Scarlett is a vocal advocate for the rights of victims of non-consensual pornography. Portions of her article were included at the beginning of this chapter. She shared this concluding perspective:

Whatever any man or woman gives you with your consent is private. We keep saying there's a risk if you send nudes that they will be leaked, but that's simply because there's little consequence to doing so.

This narrative needs to shift. You can't both expect and want private pornography from your lovers and/or friends with benefits while simultaneously having an attitude that there is not only a reasonable reason to believe that they will be stolen or leaked and distributed without your permission, but that others are entitled to their access once one person leaks them. ...

The problem with this attitude is generally that the same people who say it's your fault for ever sharing them, are the same people who want to see them spread. Really, they are just blaming you so they don't have to take responsibility for encouraging and welcoming the behavior.

Take the side of the victim. They don't need you to condescendingly warn them about how nudes can be leaked. They already know, as they have had them leaked. If you want to teach someone about online safety with private content, teach a class. Mentor some teenagers, and while you're at it, tell those teenagers not to distribute pornographic material without the subject's consent, and punish the ones that do.

I'm super proud of the majority of the responses I've gotten to sharing this [article on Medium.com]. It's been really empowering for the other women who have been affected who didn't feel able to come forward. We've still got a ways to go, but I don't regret sharing this one bit."[99]

If you would like to read Cher's full article, "Half a million people have seen me naked," you can find it on Medium.com at this address:

https://medium.com/@cherp/half-a-million-people-have-seen-me-naked-e70e8b89269c

---

[99] Scarlett, "Half a Million People Have Seen Me Naked."

Chapter 17 – Protecting Teens and Children

According to the FBI, the most common online crimes against children occur when:

- An adult forges a relationship with a young victim online and then later arranges to meet and abuse the child, or
- An adult coerces a child into producing sexually explicit images or videos through manipulation, gifts, or threats – a crime called **sextortion**.

According to the National Council for Missing & Exploited Children, child victims of online enticement range in age from one to 17 years old, with 15 being the average age. Nearly all the children reported not knowing their extorter other than from online communication. A majority, 82 percent, of the predators enticing children were males, nine percent were females, and in the other nine percent of cases the gender was unknown.[100]

> *Sextortion leads to crushing real-life consequences*
>
> The FBI reported the devastating situation that a 13-year-old girl, Chelsea (her name has been changed to protect her identity), experienced after developing an online friendship with another teenage girl named K.C. through a popular messaging app. They sent each other occasional

---

[100] "Online Enticement," National Center for Missing & Exploited Children, https://www.missingkids.org/theissues/onlineenticement.

messages and pictures of their outfits over a few weeks. One mildly revealing photo from Chelsea, however, gave K.C.– who was actually a 30-year-old Florida man named Justin Richard Testani – the opportunity he was waiting for to begin his threats.

According to the FBI in a November 10, 2020 statement posted on their website, the predator said he would share the photo and spread rumors about her to friends and family if she didn't do as he asked.

"She let her guard down," her mother said in a statement on the FBI's website. "She let her guard down because she thought it was another teenage girl."

The demands and threats escalated quickly from there. According to FBI investigators, Testani told Chelsea he would rape and kill her and her loved ones if she didn't perform the increasingly graphic and extreme acts he demanded over video call. The predator used details he'd gathered from their conversations and information she'd posted online to make his threats specific and terrifying. According to Chelsea's mother, he told her, "I know where your mom works. If you don't do what I'm telling you to do, I'll go kill her."

Testani told Chelsea he knew where she lived, where she went to school, and how to get to her friends. "She was convinced it was someone who was standing right outside the door," Chelsea's mother said. "Someone who could get to her immediately."

Testani wanted to take over one of her social media accounts so he could use it to contact her friends, giving him the ability to deceive and exploit another group of young girls.

Chelsea was desperate and terrified when she finally told her parents what was happening. Her stepfather called the police. [101]

After a sentencing hearing that lasted over a year, Testani was sentenced to 60 years in federal prison for child sexual exploitation, according to the U.S. Attorney's Office in the Middle District of Florida.

---

[101] "Sextortion: Case Highlights Growing Online Crime with Devastating Real-Life Consequences," *Federal Bureau of Investigation* (blog), November 10, 2020, https://www.fbi.gov/news/stories/sextortion-case-highlights-growing-online-crime-111020.

According to court documents and presented evidence, Testani contacted hundreds of young girls (usually between the ages of 10 and 13) across the U.S. through Instagram and Snapchat between December 2017 and January 2019.[102]

Chelsea's mother said her daughter is still dealing with depression and anxiety, has trouble concentrating in school, and experiences panic attacks. The fact that Chelsea never met Testani in person and never even saw his face only amplified her fear. This man who hurt her could be anyone, anywhere.

"That's why she went from a social butterfly to absolutely terrified to leave the house," her mother said.

So what's the most important thing parents and caregivers can do? According to the FBI statement, Chelsea herself said that it's to be available if your kids need help. If your child is afraid of getting in trouble for downloading a forbidden app or breaking another family rule, they may not ask for help if they become a victim of sextortion. This means they'll suffer alone, and the predator will be free to target another victim.

Chelsea also shared a message for young people: "Everything is not always as it seems. It is easy for people to act like someone they are not on the internet. Don't believe everything you are told. If you are put in one of these situations, one of the most important things to remember is that although they tell you they have all the power, you are the one in control. Don't be afraid to speak up. You are not alone."[103]

---

[102] "Orange City Man Who 'Sextorted' Multiple Minors Sentenced To 60 Years," *U.S. Department of Justice* (blog), August 6, 2020, https://www.justice.gov/usao-mdfl/pr/orange-city-man-who-sextorted-multiple-minors-sentenced-60-years.

[103] "Sextortion: Case Highlights Growing Online Crime with Devastating Real-Life Consequences."

Don't be afraid to call for help

Report any inappropriate contact between an adult and your child to law enforcement immediately. Notify the site they were using, too. If a young person is being exploited, they are the victim of a crime and should report it. You can help them by doing one or more of the following:

- Contact your local FBI field office at https://www.fbi.gov/contact-us/field-offices,
- Call 1-800-CALL-FBI,
- Report it online at tips.fbi.gov (https://www.fbi.gov/tips), and
- Contact your local law enforcement.

Sextortion: What parents need to know

What is sextortion?

Sextortion occurs when an adult, through threat or manipulation, coerces a minor into producing a sexually explicit image and sending it over the Internet.

Why would any child or teen agree to do such a thing?

According to the FBI, the individuals carrying out this crime are skilled and ruthless and have honed their techniques and approaches to maximize their chances at success. The entry point to a young person can be any number of mobile or online sites, applications, or games. The approach may come as compliments or flattery or the pretense of beginning a romantic relationship.

Another entry point is to offer the child something they value in exchange for taking a quick picture. This could be the possibility of a modeling contract; online game credits or codes; or money, cryptocurrency, and gift cards.

The third common point of entry is to go right to threats by either claiming they already have an image of the young person that they will distribute or threatening to harm the child or other people or things the child cares about.

Once the perpetrator has the first image, they use the threat of exposure or other harm to keep the child producing more and more explicit material.

But my child would never do that.

The FBI has interviewed victims as young as 8, and the crime affects children of both genders and crosses all ethnic and socioeconomic groups. The victims are honor-roll students, the children of teachers, student athletes, etc. The only common trait among victims is Internet access.

Why don't the victims tell someone or ask for help?

The cycle of victimization continues because the child is afraid—afraid of the repercussions threatened by the criminal and afraid they will be in trouble with their parents, guardians, or law enforcement. By the time a child is a victim, they have done something that may be generating deep feelings of shame and embarrassment. The criminal may also be telling them they have produced child pornography and will be prosecuted for it. In addition, they may fear their access to their phone or computer will be taken away from them as a result of their actions.

How do I protect the young people I know?

Information-sharing and open lines of communication are the best defense. Young people need to know this crime is happening and understand where the risks are hiding. Explain to the children in your life that people can pretend to be anyone or anything online, a stranger reaching out to them online may be doing so with bad intent, and no matter what the platform or application claims, nothing "disappears" online. If they take a photo or video, it always has the potential to become public.

The other crucial element is to keep the door open to your children so that they know they can come to you and ask for help. Let them know that your first move will be to help—always. These predators are powerful because of fear, and the victims suffer ever more negative consequences as the crime carries on over days, weeks, and months.

If you are the adult that a child trusts with this information, comfort them, help them understand they have been the victim of a crime, and help them report it to law enforcement. [104]

How to talk about sextortion with your kids

The FBI has provided the following suggestions to help parents and caregivers talk about online safety with their teens and children about online safety.

The New Version of Don't Talk to Strangers

- When you're online, has anyone you don't know ever tried to contact or talk to you?
- What did you do or what would you do if that happened?
- Why do you think someone would want to reach a kid online?
- You know, it's easy to pretend to be someone you're not online and not every person is a good person. Make sure you block or ignore anything that comes in from someone you don't know in real life.

The Power of a Picture

- Has anyone you know ever sent a picture of themselves that got passed around school or a team or club?
- What's possible anytime you send someone a picture?

---

[104] "Sextortion: What Parents, Caregivers, and Educators Need to Know," Federal Bureau of Investigation, May 30, 2019, https://www.fbi.gov/news/stories/stop-sextortion-youth-face-risk-online-090319#Resources-for%20Parents.

- What if that picture were embarrassing?
- Can you think about how someone could use that kind of picture against a person?

I'm Here to Help

- I read an article today about kids being pressured to send images and video of their bodies to a person they met online. Have you ever heard about anything like that?
- Sometimes they were being threatened and harassed—scary stuff.
- You know, if you are ever feeling like something is going on—online or off—that feels scary or wrong or over your head, my first concern is going to be helping you. You can always come to me.[105]

---

[105] "Sextortion: What Parents, Caregivers, and Educators Need to Know."

Sextortion: Ask your kids to read this

What is sextortion?

Sextortion describes a crime that happens online when an adult convinces a person who is younger than 18 to share sexual pictures or perform sexual acts on a webcam.

How does it start?

According to the FBI, sextortion can start on any site where people meet and communicate. Someone may contact you while you are playing a game online or reach out over a dating app or one of your social media accounts.

In some cases, the first contact from the criminal will be a threat. The person may claim they already have a picture or video of you that they will share if you don't send more pictures. More often, however, this crime starts when young people believe they are communicating with someone their own age who is interested in a relationship or someone who is offering something of value. The adult can use threats, gifts, money, flattery, lies, or other methods to get a young person to produce these images.

After the criminal has one or more videos or pictures, they use the threat of sharing or publishing that content to get the victim to produce more images.

The adult has committed a crime as soon as they ask a young person for a single graphic image.

Why do young people agree to do this?

The people who commit this crime have studied how to reach and target children and teens.

One person the FBI put in prison for this crime was a man in his 40s who worked as a youth minister so he could learn how teens talked to each other. Then, he created social media profiles where he pretended to be a teenage girl. This "girl" would start talking to boys online and encourage them to make videos.

Another person offered money and new smartphones to his victims.

In one case, the criminal threatened a girl—saying he would hurt her and bomb her school—if she didn't send pictures.

Other cases start with the offer of currency or credits in a video game in exchange for a quick picture.

How do you know who can be trusted online?

That's what is so hard about online connections. The FBI has found that those who commit this crime may have dozens of different online accounts and profiles and are communicating with many young people at the same time—trying to find victims.

Be extremely cautious when you are speaking with someone online who you have not met in real life. It's easy to think: I'm on my phone, in my own house, what could possibly happen? But you can very quickly give a criminal the information and material he needs to do you harm.

But how can this harm me?

It's true that these criminals don't usually meet up with kids in real life, but the victims of this crime still experience negative effects. The criminals can become vicious and non-stop with their demands, harassment, and threats. Victims report feeling scared, alone, embarrassed, anxious, and desperate. Many feel like there's no way out of the situation.

What do I do if this is happening to me?

If you are ready, reach out to the FBI at **1-800-CALL-FBI** or report the crime online at https://tips.fbi.gov. FBI agents see these cases a lot and have helped thousands of young people. The FBI wants to stop the harassment, arrest the person behind the crime, and help you get the support you need.

If you're not feeling ready to speak to the FBI, go to another trusted adult. Tell them you are being victimized online and need help. Talking about this can feel impossible, but there are people who can help. You are not the one in trouble.

How can you say I won't be in trouble?

You are not the one who is breaking the law. This situation can feel really confusing, and the criminals count on you feeling too unsure, scared, or embarrassed to tell someone. Even if this started on an app or site that you are too young to be on. Even if you felt okay about making some of the content. Even if you accepted money or a game credit or something else, you are not the one who is in trouble. Sextortion is a crime because it is illegal and wrong for an adult to ask for, pay for, or demand graphic images from a minor.

How can I help someone else who is in this situation?

If you learn a friend, classmate, or family member is being victimized, listen to them with kindness and understanding. Tell them you are sorry that this is happening to them and that you want to help. Let them know that they are the victim of a crime and have not done anything wrong. Encourage them to ask for help and see if you can help them identify a trusted adult to tell.

How do I protect myself and my friends?

Your generation can be the generation that shuts down these criminals. Awareness and sensible safety practices online, along with a willingness to ask for help, can put an end to this exploitation. The FBI agents who work on these cases want you to know these six things:

> - Be selective about what you share online. If your social media accounts are open to everyone, a predator may be able to figure out a lot of information about you.
> - Be wary of anyone you encounter for the first time online. Block or ignore messages from strangers.
> - Be aware that people can pretend to be anything or anyone online. Videos and photos are not proof that a person is who they claim to be. Images can be altered or stolen.
> - Be suspicious if you meet someone on one game or app and they ask you to start talking to them on a different platform.
> - Be in the know. Any content you create online—whether it is a text message, photo, or video—can be made public. And once you send something, you don't have any control over where it goes next.
> - Be willing to ask for help. If you are getting messages or requests online that don't seem right, block the sender, report the behavior to the site administrator, or go to an adult. If you have been victimized online, tell someone.[106]

Social media awareness

1. Make sure your children understand the difference between real friends and virtual friends.
2. Explain to your child they should never share their name, address, date of birth, or phone numbers to anyone on the internet.

---

[106] "What Kids and Teens Need to Know About Sextortion," Federal Bureau of Investigation, September 3, 2019, https://www.fbi.gov/news/stories/stop-sextortion-youth-face-risk-online-090319.

3. Explain to your child they should never send photos or videos of themselves to strangers on the internet.
4. Teach your child not to respond to mean, insulting or hurtful messages or comments.
5. For younger children, you should ensure their online friends and followers are only people you and your child actually know in real life.
6. Setting up an antivirus program and malware removal protection recommended in *Chapter 12 – Block, Remove, Backup, and Restore* will protect you and them from phishing. Explain to your child the dangers of clicking on random links that may be sent to them.
7. Make it a rule with your kids that they can't arrange to meet up with someone they met online without your knowledge and supervision.

Consider doing these 6 steps now

Here are simple, immediate steps you can take to ensure you and your child(ren) are practicing healthy online habits together.

1. Most importantly, be there for your child

Speak with your child and make sure they understand that they can come to you if they see anything inappropriate online, if anyone is treating them badly, or if they aren't sure what's right and what's wrong. The most important advice for parents is to have open and ongoing conversations about safe and appropriate online behavior.

Importantly, let them know that they will not "get in trouble" for being honest with you and that you are there to help them, no matter what the situation may be.

2. Their phone is actually your phone

Since you likely purchased or are paying the monthly service fees for your child's phone, tablet, or computer, help them understand that those devices actually belong to you (the parent), not them. You are allowing them to use the devices. As a result, you have the right to have the devices' unlock passwords. Have your child provide you with the unlock codes, write them down, and store them safely. Let them understand that, as long as they use their devices responsibly, you will let them have the appropriate level of privacy. They should, however, use their devices with the understanding that you might decide to view them at any time.

If they change their passcodes, it is their responsibility to inform you promptly. You should also confirm their passcodes occasionally in the event they inadvertently changed their codes and forgot to inform you.

3. **Practice safer browsing**

In addition to the recommendations in *Chapter 8 – Browsing*, if your family is using a shared computer, you should set up separate accounts for yourself and your child. Separate accounts can help protect your files and personal information from being accessed (and possibly deleted) by your children.

On your child's account you can adjust the settings on their internet browser to Child Safe or Child Friendly limits.

Use a password keeper for your child's online accounts, so that you can have access to their online activity if ever needed.

4. **Limit screen time**

It's a prudent habit not to let your child have phones, tablets, or laptops in their bedroom overnight, unmonitored, when they should be sleeping instead. Designate a different spot in your home for them to charge their devices overnight, not behind their closed bedroom doors.

You can determine what is reasonable and appropriate for your older children as it becomes necessary for them to do more homework on their devices.

5. Social media safety – to do

Don't let your children use their actual real name as their usernames. That information makes it too easy for someone to search for their personal information (including location) online. Have them use an alias (such as Ghost Pepper (first name: Ghost, last name: Pepper)).

For most sites, there's no benefit for using their actual date of birth in their profiles. It's important that they don't misrepresent their actual age (a 9-year-old shouldn't say they're 12 (or 18 for that matter)) but given how much data mining is performed on us, not everybody needs (or deserves) to know our true details. While keeping their birth year accurate, I recommend making their birth month and day some other easily-remembered date (such as October 31 Halloween) for social media and other non-critical accounts. For academic, medical, and other important accounts, you would use their real, valuable information.

You children should not use their face in their profile photos. Have them use a non-personal image, icon or emoji. Make it harder for random people to search for them online.

Make their social media settings private, so only Friends can see their posts. Allowing Friends of Friends to contact them is a personal decision for you to make, depending on your level of confidence your child can responsibly manage their social media. Do not let their posts be viewable by the unrestricted public.

Educate yourself about the websites, software, games, and apps that your child uses.

Check their social media and gaming profiles and posts. Have conversations about what is appropriate to say or share.

6. If your child requires a public face

It's a personal decision on whether or not you want your child to have a public-facing account. If your child requires a public face for any reason, whether for their academics, sports, or other interests, they should maintain two very separate accounts on any platform.

One account should be their personal account, set up with all of the safeguards detailed above (including an alias username and non-identifiable profile photo). They should share their personal account only with their close circle of relationships, where they can be themselves.

The other account would be their public-facing account, where the information they share is carefully curated, providing the information that is appropriate for the general public to view. They should draw a hard line on who they let into their personal account and who they deny, as some strangers (who may still be able to track down both of your child's accounts) would likely request access to both. Speak to them about the importance of setting boundaries between their personal and public faces.

If your child is already using only one account for both personal and public posting, have them create a second private account and invite only their close circle to connect there. They can continue to use the existing account as their public-facing account. They may want to consider editing or deleting past posts from that account that provide too much personal information. Review their posts with them to help decide what old posts are appropriate to continue sharing with the public.

The National Sex Offender Public Website

As a precaution, parents and caregivers should know about this website and check it to be aware if a registered sex offender may be located in their local surroundings.

This database is coordinated by the Department of Justice and enables the public to search the latest information from all 50 states, the District of Columbia, Puerto Rico, Guam, and numerous Indian tribes for the identity and location of known sex offenders. You can also search registry websites maintained by individual jurisdictions by following the links. The information contained in the national registry and the state and tribal registries is identical, but the national registry enables a search across multiple jurisdictions. The registry is available at this address:

https://www.fbi.gov/scams-and-safety/sex-offender-registry

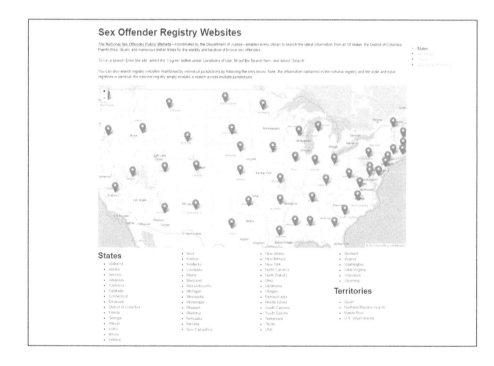

Age-appropriate education for younger children

The FBI offers age-appropriate activities to teach children in 3rd through 8th grades about online safe habits, in both English and Spanish at these addresses:

English version: https://sos.fbi.gov/en/

Spanish version: https://sos.fbi.gov/es/

Chapter 18 – Removing Your Personal Info from the Internet

Considering how much damage malicious online actors can inflict upon targets, here are several ways you can consider closing more gaps in your digital armor to protect your privacy and information. More specifically, consider taking steps to remove the abundance of information about you that exists unrestricted online. Realistically, it's not possible to make yourself a ghost, but you can diminish your visibility and reduce your digital footprint.

Be aware that removing your information from the internet takes time, so this effort is more of an on-going process, like losing weight or exercising, to get digitally healthier.

Have Google blur your home from Street View Maps

Google's Street View Maps is an excellent reconnaissance tool, and so for your privacy purposes it should be restricted as much as possible. Google Maps provide 360-degree views of probably most every street in the U.S. at this point. The general public can also upload their own regular and 360-degree images of locations, which may also include your home, so Google Street View Maps images may be the property of either Google or third parties.

Google makes it relatively easy to request blurring of images of your home, your body, or your car in images they own so the general public can't identify those details. If a third party owns an image that includes your details, the removal process is more cumbersome but still worthwhile to preserve your anonymity.

Google-owned images

https://maps.google.com

In Google Maps, enter your home address, and then click the person icon on the screen to enter Street View. In Street View, see if your home or car is identifiable. Also see if you or your family might be included in the photograph. To request blurring of the details, follow the below steps:

Go to https://maps.google.com and enter your home address. For purposes of this illustration we're looking at a random location in New York City.

Click on the person icon in the lower right corner of the map, which will show what roads are available in Google Street View.

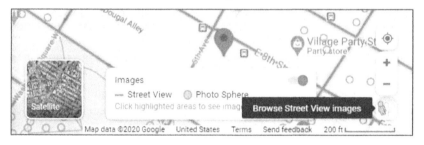

Google Street View will open. Click the ••• at the upper left for More Options, and select "Report a problem."

Request blurring of your home, car license plate, or face.

You should receive an immediate confirmation that your request has been received by Google. Google states they will contact you to let you know of any action they take. Check back in Street View in a few weeks to see if they have removed your image.

Thanks! We've received your report and will review it soon. If we find the image to be in violation of our policies we'll take the appropriate action, and will email you with the status of any changes.

Sincerely,

Google Maps team

Google Maps Home

© 2020 Google - Google Home - Google Maps Home - Privacy Policy - Google Maps Help

Third-party, Google Contributor images

According to Google Maps' privacy policy, Google automatically blurs faces and license plates from videos, but not from photos. If you find your face, license plate, or home in a user contribution and want to have the image removed, use the Report a Problem feature on the image.[107] The process is similar to the Google instructions above.

Remove your info from data brokers manually

Vermont's data broker law, which became effective January 1, 2019, governs data brokers, which it defines as companies that collect and sell or license to third parties the personal information of a consumer with whom the business does not have a direct relationship. The law requires that data brokers annually register with the Vermont Secretary of State. To give a sense of how prevalent this activity is, as of November 2020, there were 277 data

---

[107] "Maps User Contributed Content Policy: Privacy," Google Support, https://support.google.com/contributionpolicy/answer/7401426?hl=en&ref_topic=7422769.

brokers registered in Vermont[108], and it's fair to assume those companies are active nationwide or even globally.

I worked to remove my own, my wife's and my adult daughter's information from several data broker sites and speaking from personal experience, it's a time-consuming and frustrating process. That being said, removing personal data from data broker sites is important to make it more difficult for strangers to find your personal information.

There is also a paid service available that will remove your information from data broker sites on an on-going basis (more on that below).

Here are opt-out addresses for some of the most popular data brokers that you can contact directly:

BeenVerified: https://www.beenverified.com/app/optout/search

CheckPeople: https://checkpeople.com/do-not-sell-info

Instant Checkmate: https://www.instantcheckmate.com/opt-out/

Intelius: https://www.intelius.com/opt-out/

PeekYou: https://www.peekyou.com/about/contact/optout/

PeopleFinders: https://www.peoplefinders.com/opt-out

Pipl: https://pipl.com/personal-information-removal-request

Radaris: https://radaris.com/page/how-to-remove

Spokeo: https://www.spokeo.com/optout

USA People Search: https://www.usa-people-search.com/manage

USSearch: https://www.ussearch.com/opt-out/submit/

---

[108] "Data Broker Search," Vermont Secretary of State: Corporations Division, https://bizfilings.vermont.gov/online/DatabrokerInquire/DataBrokerSearch.

Consider using a paid removal service to get the job done

DeleteMe

https://www.joindeleteme.com

After deciding that: (i) my time was valuable and worth some amount of money, (ii) avoiding unnecessary frustration was important to my mental wellbeing, and (iii) I really do not want my, my wife's or my children's personal information freely and easily available on the internet, I decided to subscribe to the paid data removal service DeleteMe. I decided that this was a justifiable expense to add to my cyber security budget (which otherwise isn't that significant) for the outsized benefit I expect to receive. As more and more of our online lives are connected, analyzed, and targeted by sophisticated marketing (whether for commercial, political or other agendas) I want to make my family as opaque as possible to prying eyes.

In my search for a data removal service, I have not found comparable services to DeleteMe, which uses actual human beings for their data removal processes, not merely relying on bots or apps to request removal from sites. DeleteMe points out that while some sites remove your information quickly others can take days or weeks.

DeleteMe currently removes data from 41 data broker sites (listed below), which are way more than I care to deal with personally. Importantly, DeleteMe reviews these sites quarterly (so 4 times a year) for any new information that may be added about my family. The service will provide regular reporting on your data removal status.

The cost may cause someone to pause, but I believe it's well worth it for the privacy it affords. The standard plan for 1 person is $130 per year ($10.75 per month), $230 for 2 people for 1 year ($9.54 per person per month), or $350 for 2 people for 2 years ($7.24 per person per month).

Here also is an affiliate link that will apply a 20% off discount from DeleteMe's standard pricing, I hope it helps!

https://joindeleteme.com/refer?coupon=RFR-115917-RMHRRR

Personally, I decided to cancel an online entertainment subscription that was about the same cost and replace it with this service for the benefits received.

The 41 data broker sites that DeleteMe removes your personal data from include:

411.com	emailfinder.com	phonesbook.com
addresses.com	freephonetracer.com	premium.whitepages.com
advanced-people-search.com	grey-pages.com	privateeye.com
	hauziz.com	publicrecords.com
advancedbackgroundchecks.com	identitypi.com	publicrecordsnow.com
	instantcheckmate.com	spokeo.com
anywho.com	intelius.com	thepublicrecords.com
archives.com	mylife.com	theidentitypages.com
beenverified.com	neighbor.report	truthfinder.com
checkthem.com	nuwber.com	ussearch.com
clustrmaps.com	people.yellowpages.com	usa-people-search.com
cyberbackgroundchecks.com	peoplefinders.com	whitepages.com
dexknows.com	peoplelooker.com	xlek.com
easybackgroundchecks.com	peoplelookup.com	zabasearch.com
	peoplesmart.com	

Chapter 19 – Identity Theft

Well beyond the financial damage that identity theft inflicts on victims, the emotional, mental, and physical harm may be severe for the targeted victim as well as their family, friends, co-workers, classmates, and other relationships. According to the Identity Theft Resource Center, a non-profit organization established to support victims of identity theft in resolving their cases, "the emotional impacts of identity crime have left victims with overwhelmingly negative feelings about their situation." Respondents reported that they felt worried, angry and frustrated (each at 85 percent); violated (83 percent); that they could not trust others and felt unsafe (both 69 percent); a sense of powerlessness or helplessness (67 percent); sad or depressed (59 percent) and betrayed (55 percent).

Additionally, the Center reported, "The negative emotional impacts had very real physical consequences." Of the individuals that have responded, 84 percent reported issues with their sleep habits; 77 percent reported increased stress levels; 63 had problems with their concentration; 56 had persistent aches, pains, headaches and/or cramps and the same percentage experienced stomach issues; 54 percent had increased fatigue or decreased energy and 50 percent reported that they had lost interest in activities or hobbies they once enjoyed.[109]

It is far from a victimless crime

Victims of identity theft can be harmed in several ways. When someone assumes your name and credentials, they can:

---

[109] "Identity Theft: The Aftermath Study," *Identity Theft Resource Center* (blog), https://www.idtheftcenter.org/identity-theft-aftermath-study/.

Exploit your credit. With your Social Security number, a thief can easily open new accounts, ranging from credit cards to services to mortgages to personal and business loans. Damaged credit ratings will also make premiums for things such as auto and homeowners' insurance more expensive.

Create tax liabilities. If someone uses your SSN on a job application, collects income and doesn't pay taxes that burden will by default fall to you. Also, thieves sometimes file fake tax returns in a person's name, claiming a hefty tax refund. By the time the victim discovers the government paid an illegitimate payment to a stranger, the money has disappeared, leaving you to clean up the damage.

Hurt your job prospects. The Fair Credit Reporting Act requires prospective employers to obtain a hiring candidate's written consent before obtaining their credit history. Although some states restrict employers from using credit reports for employment decisions, employers have full discretion on whether or not they choose to hire a person. Could an applicant's bad credit report influence a prospective employer's decision? Possibly. Employers are not required to explain the reasons for declining a candidate, so you might never know if bad credit was a factor.

Hurt your healthcare. Medical identity theft is when someone steals or uses your personal information to obtain medical treatment, and submit fraudulent health insurance claims without your authorization. Medical identity theft can disrupt your medical care when another person's medical treatments are added erroneously to your health history.

Hurt your children. Child identity theft occurs when someone uses a child's Social Security number to commit fraud, including opening credit accounts, taking out loans or applying for government benefits or a job. Because children typically have clean credit records and don't apply for credit until they are older, such as for student loans, this identity theft can go on for years. According to research firm Javelin Strategy & Research, more than 1 million children were victims of identity fraud in 2017, resulting in losses of $2.6 billion and over $540 million in out-of-pocket costs to families.[110]

Cost you time, money, and energy. Repairing identity theft is a laborious, stressful, time-consuming process. Your labor, stress, and time are what is going to be expended, as well as those people close to you who get involved in helping you resolve it.

So, what to do?

Check your credit reports regularly, at least annually.

https://www.annualcreditreport.com/

Get your free credit reports from Equifax, Experian, and TransUnion. Review your reports. Make note of any account or transaction you don't recognize. This will help you report the theft to the FTC and the police.

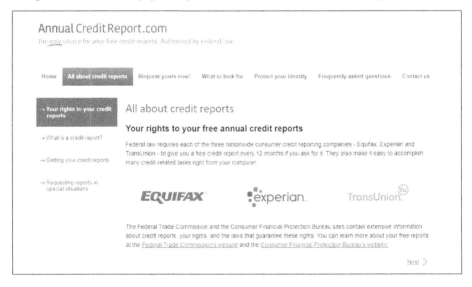

---

[110] Al Pascual and Kyle Marchini, "2018 Child Identity Fraud Study," Javelin, April 24, 2018, https://www.javelinstrategy.com/coverage-area/2018-child-identity-fraud-study.

Place a fraud alert on your credit reports

Place a free, one-year fraud alert by contacting one of the three credit bureaus. That company must tell the other two. A fraud alert is free. It will make it harder for someone to open new accounts in your name. When you have an alert on your report, a business must verify your identity before it issues new credit in your name. You can renew the fraud alert after one year. You'll get a letter from each credit bureau. It will confirm that they placed a fraud alert on your file.

https://www.equifax.com/personal/

Phone: 800-685-1111

https://www.experian.com/

Phone: 888-EXPERIAN (888-397-3742)

https://www.transunion.com/

Phone: 888-909-8872

Pay attention to the bills you receive

In the constant flow of information we receive, it's easy to let microtransactions or vague recurring transactions slip past on our credit cards, which can be indicative of larger crimes.

Protect your privacy online.

As previously covered in earlier chapters.

Identity theft recovery steps

According to the Federal Trade Commission (FTC), if your identity has been stolen there are important action steps to take immediately. A summary of these steps are provide below. A much more detailed action plan with steps to take and authorities to contact is provided in this book's Appendix. The action plan in the Appendix is laborious and provides specific instructions to help you reclaim your data and identity. I truly hope you never have to use it.

What's important to note in this extremely brief summary is how many meaningful, time-consuming actions may need to be taken on your part to recover your identity. I hope this list underscores why all of the healthy habits we covered in previous chapters should be not only considered but actually put into action to keep your data private.

If your identity is stolen, do these right away
1. Call the companies where you know fraud occurred.
2. Place a fraud alert and get your credit reports.
3. Report identity theft to the FTC.
4. File a report with your local police department.

What to do next - Begin to repair the damage.
5. Close new accounts opened in your name.
6. Remove bogus charges from your accounts.
7. Correct your credit report.
8. Consider adding an extended fraud alert or credit freeze.
9. Review your credit reports often.

Other possible steps

10. Report a misused Social Security number.
11. Stop debt collectors from trying to collect debts you don't owe.
12. Replace government-issued IDs.
13. Clear your name of criminal charges.

For certain types of accounts, you might have to contact additional offices.

14. Utilities
15. Phones
16. Government benefits
17. Checking accounts
18. Student loans
19. Apartment or House Rentals
20. Investment accounts
21. Bankruptcy filed in your name

Special forms of identity theft requiring additional steps

22. Tax Identity Theft
23. Child Identity Theft
24. Medical Identity Theft

Section IV – Protect Your Career

Section Table of Contents

Topic	**Page**
Chapter 20 – Separate Your Work Life from Your Personal Life	293
HR protects the company, not you	293
Use separate devices	294
Everything is being monitored	294
The data on company devices belong to your employer	295
Chapter 21 – Job Searches and Career Tools	297
Identify sales robots and fake friends on LinkedIn	297
Job searching	298
Get past screening robots	299
Chapter 22 – Online Meetings	301
This really could have been an email	301
Safety steps for meeting organizers	301
Safety steps for attendees	303
Which video call services to avoid	306
Protect your recorded meetings	307

Chapter 20 – Separate Your Work Life from Your Personal Life

I've been on both sides of the hiring and firing process over the years and, not surprisingly, the attitudes on each side of the employer/employee relationship are very different.

HR protects the company, not you

A company's human resources department is there to protect the company, they're not there to protect you. When there are employment disputes, human resources will ultimately take the actions that are in the company's best interests and reduce the company's risks. If you can be treated well in the resolution, all the better. If you can't be treated as well as you would like, it's wise to position yourself (in advance) with the least personal risk as possible, including making sure your personal digital life is organized and under your control.

When I was an employee, I hadn't given much thought to using my company-issued laptop and mobile phone as "my" computer and "my" phone, meaning I used them for most everything in both my work and personal life. I was always careful not to use either in violation of common sense when web browsing, writing emails or anything else, knowing that the company was monitoring everyone's computer usage. I did, however, likely use them for more of my personal life than was prudent. Paying bills, bookmarking vegetarian chili recipes, checking Facebook or my personal Gmail account were everyday activities I would slip into my hours at the office. When I left a company, like everyone else I dutifully turned in my laptop and phone. Fortunately, because I never did anything inappropriate, I had nothing to fear.

On the other hand, when I was in management, we once had the difficult task of terminating a wayward employee for dereliction of duty and some severe lapses in judgment. The company took possession of that person's laptop and mobile phone and had our IT person sift through them for any files or emails that would be of concern to the company. Every file, including browser histories (and they were extensive), on the devices was reviewed since they were, after all, the company's property.

It's important to recognize which side of the employer/employee relationship you are on so you can fulfill your duties accordingly.

Use separate devices

If at all possible, you should try to use your company-issued computer and/or phone solely for your work responsibilities and a completely separate computer and phone (that you rightfully own) for everything else. It's the best way to not cross-contaminate your two very important worlds. You should assume that everything you do on your company-issued devices are monitored by your company, backed up and documented for future reference. Clearly, there is a cost to purchase a separate computer, tablet, iPad or ChromeBook for your personal use but if at all possible this important step can provide important personal protection. If you are unable to have a separate computer, try to use your personal mobile phone for your personal activity, emails and browsing. It's not a guarantee of privacy (especially if you use your personal device on the company's WiFi) but it's much better than not doing so.

Everything is being monitored

You should assume that everything you do while connected to your employer's network (both on-site and remotely) is being logged by your company, and can be retrieved in the company's log files.

Be further aware that the sites you visit could unintentionally go against the company's usage policies so constant diligence and caution is wise.

Also assume that every keystroke and mouse click you make, even if working offline, are still being recorded by your devices, with the surveillance to be uploaded to the company's servers the next time you connect to the internet.

The data on company devices belong to your employer

If you haven't backed up your personal data to somewhere you control, should you ever get terminated or laid off and your devices are taken back by the company you could lose your important documents if they reside only on that device. I've yet to see a company that would grant an imminently departing employee the time (or continued access) to back up their personal files off their devices.

Chapter 21 – Job Searches and Career Tools

Identify sales robots and fake friends on LinkedIn

Not too long ago I added a piece of digital bait to my LinkedIn profile to test if the "new friend" invitations I regularly receive were being sent to me by real people or automated robots. The results were eye-opening.

I receive anywhere from one to a few invitations a day, and roughly half of those are from 3rd hand connections, meaning they don't know me or anyone else I'm connected to on LinkedIn. Oftentimes the invitations don't include a message, just a connection request so there's no context and I haven't met the individuals previously. While I'd like to think that I'm sooooo interesting a human being that strangers from around the world flock to me, in reality I don't know why strangers from China, the Middle East, Africa and randomly across the U.S. might send me connection invites.

More and more, companies and salespeople are using automated programs to scrub Linkedin for leads. To test if any of my connection requests were automated, I added an emoji icon before my first name in my professional profile. To insert the graphic, I edited my profile name using the LinkedIn app on my mobile phone, which allowed me to use the on-screen keyboard with emojis. I chose a globe because, yeah, I'm so worldly or something like that. It seemed more appropriate than the beer mug or smiley face choices. For good measure, I also added a different emoji, a blue map, at the end of my headline to see if that may get picked up by any automation.

Soon enough, about 1 out of every 5 or 7 new invitations I received said something along the lines of "Hi there 🌐 Daniel Farber, I work in the IT industry and am interested in connecting. Any interest?"

Ummm... no.

The connection invites continue to trickle in day after day. Adding an emoji at the beginning of my first name tells me which ones I can ignore since they truly are cold calls and I'm just an automated keyword search.

Job searching

It's tough trying to find a job through online resources. LinkedIn, Indeed, ZipRecruiter, Monster.com, and the countless company-specific job boards offer thousands of "opportunities" but it's hard to tell what's real, what's real for you, and what's never going to materialize.

On the flip side, from the recruiters' standpoint, they are deluged with electronic resumes and cover letters from a spectrum of qualified, somewhat qualified, and less-than-qualified candidates that may or may not be a fit for the role. To sort through the sheer volume they sometimes encounter, it makes efficient sense for hiring managers or their outsourced employment service providers to automate the initial screening process.

One executive I know who heads up a research division of a well-respected human rights organization needed to hire one entry level office assistant. His organization posted the job opening on their website. He told me that he received over 500 resumes from hopeful candidates because they wanted to be associated with that organization at any level.

I've read estimates that say general job seekers have only a 5 percent chance of getting an interview for an online job posting. Is it 5 or 7 or 10 percent? Or 2? It depends on the situation but realistically whatever the odds are, they're incredibly low. A 5 percent likelihood means that someone who sends out 100 proper resumes might get 5 interviews out of the effort. Depressing odds at best.

Today's recruiting landscape is heavily automated, which makes it more difficult for the vast majority of people seeking opportunities. Knowing how the screening process works is important, here are ways one can try to improve their chances of rising to the top of the candidate pile by playing to those rules of engagement.

Get past screening robots

Ultimately, the hiring decisions will be made by living, breathing people but, to get to them, candidates have to do the dance of getting through the algorithms. It's not unreasonable to make a screening strategy part of one's job search. I've heard many recruiting consultants recommend that candidates weave key words and phrases found in specific job postings into the resume they submit to that specific company, which makes sense. The hiring manager after all would plug keywords into the screening program to sift through the incoming resumes.

I recommend taking that customized approach a step further (actually, a few steps further) and not only weave in keywords (which takes a long time to edit and craft into a resume) and instead inject the entire job description into your customized resume and cover letter. Again, the objective is to connect with a real human being, and that requires getting past an algorithm which has no feelings, so don't feel too bad about outwitting a robot. It's like a digital chess game.

Assuming your resume is formatted in Microsoft Word or similar program where you have the ability to provide detailed formatting, if you would like to bypass some of the screening robots, try these steps:

1. Copy the entire job posting text (including job title, responsibilities, and qualifications) and paste it as plain text (without line breaks so it is one long wrapped paragraph) at the bottom (not the footer) of both your resume and cover letter.

2. Change that additional text to 1-point font and make the color white so it appears invisible. By making the font 1 point it should not alter your overall page length. Adjust line spacing if necessary.

3. Rename and save your resume and cover letter as PDF documents specific to that particular job opportunity. You've essentially added your own version of metadata into your documents, which will hopefully be read by screening programs as matching keywords to that job search, and add your application to the shorter list of candidates for review.

4. Some recruiting sites may automatically upload resumes and cover letters into form fields. If that happens to your documents, the job descriptions may appear at the very bottom of the standardized form, but let's assume that if you are a qualified candidate the human recruiter will not mind to meet. They may just assume it was a formatting error. Or maybe they will be impressed with your resourcefulness in bypassing their screening program. It's impossible to predict. Either way, hopefully you'll have achieved your goal of getting past screening robots.

Chapter 22 – Online Meetings

From UrbanDictionary.com:

Zoombomb – The act of performing a silly or mischievous act in the background of someone's video conference. Can be contacted to z-bomb. Similar to photo bombing. Originated from the CoViD-19 quarantine era where schools and employers were using Zoom to conduct classes and business from home. [111]

Like the Zoom-related scam we mentioned in *Chapter 4 – Email Safety*, be conscientious when clicking meeting links and confirm the link is from someone you trust.

This really could have been an email

Now that so much of the world has gone virtual working and learning from home, the millions of daily video calls leave unsuspecting users open to snooping, surveillance, harassment, invasion, and disruption. As time goes on the list will get longer as troublemakers develop new ways to exploit meetings as workers spend more and more time in video calls that really could have been emails.

Safety steps for meeting organizers

For maximum security and personal privacy consider adding some or all of the following steps to your video call habits:

---

[111] Lyfesavr, "Urban Dictionary: Zoom Bomb," Urban Dictionary, April 1, 2020, https://www.urbandictionary.com/define.php?term=Zoom%20bomb.

Require pre-registration for public calls

If you are advertising a public video call or conference call, don't include the meeting link in the initial announcement. Instead, require users to register, and then inform the registered, vetted users that you will be sending them the live meeting link as close to the meeting date and time as possible, which will help control your information being put out in the wild.

Use a temporary meeting ID

If you are the person responsible for scheduling a video call or conference call, it's safest to use a temporary meeting ID. If you use your account's default meeting ID and an unauthorized person gains access, they can always sign in again to your default ID during your future meeting if they seek to harass you further.

Require a meeting passcode

Have the meetings you organize require users enter a passcode for entry, making it harder for drive-by Zoombombing. The Electronic Frontier Foundation, a nonprofit focused on digital civil liberties, advises meeting organizers to be aware that meeting passcodes may automatically be included in meeting invitations by default depending on the platform being used. So if you are posting a meeting publicly, such as in a newsletter or on social media, you should ensure the passcode is not shared to the general public in the invitation link. You can send registered, approved attendees the passcode separately.[112]

---

[112] Gennie Gebhart and Rory Mir, "Harden Your Zoom Settings to Protect Your Privacy and Avoid Trolls," *Electronic Frontier Foundation* (blog), April 10, 2020, https://www.eff.org/deeplinks/2020/04/harden-your-zoom-settings-protect-your-privacy-and-avoid-trolls.

Use a waiting room

Making users wait in a virtual waiting room until the host admits them into the main meeting is also a good crowd control mechanism.

Designate co-hosts

You can designate co-hosts for a meeting in your meeting settings. Co-hosts can assist with admitting people into the meeting, responding to chats, and moderate attendees to run your meeting efficiently.

Restrict screen sharing

As meeting host, you can decide if allowing participants to have the ability to share their screen. For a meeting with the general public, you should restrict meeting settings to allow only the hosts or co-hosts to share their screens during the meeting.

Decide what to save

Depending on the nature of your meeting, decide if auto-saving the video recording, audio recording or even the group chat is appropriate for your needs. Select your meeting settings accordingly.

Safety steps for attendees

Whether you are in a private work meeting or one open to the general public, the following steps are good habits to keep in mind to protect your privacy.

Act like your webcam and microphone are always on

Even when they're off during your meetings, act like they are on. Social media has been more than gleeful to broadcast to the world the momentary yet hugely embarrassing missteps unwitting Zoom users have made on video calls, ranging from not wearing pants in view of the camera (to either the dismay or laughter of the other participants); using the bathroom;

talking to their parents, pets, or plants; to any number of other previously unimaginable situations. In certain instances, the meeting participant's behavior was so out of line they ended up getting fired.

Mute your microphone and turn off your webcam when possible

Depending on your meeting, less is more. Always. Particularly for public meetings, unless your smiling face is required, keeping your camera off by default is a good habit.

Assume private chats are not private

Conversations that you have directly with another meeting participant through the group chat, even when it is marked "private" may not necessarily be shielded from the moderators. Assume that your conversation is being monitored, so don't conduct "private" chats on a work call that may be considered inappropriate or NSFW.

Clean your room

With high definition cameras being fairly standard for computers, tablets and phones, the details in your background can be zoomed in on and magnified by snooping observers. Videos can also be recorded or captured in screenshots for more thorough investigation offline. Do an audit of your background and see if there are any details that you don't want prying eyes to look at or read.

Consider using a virtual background

Large and small personal details can sometimes be gleaned from a meeting attendee's surroundings, ranging from clues to their physical location (if there are windows visible), identity of family members (including their children) from photos on the wall or shelf, and other specifics that you may not want the general public to know. Virtual backgrounds, or images that mask your actual background view, can be selected in your meeting settings. For public situations, consider turning it on.

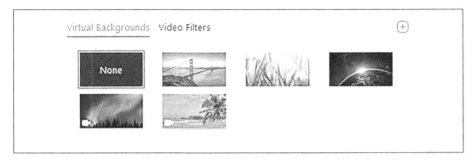

These are the default virtual backgrounds available in Zoom's settings. Other platforms offer similar ways to hide your real-life backgrounds.

Mask your profile and screen name

For public chats, consider changing your display name to something anonymous. Similarly, you may consider removing your profile photo from your account. When you turn off your webcam, some meeting platforms will display your profile photo in place of your live view. Removing your photo should show just a black or blank screen to keep you anonymous.

Which video call services to avoid

Mozilla, the creators of the Firefox browser, surveyed 18 video call apps on their level of encryption, security, privacy, password requirements, and vulnerability management. Of the 15 providers reviewed, three failed to meet their minimum standards and should be avoided. Keep in mind, minimum standards are not a high bar to meet so the other 12 that passed have varying levels of robustness, but still are deemed reliable by Mozilla.

The three apps (and their publishers) that **didn't pass** review are, in alphabetical order:

- Discord (Discord)
- Doxy.me (Doxy.me)
- Houseparty (by Epic Games)

The 15 that **met Mozilla's minimum standards** (and their publishers) are, in alphabetical order:

- BlueJeans (Verizon)
- Duo / Hangouts / Meet apps (Google)
- FaceTime (Apple)
- Signal (Signal Technology Foundation)
- Jitsi Meet (8x8)
- Messenger / Messenger Kids (Facebook)
- Skype (Microsoft)
- Teams (Microsoft)
- GoToMeeting (LogMeIn)
- Webex (Cisco)
- WhatsApp (Facebook)
- Zoom (by Zoom)[113]

---

[113] "*Privacy Not Included: A Buyer's Guide for Connected Products," Mozilla, n.d., https://foundation.mozilla.org/en/privacynotincluded/categories/video-call-apps/.

Protect your recorded meetings

Oftentimes video calls and conference calls are recorded, which can be both helpful and dangerous if you're not careful. It's safest to store your recordings on a computer's hard drive rather than the cloud. In early 2020, Zoom had a data flaw where some calls were stored on popular cloud services. Hackers were able to search those services for files that used Zoom's standard naming rules and **gained access to recorded meeting files**. Zoom has since fixed that particular issue. Hackers were actively looking for meeting recordings so that debacle is a good reminder to keep your sensitive files safely locked away.

Zoom allows you to limit who can access recordings to authenticated users with a passcode that you've provided. When you're done sharing, toggle the sharing option off. If you have to share recordings or other files with other people, cloud services such as Google Drive, SharePoint, and OneDrive allow you to set specific user permissions on who can access, read, and edit files. You can also disable file downloads.

The Wrap Up

Congratulations on reading this sentence! Hopefully that means you've perused most of this guide and – even more hopefully – you've taken some of the steps herein to protect yourself, your loved ones, and your work from online actors who might seek to do you harm.

I'm proud of you.

Really, I am!

Taking care of your digital life is in certain ways similar to taking care of your body and your home. Some things require regular maintenance, and others ought to be checked in on every so often. I hope you'll make your online safety and wellbeing a regular part of your self-care. Having read and followed this guide is a huge step in that on-going direction. I am genuinely pleased to know that more and more individuals like yourself are taking their personal cyber security seriously, because that ultimately makes all of us and those we care about safer.

Daniel Farber Huang

Appendix

Identity Theft Recovery Action Plan

According to the Federal Trade Commission, if your identity has been stolen here are the action steps to take immediately:

Do These Right Away

Are you dealing with tax, medical, or child identity theft? See: Special forms of identity theft

Step 1: Call the companies where you know fraud occurred.

- ☐ Call the fraud department. Explain that someone stole your identity.

- ☐ Ask them to close or freeze the accounts. Then, no one can add new charges unless you agree.

- ☐ Change logins, passwords and PINS for your accounts.

Step 2: Place a fraud alert and get your credit reports.

- ☐ Place a free, one-year fraud alert by contacting one of the three credit bureaus. That company must tell the other two. A fraud alert is free. It will make it harder for someone to open new accounts in your name. When you have an alert on your report, a business must verify your identity before it issues new credit in your name. You can renew the fraud alert after one year. You'll get a letter from each credit bureau. It will confirm that they placed a fraud alert on your file.

- [ ] The three credit reporting companies are:

- o Equifax
    - https://www.equifax.com/personal/
    - Phone: 800-685-1111

- o Experian
    - https://www.experian.com/
    - Phone: 888-EXPERIAN (888-397-3742)

- o Transunion
    - https://www.transunion.com/
    - Phone: 888-909-8872

- [ ] Get your free credit reports from Equifax, Experian, and TransUnion by going to AnnualCreditReport
    - o https://www.annualcreditreport.com/index.action

- [ ] Review your reports. Make note of any account or transaction you don't recognize. This will help you report the theft to the FTC and the police.

Step 3: Report identity theft to the FTC.

☐ Create an account and provide your information to the FTC at https://www.IdentityTheft.gov (or call 1-877-438-4338). Include as many details as possible. Based on the information you enter, IdentityTheft.gov will create your Identity Theft Report and recovery plan. Your identity theft report proves to businesses that someone stole your identity. It also guarantees you certain rights.

Step 4: File a report with your local police department.

☐ Go to your local police office with:
- a copy of your FTC Identity Theft Report
- a government-issued ID with a photo
- proof of your address (mortgage statement, rental agreement, or utilities bill)
- any other proof you have of the theft (bills, IRS notices, etc.)

☐ Tell the police someone stole your identity and you need to file a report.

☐ Ask for a copy of the police report. You may need this to complete other steps.

What To Do Next - Begin to repair the damage.

Close new accounts opened in your name.

☐ Now that you have an FTC Identity Theft Report, call the fraud department of each business where an account was opened. Explain that someone stole your identity. Ask the business to close the account.

☐ Ask the business to send you a letter confirming that:
- the fraudulent account isn't yours
- you aren't liable for it
- it was removed from your credit report
- Keep this letter. Use it if the account appears on your credit report later on.
- The business may require you to send them a copy of your FTC Identity Theft Report or complete a special dispute form. This sample letter can help.

☐ Write down who you contacted and when.

Remove bogus charges from your accounts.

☐ Call the fraud department of each business.
- Explain that someone stole your identity. Tell them which charges are fraudulent. Ask the business to remove them.
- Ask the business to send you a letter confirming they removed the fraudulent charges. Keep this letter. Use it if this account appears on your credit report later on.
- The business may require you to send them a copy of your FTC Identity Theft Report or complete a special dispute form.

☐ Write down who you contacted and when.

Correct your credit report.

☐ Write to each of the three credit bureaus. Include a copy of your FTC Identity Theft Report and proof of your identity, like your name, address, and Social Security number. Explain which information on your report came from identity theft. Ask them to block that information.

- Equifax.com
    - P.O. Box 105069, Atlanta, GA 30348-5069.
    - Tel: 1-800-525-6285
- Experian.com
    - P.O. Box 9554, Allen, TX 75013.
    - Tel: 1-888-397-3742
- TransUnion.com, Fraud Victim Assistance Department
    - P.O. Box 2000, Chester, PA 19016.
    - Tel: 1-800-680-7289

- If someone steals your identity, you have the right to remove fraudulent information from your credit report. This is called blocking. Once the information is blocked, it won't show up on your credit report, and companies can't try to collect the debt from you. If you have an FTC Identity Theft Report, credit bureaus must honor your request to block this information.
- If you don't have an FTC Identity Theft Report, you still can dispute incorrect information in your credit file. It can take longer, and there's no guarantee that the credit bureaus will remove the information.

Consider adding an extended fraud alert or credit freeze.

Extended fraud alerts and credit freezes can help prevent further misuse of your personal information. There are important differences. This chart can help you decide which might be right for you.

Extended Fraud Alert	Credit Freeze
Lets you have access to your credit report as long as companies take steps to verify your identity.	Stops all access to your credit report unless you lift or remove it.
Free to place and remove. Available if someone stole your identity.	Free to place and remove. Available to anyone.
Lasts for 7 years.	Lasts until you lift or remove it.
Set it by contacting each of the three credit bureaus: Report that someone stole your identity. Request an extended fraud alert. Complete any necessary forms and send a copy of your FTC Identity Theft Report.	Set it by contacting each of the three credit bureaus.

Review your credit reports often.

Other Possible Steps

Depending on your situation, you might need to take additional steps.

Report a misused Social Security number.

☐ Get a replacement card if your social security card has been lost or stolen.

☐ Do you think someone else is using your Social Security number for work? Review your Social Security work history by creating an account at socialsecurity.gov/myaccount. If you find errors, contact your local SSA office.

Stop debt collectors from trying to collect debts you don't owe.

☐ Write to the debt collector within 30 days of getting the collection letter. Tell the debt collector someone stole your identity, and you don't owe the debt. Send copies of your Identity Theft Report and any other documents that detail the theft.

☐ Contact the business where the fraudulent account was opened. Explain that this is not your debt. Tell them to stop reporting this debt to the credit bureaus. Ask for information about the debt, and how it happened. The business must give you details if you ask. For example, if someone opened a credit card in your name, ask for a copy of the application and the applicant's signature.

☐ If you haven't already, ask the credit bureaus to block information about this debt from your credit report.

☐ Write down who you contacted and when. Keep copies of any letters you send.

Replace government-issued IDs.

☐ Driver's license lost or stolen? Contact the nearest Department of Motor Vehicles branch to report it. The state might flag your license number in case someone else tries to use it, or they might suggest that you apply for a replacement license.

☐ Passport lost or stolen? Call the U.S. State Department at 1-877-487-2778. You can also apply for a replacement passport at some post office branches. Call ahead to inquire.

Clear your name of criminal charges.

☐ If someone is arrested and uses your name or personal information, contact the law enforcement agency that arrested the thief. You may need to check court records to find out where the thief was arrested.
- File a report about the impersonation. Give copies of your fingerprints, photograph, and identifying documents.
- Ask the law enforcement agency to:
  - compare your information to the imposter's
  - change all records from your name to the imposter's name (if you know it)
  - give you a "clearance letter" or "certificate of release" to declare
  - your innocence
  - Keep the clearance letter or "certificate of release" with you at all times.
- Write down who you contacted and when.

☐ If a court prosecutes an identity thief using your name, contact the court where the arrest or conviction happened.
- Ask the district attorney for records to help you clear your name in court records.
- Provide proof of your identity.

- Ask the court for a "certificate of clearance" that declares you are innocent.
- Keep the "certificate of clearance" with you at all times.

☐ Contact your state Attorney General.
- Ask if your state has an "identity theft passport" (a tool you can use to resolve financial issues related to the identity theft) or some other special help for identity theft victims. If you get an identity theft passport, keep it with you at all times.

☐ Consider hiring a criminal defense lawyer. The American Bar Association can help you find a lawyer.

☐ Ask the law enforcement agency that arrested the thief which information brokers buy their records. Information brokers buy criminal records and sell information to employers and debt collectors.
- Write to the brokers. Ask them to remove errors from your file.

☐ Write down who you contacted and when. Keep copies of any letters you send.

Steps for Certain Accounts

For certain types of accounts, you might have to contact additional offices.

☐ **Utilities**
- o If someone used your information to get cable, electric, water, or other similar services, contact the service provider. Tell them someone stole your identity. Ask them to close the account.
- o For additional help, contact your state Public Utility Commission and explain the situation.
- o Write down who you contacted and when. Keep copies of any letters you send.

☐ **Phones**
- o Contact the National Consumer Telecom and Utilities Exchange and request your NCTUE Data Report. The NCTUE data report is a record of all telecommunication, pay TV and utility accounts reported by exchange members, including information about your account history, unpaid accounts and customer service applications. Review it for any accounts you don't recognize.
- o https://www.nctue.com, Tel: 1-866-349-5185
- o If the service provider doesn't resolve the problem, file a complaint with the Federal Communications Commission at 1-888-225-5322.

☐ **Government benefits**
- o Contact the agency that issued the government benefit and explain that someone stole your identity. Ask what you need to do to fix the problem.
- o If you stopped receiving your benefits because of the identity theft, ask what you need to do to get them

reinstated. You may need to appear in person or send something in writing.
- Make a note of who you contacted and when.

☐ **Checking accounts**
- Do you think someone opened a checking account in your name? Order a free copy of your ChexSystems report, which compiles information about your checking accounts.
    - To get your report, contact ChexSystems at 1-800-428-9623. Or visit their website.
- Then contact every financial institution where a new account was opened. Ask them to close the accounts.
- If someone is writing bad checks against your account, contact your financial institution. Ask them to stop payment on stolen checks and close your account. Ask them to report the theft to its check verification system. The check verification system will tell businesses to refuse the stolen checks.
- Also, contact any business that took the bad check. Explain that someone stole your identity. Act quickly, before they start collection action against you.
- You also can contact check verification companies. Report that your checks were stolen. Ask them to tell businesses to refuse the stolen checks.
    - Telecheck 1-800-710-9898
    - Certegy 1-800-437-5120
- If a business rejects your checks, ask the business for an explanation. The business must tell you what information led them to reject your check.
- Write down who you contacted and when. Keep copies of any letters you send.

- ☐ **Student loans**
    - ○ Contact the school or program that opened the loan. Explain the situation. Ask them to close the loan, and send you a letter that says you aren't responsible for the loan.
    - ○ If this is a federal student loan, contact the U.S. Department of Education Office of Inspector General hotline at 1-800-MISUSED (1-800-647-8733).
    - ○ If these steps don't resolve your situation, contact the U.S. Department of Education Federal Student Aid Ombudsman at 1-877-557-2575 or online.
    - ○ Write down who you contacted and when. Keep copies of any letters you send.
- ☐ **Apartment or House Rentals**
    - ○ Ask the landlord who rented the property to the identity thief what tenant history services they use. Contact those companies. Ask for a copy of your tenant history report, and ask what steps you need to take to correct fraudulent information in the report.
        - ▪ What's a tenant history report? There are several companies that collect and sell information about renters – such as how often a renter was late or if a renter has ever been evicted. If someone leased an apartment in your name, you'll want to correct any errors in your tenant history reports.
    - ○ Write down who you contacted and when. Keep copies of any letters you send.

☐ **Investment accounts**
- o Call your broker or account manager, and describe the situation.
- o Write down who you contacted and when. Keep copies of any letters you send.

☐ **Bankruptcy filed in your name**
- o Write to the U.S. Trustee in the region where the bankruptcy was filed. Describe the situation and provide proof of your identity. The U.S. Trustee Program refers cases of suspected bankruptcy fraud to the U.S. Attorney's Office for possible prosecution. The U.S. Trustee can't give you legal help, so you may need to hire an attorney.
- o Consider hiring an attorney. The American Bar Association or a local legal services provider can help you find a lawyer. An attorney can explain to the court that the bankruptcy filing was fraudulent.
- o Write down who you contacted and when. Keep copies of any letters you send.

Special Forms of Identity Theft

Tax Identity Theft

☐ If you get an IRS notice in the mail that says someone used your Social Security number to get a tax refund, follow the instructions provided in the letter.

☐ Did the notice say you were paid by an employer you don't know? Send a letter to the employer too, explaining that someone stole your identity and that you don't work for the employer.

☐ Complete IRS Identity Theft Affidavit (Form 14039). Mail or fax the form according to the instructions.

☐ File your tax return, and pay any taxes you owe. You might have to mail paper tax returns.

☐ Write down who you contacted and when. Keep copies of any letters you send.

☐ If these steps don't resolve your situation, contact the Internal Revenue Service for specialized assistance at 1-800-908-4490.

☐ Place a fraud alert. Contact one of the three credit bureaus. That company must tell the other two.
- Equifax
  - https://www.equifax.com/personal/
  - Phone: 800-685-1111
- Experian
  - https://www.experian.com/
  - Phone: 888-EXPERIAN (888-397-3742)

- Transunion
    - https://www.transunion.com/
    - Phone: 888-909-8872

☐ Get your free credit reports from Equifax, Experian, and TransUnion. Go to https://www.annualcreditreport.com or call 1-877-322-8228. Review your reports. If you find any accounts or charges you don't recognize, follow the steps in What to Do Next.

Child Identity Theft

☐ Did someone use your child's information to commit fraud? Call the company where the fraud occurred.
- Explain that someone stole your child's identity and opened a fraudulent account. Explain that your child is a minor, and cannot enter into legal contracts.
- Ask them to close the fraudulent account and send you a letter confirming that your child isn't liable for the account.
- Send a follow-up letter and include your child's FTC Identity Theft Report and a copy of your child's birth certificate.
- Make a note of who you contacted and when.

☐ Generally, children won't have credit reports – unless someone is using their information for fraud. To find out if your child has a credit report, request a manual search for your child's Social Security number. Each credit bureau has its own process for this:

☐ If a credit bureau has a credit report for your child, they will send you a copy of the report. To remove fraudulent accounts, follow the instructions provided with the credit report.

☐ Request a free credit freeze, also known as a security freeze, to make it harder for someone to open new accounts in your child's name. Contact each credit bureau separately and follow its instructions for placing a freeze for a minor:

☐ Did someone file taxes using your child's Social Security number? Complete IRS Identity Theft Affidavit (Form 14039). Mail or fax the form according to the instructions. If that doesn't resolve the problem, contact the IRS for specialized assistance at 1-800-908-4490.

Medical Identity Theft

☐ If you suspect that someone used your information to get medical services, get copies of your medical records. Federal law gives you the right to know what's in your medical files.

- Contact each doctor, clinic, hospital, pharmacy, laboratory, and health plan where the thief may have used your information. Ask for copies of your medical records.
- Complete the providers' records request forms and pay any fees required to get copies of your records.
- Check your state's health privacy laws. Some state laws make it easier to get copies of your medical records.

☐ Did your provider refuse to give you copies of the records to protect the identity thief's privacy rights? You can appeal. Contact the person listed in your provider's Notice of Privacy Practices, the patient representative, or the ombudsman. Explain the situation and ask for your file.

☐ If the provider refuses to provide your records within 30 days of your written request, you may complain to the U.S. Department of Health and Human Services Office for Civil Rights.

- ☐ Review your medical records, and report any errors to your health care provider.
  - ○ Write to your health care provider to report mistakes in your medical records.
  - ○ Include a copy of the medical record showing the mistake.
  - ○ Explain why this is a mistake, and how to correct it.
  - ○ Include a copy of your FTC Identity Theft Report.
  - ○ Send the letter by certified mail, and ask for a return receipt.
- ☐ Your health care provider should respond to your letter within 30 days. Ask the provider to fix the mistake and notify other health care providers who may have the same mistake in their records.
- ☐ Notify your health insurer.
  - ○ Send your FTC Identity Theft Report to your health insurer's fraud department. Tell them about any errors in your medical records.
- ☐ If there are medical billing errors on your credit report, notify all three credit reporting companies by following the steps under What to Do Next.
- ☐ Write down who you contacted and when. Keep copies of any letters you send.

Acknowledgements

This book (and the preceding years building up to its publication) would not have been possible without the support, assistance and encouragement of my wife, Theresa Menders, and my children Quincy Huang, Christian Menders Huang, Alexander Huang-Menders, and Celeste Huang-Menders. Thank you, to each of you.

Of course, thank you to my sisters and brothers and their partners, Elizabeth Majorczyk and Tomasz Majorczyk, Christina Huang, Henry Huang, Grace Weidmann and Richard Weidmann, Joy Huang, Andrew Huang and Daisy Huang, Glory Huang, David Huang and Alana Evans, James Huang and Elizabeth Sandy. And my parents, Dr. Chen-Ya Huang and Dr. Mona Huang. Marie Louise Menders is a continual inspiration. And although too numerous to mention here, to my nieces and nephews: know that each of you are appreciated.

There have been many individuals who have provided input, experiences, collaboration and just plain camaraderie necessary to accumulate the collective knowledge and perspective that a book of this nature requires. I would like to thank the following individuals (alphabetically) for their wisdom, support and friendship:

Paul Aris at Janney Montgomery Scott LLC; Dan Bauer at Dan Bauer Public Relations and Communications; Urvish Bidkar at Aspire Macro, LLC; Adem Carroll at Justice For All; the inimitable David Colbert; Loren Danzis at Fox Rothschild LLP; Christopher DelCol at Guidance Point Advisors, LLC; Fred Dellis at Dellis Automotive Group; John DeLorenzo at Aimers; Peter Egbert at PM&E Structures, Inc.; Rehana Farrell at Youth, Inc.; Lisa Graf at Chandler Admissions Advisors; Sir Mark Fehrs Haukohl at The Vero Group; Nina Garćia Wright at Pacific Branch Co.; Dr. William Hawkey at The Pennington School; Janie Hermann at the Princeton Public Library; Stephanie Hessler at Proctor Gallagher Institute; Donald Hofmann at Crystal Ridge Partners; Will Hogan at Bequia Securities, LLC; J. Samuel Houser at The George School; the incomparable Lisa Ilaria; Leslie Jackson at OP/TECH USA; Terry Jackson at OP/TECH USA; Dahlia Kang at Autism Speaks; the dauntless Mohammed Khalidi; Kristina Kohl at HRComputes; the insightful Andrew Kwee; Stephanie Landers at Princeton University's Keller Center for Innovation; Jennifer Loo at New Hope Partners LLC; Simon Milne at ENTHEOS Group; Michelle Morrison at Princeton Montessori School; Sunanda Nair-Bidkar at the Institute for New Economic Thinking; Swati Navani at Seattle Genetics; Vinay Navani at WilkinGuttenplan; Andrew Noble at ABCO Systems Inc.; Christopher Pace at First Republic Bank; Bridget Piraino at Anova; the extraordinary Robert Rivett; Devron Robinson at Berkshire Bank; Jordan Robinson at Fairview Capital Group; Jamie Schnitzer at Sanofi Genzyme; Khurram Rumi Shahzad at New Hope Partners LLC; Professor Sallie Sharp at Harvard University; Dr. Christopher Speller at SSB Stellar Solutions Inc.; Seth Weisberg at ABCO Systems Inc.; Kevin Widrow at Le Mas Perreal, Provence; Daisy M. Wong at Edward & Frank Lee, Inc.; Michael Wyrick at TEI Logistics; Yuki Zhang at Otsuka Pharmaceutical Companies.

Thank you, everyone, for being you.

About the Author

Daniel Farber Huang is a strategic consultant and advisor on cyber security and other risk mitigation issues to a broad array of companies and organizations, ranging from entrepreneurial start-ups to multi-national corporations. He has worked closely with numerous federal, state, and local law enforcement agencies across the U.S. on providing solutions to their mobile technology requirements. Daniel has focused on providing hardware and software solutions to federal field agents, the police, and other authorities to support them in fulfilling their duties.

Before founding his own independent advisory firm, Daniel worked for Goldman, Sachs & Co., Merrill Lynch and other major investment banks advising a corporations and investors on domestic and international corporate finance transactions. He was actively involved in capital raising engagements encompassing in excess of $10 billion. Daniel has advised a wide range of investment sponsors and strategies, including private equity, venture capital, infrastructure, real estate, emerging markets, hedge funds and specialized situations. Daniel is an Advisor to Princeton University's Keller Center for Innovation in Engineering Education, where he advises startups founders on business best practices.

Outside of his consulting work, Daniel is a journalist and documentary photographer focused on women's and children's issue and the alleviation of poverty around the world. Daniel is a co-founder of The Power of Faces, a major portrait project raising awareness of the global refugee crisis. As an independent humanitarian advocate, Daniel has documented refugee camps around the world, and has actively raised awareness through multiple Talks on TED.com and other platforms. His documentary work has been exhibited at Amnesty International, the Middle East Institute, and numerous universities and colleges. His work is included in the permanent collections of The International Center of Photography, The Museum of the City of New York, New-York Historical Society, Museum of Chinese in the Americas, New York City Fire Museum and other institutions.

Daniel is a National Member of The Explorers Club, a multidisciplinary professional society dedicated to the advancement of field research and the ideal that it is vital to preserve the instinct to explore. He is a Brand Ambassador for OP/TECH USA camera accessories. Daniel is an Ambassador for the Wharton Alumni Social Impact Club.

Daniel earned his Master's degree (A.L.M.) in Journalism and a Certificate in International Security from Harvard University, an M.B.A. from The Wharton School, University of Pennsylvania in Finance and Entrepreneurial Management, and a B.A. from New York University in Economics.

Bibliography

Abnormal Security. "Zoom Phishing," April 21, 2020. https://abnormalsecurity.com/blog/abnormal-attack-stories-zoom-phishing/.

Amer, Pakinam. "Deepfakes Are Getting Better. Should We Be Worried?" Boston Globe, December 13, 2019. https://www.bostonglobe.com/2019/12/13/opinion/deepfakes-are-coming-what-do-we-do/.

Angwin, Julia. "How Journalists Fought Back Against Crippling Email and Subscription Bombs." WIRED, November 9, 2017. https://www.wired.com/story/how-journalists-fought-back-against-crippling-email-bombs/.

Anon, Dennis. "How Cookies Track You around the Web & How to Stop Them." Privacy.Net (blog), February 24, 2018. https://privacy.net/stop-cookies-tracking/.

Anonymous. "How a Group of Online Misogynists Tried to Ruin My Professional Life." Women's Media Center (blog), March 31, 2016. https://womensmediacenter.com/speech-project/how-a-group-of-online-misogynists-tried-to-ruin-my-professional-life.

Ayyub, Rana. "I Was The Victim Of A Deepfake Porn Plot Intended To Silence Me." Huffington Post UK, November 21, 2018. https://www.huffingtonpost.co.uk/entry/deepfake-porn_uk_5bf2c126e4b0f32bd58ba316.

BBC News, sec. Trending. "Punctuation Protest against Far Right Trolls on Twitter." June 8, 2016. https://www.bbc.com/news/blogs-trending-36470879.

BBC News. "Cyber Attacks Briefly Knock out Top Sites," October 21, 2016. https://www.bbc.com/news/technology-37728015.

Bradford, Alina. "8 Red Flags Someone's Tracking Your Cell Phone." Reader's Digest, September 26, 2020. https://www.rd.com/article/red-flags-someones-tracking-your-cell-phone/.

Chandler, Daniel, and Rod Munday. "Sealioning." In A Dictionary of Social Media, 2016th ed. Oxford University Press, 2016. https://www.oxfordreference.com/view/10.1093/acref/9780191803093.001.0001/acref-9780191803093-e-1257.

Childnet. "About Project DeSHAME." Childnet International. http://www.childnet.com/our-projects/project-deshame/about-project-deshame.

Committee to Protect Journalists. "Digital Safety: Protecting against Targeted Online Attacks," September 28, 2020. https://cpj.org/2020/05/digital-safety-protecting-against-targeted-online-attacks/.

Committee to Protect Journalists. "Psychological Safety: Online Harassment and How to Protect Your Mental Health," September 4, 2019. https://cpj.org/2019/09/psychological-safety-online-harassment-emotional-health-journalists/.

Crawley, Kim. "Bluetooth Security Risks Explained." AT&T Cybersecurity (blog), June 11, 2020. https://cybersecurity.att.com/blogs/security-essentials/bluetooth-security-risks-explained.

Cyber Civil Rights Initiative. "46 States + DC + One Territory NOW Have Revenge Porn Laws," n.d. https://www.cybercivilrights.org/revenge-porn-laws/.

Cyber Civil Rights Initiative. "Definitions." https://www.cybercivilrights.org/definitions/.

Cyberbullying Research Center. "What Is Cyberbullying?," December 23, 2014. https://cyberbullying.org/what-is-cyberbullying.

Desai, Deepen. "30,000 Percent Increase in COVID-19-Themed Attacks." https://www.zscaler.com/blogs/research/30000-percent-increase-covid-19-themed-attacks.

Desal, Shivang. "Android App Offers Coronavirus Mask, Delivers Trojan." Zscaler (blog). https://www.zscaler.com/blogs/research/new-android-app-offers-coronavirus-safety-mask-delivers-sms-trojan.

DuckDuckGo Help Pages. "DuckDuckGo Help Pages: Results, Sources." https://help.duckduckgo.com/duckduckgo-help-pages/results/sources/.

Elder, Miriam. "Hacked Emails Allege Russian Youth Group Nashi Paying Bloggers." The Guardian, February 7, 2012, sec. World news. http://www.theguardian.com/world/2012/feb/07/hacked-emails-nashi-putin-bloggers.

Federal Bureau of Investigation. "Cyber Crime." https://www.fbi.gov/investigate/cyber.

Federal Bureau of Investigation. "Sextortion: Case Highlights Growing Online Crime with Devastating Real-Life Consequences," November 10, 2020. https://www.fbi.gov/news/stories/sextortion-case-highlights-growing-online-crime-111020.

Federal Bureau of Investigation. "Sextortion: What Parents, Caregivers, and Educators Need to Know," May 30, 2019. https://www.fbi.gov/news/stories/stop-sextortion-youth-face-risk-online-090319#Resources-for%20Parents.

Federal Bureau of Investigation. "What Kids and Teens Need to Know About Sextortion," September 3, 2019. https://www.fbi.gov/news/stories/stop-sextortion-youth-face-risk-online-090319.

Filipovic, Jill. "Let's Be Real: Online Harassment Isn't 'Virtual' For Women." Talking Points Memo, January 10, 2014. https://talkingpointsmemo.com/cafe/let-s-be-real-online-harassment-isn-t-virtual-for-women.

Fleishman, Cooper, and Anthony Smith. "'Coincidence Detector': The Google Chrome Extension White Supremacists Use to Track Jews." Mic, June 2, 2016. https://www.mic.com/articles/145105/coincidence-detector-the-google-extension-white-supremacists-use-to-track-jews.

Friedberg, Brian, Gabrielle Lim, and Joan Donovan. "Space Invaders: The Networked Terrain of Zoom Bombing." Technology and Social Change Research Project, June 9, 2020. https://doi.org/10.37016/TASC-2020-02.

Gebhart, Gennie, and Rory Mir. "Harden Your Zoom Settings to Protect Your Privacy and Avoid Trolls." Electronic Frontier Foundation (blog), April 10, 2020. https://www.eff.org/deeplinks/2020/04/harden-your-zoom-settings-protect-your-privacy-and-avoid-trolls.

Germain, Thomas. "How to Protect Phone Privacy and Security During a Protest." Consumer Reports, June 3, 2020. https://www.consumerreports.org/privacy/protect-phone-privacy-security-during-a-protest/.

Gonzales, Laurence. Deep Survival: Who Lives, Who Dies, and Why. W. W. Norton & Company, 2017.

Google Support. "Maps User Contributed Content Policy: Privacy." https://support.google.com/contributionpolicy/answer/7401426?hl=en&ref_topic=7422769.

HeartMob. "Join the Movement to End Online Harassment." https://www.iheartmob.org.

Hesse, Brendan. "Beware Coronavirus-Themed Malware Disguised as Excel Spreadsheets." Lifehacker, May 22, 2020. https://lifehacker.com/beware-coronavirus-themed-malware-disguised-as-excel-sp-1843613107.

Hesse, Brendan. "How to Spot Scam IOS Apps That Sucker You into Making Expensive Purchases." Lifehacker, August 8, 2019. https://lifehacker.com/how-to-spot-scam-ios-apps-that-sucker-you-into-making-e-1837053973.

HTML.com. "What Is Doxing? (And Why Is It So Scary?): An Infographic." https://html.com/blog/doxing/.

IC Off The Record. "NSA Ant Catalog - USB." https://nsa.gov1.info/dni/nsa-ant-catalog/usb/index.html.

Identity Theft Resource Center. "Identity Theft: The Aftermath Study." https://www.idtheftcenter.org/identity-theft-aftermath-study/.

Jacobson, Roni. "I've Had a Cyberstalker Since I Was 12." WIRED, February 29, 2016. https://www.wired.com/2016/02/ive-had-a-cyberstalker-since-i-was-12/.

Jareth. "Phishing vs Spear Phishing vs Whaling Attacks." Emsisoft (blog), February 19, 2019. https://blog.emsisoft.com/en/32736/phishing-vs-spear-phishing-vs-whaling-attacks/.

Jeffries, Adrianne. "Meet 'swatting,' the Dangerous Prank That Could Get Someone Killed." The Verge, April 23, 2013. https://www.theverge.com/2013/4/23/4253014/swatting-911-prank-wont-stop-hackers-celebrities.

Jensen, K Thor. "Stalker Finds Japanese Idol's Home from Reflections in Her Pupils." Newsweek, October 10, 2019. https://www.newsweek.com/stalker-finds-idol-reflection-pupils-1464373.

Keheley, Paulette. "How Many Pages In A Gigabyte? A Litigator's Guide." Digital WarRoom (blog), April 2, 2020. https://www.digitalwarroom.com/blog/how-many-pages-in-a-gigabyte.

Kessler, Sarah. "Why Online Harassment Is Still Ruining Lives—And How We Can Stop It." Fast Company, June 3, 2015. https://www.fastcompany.com/3046772/why-online-harassment-is-still-ruining-lives-and-how-we-can-stop-it.

Konnikova, Maria. The Confidence Game: Why We Fall for It . . . Every Time. Penguin Books, 2017.

Lazarus, David. "Column: Whatever You Do, Don't Say Yes When This Chatbot Asks, 'Can You Hear Me?'" Los Angeles Times, March 24, 217AD. https://www.latimes.com/business/lazarus/la-fi-lazarus-chatbot-phone-scam-20170324-story.html.

Legal Information Institute. "18 U.S. Code § 2261A - Stalking," n.d. https://www.law.cornell.edu/uscode/text/18/2261A.

Levitt, Steven D., and Stephen J. Dubner. Think Like a Freak: The Authors of Freakonomics Offer to Retrain Your Brain. William Morrow Paperbacks, 2015.

Lexico Dictionaries | English. "Threat | Definition of Threat by Oxford Dictionary on Lexico.Com Also Meaning of Threat." https://www.lexico.com/en/definition/threat.

Lorenz, Taylor. "'Zoombombing': When Video Conferences Go Wrong." The New York Times, March 20, 2020, sec. Style. https://www.nytimes.com/2020/03/20/style/zoombombing-zoom-trolling.html.

Lyfesavr. "Urban Dictionary: Zoom Bomb." Urban Dictionary, April 1, 2020. https://www.urbandictionary.com/define.php?term=Zoom%20bomb.

Morris, David Z. "Bestselling Feminist Author Jessica Valenti Quits Social Media After Rape and Death Threats Directed at Daughter." Fortune, July 31, 2016. https://fortune.com/2016/07/31/bestselling-feminist-author-jessica-valenti-quits-social-media-after-rape-and-death-threats-directed-at-daughter/.

Mozilla. "*Privacy Not Included: A Buyer's Guide for Connected Products," n.d. https://foundation.mozilla.org/en/privacynotincluded/categories/video-call-apps/.

Mozilla. "Seven of the Best Browsers in Direct Comparison." https://www.mozilla.org/en-US/firefox/browsers/compare/.

Mozilla. "The Ad Blocker - a Secret Weapon against Annoying Ads." https://www.mozilla.org/en-US/firefox/features/adblocker/.

National Center for Missing & Exploited Children. "Online Enticement." https://www.missingkids.org/theissues/onlineenticement.

NPR.org. "Jewish Reporters Harassed By Trump's Anti-Semitic Supporters," July 6, 2016. https://www.npr.org/2016/07/06/484987245/jewish-reporters-harassed-by-trumps-anti-semitic-supporters.

Pascual, Al, and Kyle Marchini. "2018 Child Identity Fraud Study." Javelin, April 24, 2018. https://www.javelinstrategy.com/coverage-area/2018-child-identity-fraud-study.

PEN America, Online Harassment Field Manual. "Defining 'Online Abuse': A Glossary of Terms." https://onlineharassmentfieldmanual.pen.org/defining-online-harassment-a-glossary-of-terms/.

PEN America, Online Harassment Field Manual. "Documenting Online Harassment." https://onlineharassmentfieldmanual.pen.org/documenting-online-harassment/.

PEN America, Online Harassment Field Manual. "Fight Back/Write Back." https://onlineharassmentfieldmanual.pen.org/fight-back-write-back/.

PEN America, Online Harassment Field Manual. "Guidelines for Talking to Employers about Abuse." https://onlineharassmentfieldmanual.pen.org/guidelines-for-talking-to-employers-and-professional-contacts/.

PEN America, Online Harassment Field Manual. "Guidelines for Talking to Friends and Allies." https://onlineharassmentfieldmanual.pen.org/guidelines-for-talking-to-friends-and-loved-ones/.

PEN America, Online Harassment Field Manual. "Legal Considerations." https://onlineharassmentfieldmanual.pen.org/legal-considerations/.

PEN America, Online Harassment Field Manual. "Legal Resources for Writers & Journalists." https://onlineharassmentfieldmanual.pen.org/legal-resources-for-writers-and-journalists/.

PEN America, Online Harassment Field Manual. "Protecting from Doxing." https://onlineharassmentfieldmanual.pen.org/protecting-information-from-doxing/.

PEN America, Online Harassment Field Manual. "Protecting from Hacking and Impersonation." https://onlineharassmentfieldmanual.pen.org/protecting-from-hacking-impersonation/.

PEN America, Online Harassment Field Manual. "Reporting to Law Enforcement." https://onlineharassmentfieldmanual.pen.org/reporting-to-law-enforcement/.

PEN America, Online Harassment Field Manual. "Reporting to Platforms." https://onlineharassmentfieldmanual.pen.org/reporting-online-harassment-to-platforms/.

retruster. "Protect Your Users against Phishing Emails, Ransomware & Fraud." https://retruster.com.

Rogers, Katie. "Leslie Jones, Star of 'Ghostbusters,' Becomes a Target of Online Trolls." The New York Times, July 19, 2016, sec. Movies. https://www.nytimes.com/2016/07/20/movies/leslie-jones-star-of-ghostbusters-becomes-a-target-of-online-trolls.html.

Rosenblatt, Kalhan. "New Jersey Family to Sue School District after 12-Year-Old Daughter's Suicide." NBC News, August 1, 2017. https://www.nbcnews.com/news/us-news/new-jersey-family-sue-school-district-after-12-year-old-n788506.

Sample, Ian. "What Are Deepfakes – and How Can You Spot Them?" The Guardian, January 13, 2020, sec. News. https://www.theguardian.com/technology/2020/jan/13/what-are-deepfakes-and-how-can-you-spot-them.

Sanger, David E. The Perfect Weapon: War, Sabotage, and Fear in the Cyber Age. Broadway Books, 2019.

Sarkeesian, Anita. "Anita Sarkeesian's Guide to Internetting While Female." Marie Claire, February 20, 2015. https://www.marieclaire.com/culture/news/a13403/online-harassment-terms-fight-back/.

Satter, Raphael, Jeff Donn, and Nataliya Vasilyeva. "Russian Hackers Fancy Bear Targeted Hundreds of Journalists." Associated Press, December 22, 2017. https://apnews.com/article/c3b26c647e794073b7626befa146caad.

Scarlett, Cher. "Half a Million People Have Seen Me Naked." Medium, October 2, 2018. https://medium.com/@cherp/half-a-million-people-have-seen-me-naked-e70e8b89269c.

Seltzer, Sarah. "Beyond Mansplaining: A New Lexicon of Misogynist Trolling Behaviors." Flavorwire, March 24, 2015. https://www.flavorwire.com/511063/beyond-mansplaining-a-new-lexicon-of-misogynist-trolling-behaviors.

StatCounter GlobalStats. "Desktop Browser Market Share Worldwide." https://gs.statcounter.com/browser-market-share/desktop/worldwide.

Talbot, Margaret. "The Attorney Fighting Revenge Porn." The New Yorker, November 28, 2016. https://www.newyorker.com/magazine/2016/12/05/the-attorney-fighting-revenge-porn.

Team Password. "Top 50 Worst Passwords of 2019," December 18, 2019. https://www.teampassword.com/blog/top-50-worst-passwords-of-2019.

Totem Project. "Totem Project." https://learn.totem-project.org/.

U.S. Department of Justice. "Orange City Man Who 'Sextorted' Multiple Minors Sentenced To 60 Years," August 6, 2020. https://www.justice.gov/usao-mdfl/pr/orange-city-man-who-sextorted-multiple-minors-sentenced-60-years.

Valenti, Jessica. "Insults and Rape Threats. Writers Shouldn't Have to Deal with This | Jessica Valenti." The Guardian, April 14, 2016, sec. Technology. https://www.theguardian.com/commentisfree/2016/apr/14/insults-rape-threats-writers-online-harassment.

Vermont Secretary of State: Corporations Division. "Data Broker Search." https://bizfilings.vermont.gov/online/DatabrokerInquire/DataBrokerSearch.

West, Lindy. "What Happened When I Confronted My Cruellest Troll." The Guardian, February 2, 2015, sec. Society. http://www.theguardian.com/society/2015/feb/02/what-happened-confronted-cruellest-troll-lindy-west.

Whitman, Ryan. "Judge: Police Can't Force You to Unlock Phone With Fingerprint or Face ID - ExtremeTech." ExtremeTech (blog), January 15, 2019. https://www.extremetech.com/mobile/283795-judge-police-cant-force-you-to-unlock-phone-with-fingerprint-or-face-id.

Without My Consent. "Without My Consent." https://withoutmyconsent.org/.

Women's Media Center. "Online Abuse 101." https://womensmediacenter.com/speech-project/online-abuse-101.

Woolley, Samuel C., and Philip N. Howard. "Computational Propaganda Worldwide: Executive Summary." Computational Propaganda Research Project. University of Oxford, Oxford Internet Institute, n.d.

Zeltser, Lenny. "Network DDoS Incident Response Cheat Sheet." Lenny Zeltser (blog), September 23, 2016. https://zeltser.com/ddos-incident-cheat-sheet/.

Zhang, Xiaolu, Ibrahim Baggili, and Frank Breitinger. "Breaking into the Vault: Privacy, Security and Forensic Analysis of Android Vault Applications." Computers & Security 70 (September 2017): 516–31. https://www.sciencedirect.com/science/article/pii/S0167404817301529.

Index

1Password 52
2-factor authentication . 14, 57, 58, 59
911 .... 183, 200, 243
Abnormal Security 38
accounts payable 29, 30
accounts receivable 29
Adobe PDF124, 183, 227, 237, 246, 300
Adobe Photoshop 172, 234
Advanced Network Technology division 13
air gap 12
algorithm 16
AllMyTweets.net 156, 228
Amazon S3 Glacier 142
American Bar Association .321, 325
American Civil Liberties Union ..109
Anita Sarkeesian 187
antivirus program 139
antivirus programs 137, 139, 270
Apple AirDrop 24
Apple App Store 94, 99, 101, 254
Apple FaceTime 306
Apple FileVault 133
Apple Find My app 97
Apple iCloud 97, 100, 107, 141, 142
Apple iMessage 107
Apple MacBooks 133

Apple macOS Recovery 143
Archive Today 236
Astroturfing 186
Avast Antivirus 139
AVG Antivirus 139
Ayyub, Rana 190
Backblaze 141
bank account number 29
Bank of America 58, 59
Batman 182
battery power 104
BitDefender 139, 140
Blizzard *241*
BlueBugging 23
BlueJacking 23
BlueSmacking 23
BlueSnarfing 23
Bluetooth 8, 22, 23, 24, 148
bots 16, 67, 297, 299, 300
Brave Browser 81, 85
British Broadcasting Company ..192
Brown, Michael 193
burabura 129
Burner App 176
burner phone 175
Caller ID 115
Ccleaner 144
Certegy 323
charger cables 13

345

ChexSystems 323
child identity theft.... 286, 290, 327
Cisco Webex 306
CleanMyMac 144
climate change 35
Comcast..................................... 33
computational propaganda . 67, 68
concern trolling 186
conference calls 302
Consumer privacy laws 68
ContactOut.............................. 229
cookies ... 16, 81, 82, 84, 87, 88, 89, 91, 92, 93
CopyByte 244
counterspeech 186, 189, 197
CoverMe 102, 255
COVID-19 .... 35, 36, 37, 38
credit freeze 289, 317, 318, 328
credit rating............................ 286
credit reports .. 286, 287, 288, 289, 313, 314, 316, 317, 318, 319, 327, 329
cross-platform harassment 187
cryptocurrency 262
Cyber Civil Rights Initiative...... 194, 195, 197, 243, 244, 245
cyberbullying 188
cyber-mob attacks 188
cybersexual abuse 193
cyberstalking 189
Cydia....................................... 104
Daily Beast.............................. 196
Dark Web 58, 87
data brokers 64, 79, 280, 281
David Sanger 12
de Saint-Exupéry, Antoine 129
deadnaming 194
debt collectors 290, 319, 321

Deep Survival............................ 129
deepfake 190
default PIN code 24, 110, 111
DeleteMe 64, 282, 283
denial of access 190
denial of service attack 191, 192
Department of Motor Vehicles 319
DHL.......................... 119, 120, 122
Digital WarRoom 70
Discord 306
distributed denial of service attack 191, 192
Do Not Call Registry 116, 117
dog whistling 192
dogpiling................................. 188
doxing188, 193, 197, 200, 225, 248
Doxy.me 306
Dubner, Stephen J. 26, 27
DuckDuckGo 88, 253, 254
Dust 107
Electronic Frontier Foundation 302
email filters 40
Emsisoft.............................. 34, 35
encryption 3, 133, 134, 135
Equifax.......287, 314, 317, 326, 327
Etsy 192
Exchangeable Image File Format 172, 173, 233
Experian 287, 314, 317, 326, 327
FACC 35
Facebook 47, 52, 54, 68, 70, 71, 76, 77, 78, 82, 85, 107, 108, 155, 172, 174, 177, 185, 187, 189, 202, 203, 293, 306
Facebook Messenger 107, 185, 306
Facebook Messenger Kids 306
facial recognition 14, 110, 112, 113
factory reset 110, 113, 114

Fair Credit Reporting Act 286
false positive 27
false reporting 190
Fancy Bear 196
fearware 15, 35, 38
Federal Bureau of Investigation 18, 45, 259, 260, 261, 262, 263, 264, 266, 267, 268, 275
Federal Trade Commission 116, 287, 289, 313, 314, 315, 316, 317, 318, 327, 329
FedEx Office 55
Fifth Amendment 112
Filipovic, Jill 195
fingerprints ... 14, 99, 110, 112, 113
firewall 19
firmware 21
flooding 191
Florida, Middle District of 260
fraud alert 288, 289, 313, 317, 318, 326
Freakonomics 26
gender-based harassment 193
Ghostery 90, 91
gift cards 28, 116, 262
GitHub 192
Gladwell, Malcolm 129
Goldberg, Carrie 197
Gonzales, Laurence 129
Google Alerts 181, 226
Google Calendar 142
Google Chrome .. 63, 65, 81, 83, 84, 86, 92, 192, 229, 230
Google Contacts 142
Google Contributor 280
Google Drive 101, 108, 142, 307
Google Duo 306
Google Earth 86, 158, 162

Google Find My Device 98
Google Gmail 40, 41, 43, 44, 70, 142, 148, 293
Google Hangouts 306
Google Maps 86, 158, 160, 162, 164, 277, 278, 280
Google Maps Satellite View 86, 158, 164
Google Maps Street View .. 86, 158, 160, 162, 164, 232, 277, 278, 279, 280
Google Meet 306
Google One 142
Google Outdated Content Removal 247
Google Photos 142
Google Play Store ... 94, 98, 99, 100
Google Takeout 78
Google Voice 175
GoToMeeting 306
guest WiFi 20
hacking 196
hateful speech 196
HaveIBeenPwned 48, 50
Hilton Hotels 54
Hilton, Paris 54
hotel business office 55
hotspot 145
Houseparty 306
Huffington Post 190
human resources 293
Human Resources 38
Hushed App 176
identity theft 120, 124, 248, 285, 287, 289, 290, 313, 315, 316, 317, 318, 319, 321, 322, 326, 327, 328, 329
Identity Theft Resource Center 285

Imgur 202, 204, 240, 241
Incognito mode 83, 84
Indeed 298
InPrivate mode......................... 83
Instagram 155, 172, 174, 177, 178, 185, 202, 206, 208, 209, 261
Internal Revenue Service 115, 116, 130, 315, 326, 328
Internet Crime Complaint Center 45
invoices 30
IP address 16, 146
Iran 12
Israeli intelligence 12
jailbreaking............................. 104
Javelin Strategy & Research 286
Jitsi Meet................................ 306
Jones, Leslie........................... 197
Keepsafe......................... 102, 255
Konnikova, Maria 125
LastPass............................. 51, 52
law enforcement... iii, 6, 25, 45, 87, 109, 112, 117, 119, 120, 122, 123, 124, 127, 128, 130, 133, 146, 180, 182, 183, 184, 190, 193, 195, 197, 200, 227, 230, 240, 242, 243, 245, 260, 262, 263, 264, 287, 289, 314, 315, 320, 321, 333
Lessin, Jessica 201
Levitt, Steven D. 26, 27
LGBTQIA+ 193, 194
Lifehacker.com......................... 99
LinkedIn 229, 297, 298
location sharing................ 105, 171
lollipopping 194
Los Angeles Times 117
malware 15, 37, 137, 139, 140

malware removal 105, 137, 138, 139, 140, 141, 270
Malwarebytes 140
Mandel, Bethany..................... 189
mass report 190
Matsuoka, Ena 157
medical identity theft.............. 286
Medium.com.... 239, 242, 257, 258
mental health 180, 195
message bombing 191
metadata...172, 173, 227, 233, 300
microphone.9, 10, 11, 89, 303, 304
Microsoft Bing... 81, 225, 231, 247, 254
Microsoft Edge 81, 86
Microsoft OneDrive.......... 142, 307
Microsoft Outlook................ 32, 33
Microsoft Safety Scanner 140
Microsoft Skype 121, 122, 125, 128, 306
Microsoft Store 94
Microsoft Teams 306
Microsoft Windows BitLocker.. 134
Microsoft Windows recovery... 143
Microsoft Word................. 70, 299
Middle East 12
Monster.com........................... 298
Mozilla Firefox....63, 65, 81, 85, 90, 306
Mozilla Firefox Focus 85
Mozilla Firefox Monitor 49
Nashi 186
National Consumer Telecom and Utilities Exchange 322
National Council for Missing & Exploited Children 259
National Security Administration 13

National Security Administration ANT catalog 13
National Sex Offender Public Website 274
New York Times 193, 196, 197, 201
New York University School of Law 195
newly registered domains 36
Nigerian email scams 26, 27
non-consensual pornography .. 153, 225, 239, 248, 253
NordVPN 147
Norton 360 Deluxe 63, 138
Norton Secure VPN 148
Office for Civil Rights 328
online game credits 262
online impersonation 198
Ookla Speedtest 22
outrage/shame mobs 188
Overwatch 241
Oxford Dictionary of Social Media 187
Oxford Internet Institute 68
password keeper 19, 51, 52, 55, 84, 89, 271
PEN America 182, 183, 184, 185, 186, 191, 193, 195, 196, 199, 200, 201
PermissionDog 100
phishing ... ii, 15, 25, 26, 28, 31, 34, 35, 36, 38, 81, 139, 174, 199, 270
Photo Exif Editor 173
Photo Investigator 174
Photo Locker 103, 256
political elections 35
portable disk drive 3
predators i, 259, 260, 261, 263, 269
Privacy Badger 90
Privacy.net 82
Private Internet Access 147
ProPublica.com 191
Protonmail 44
public computers 55
public WiFi 145, 146
purchase orders 29
PureVPN 147
pwned 47
ransomware ... 15, 25, 37, 137, 139, 141
Reader's Digest 104, 105
reboot your router 21
Reddit 187, 192, 202, 210
Retruster 25
revenge porn ... 184, 195, 197, 198, 202, 225, 239
reverse image lookups 230
Ricochet 189
rooting 104
Russian intelligence 12
Russian reporters 196
Russian troll farms 196
Safari . 63, 65, 81, 84, 143, 253, 254
Sarkeesian, Anita 187
Scarlett, Cher ... 239, 240, 242, 257, 258
Scientific American 189
screenshot ... ii, 107, 180, 183, 202, 227, 233, 235, 246, 304
Seagate 34
sealioning 187
secret questions 54, 55
sextortion 194, 243, 259, 260, 261, 262, 264, 265, 266, 268, 269
SharePoint 307
Signal 106, 173, 306

349

SIM card 110, 111
SIPRNet.. 12
Snagit...................................... 236
Snapchat..... 35, 178, 202, 212, 261
social media trackers 82, 84
Social Security number 59, 286, 290, 317, 319, 326, 327, 328
SoundCloud 192
spam filters............................... 40
spear phishing 28
SplashData, Inc........................ 53
spoofing............15, 30, 32, 42, 120
Spotify 192
spyware....14, 15, 83, 93, 104, 105, 133, 137, 139
Statcounter.com 83
student loans 290, 324
SuperAntiSpyware................... 140
Superuser 104
swatting................................. 200
Swisher, Kara.......................... 201
Telecheck 323
Testani, Justin Richard 260, 261
text messages...14, 23, 37, 57, 107, 110, 246, 269
The Confidence Game 125
The Little Prince 129
The Perfect Weapon................... 12
Think Like a Freak...................... 26
threats...................... 174, 199, 200
TikTok 155, 174, 178
Tile tracker 148, 149
TinEye.................................... 232
Tokyo Metropolitan Police........ 157
Tor Browser............................... 87
Tor Project................................. 87
tracking pixels 16, 43, 82
TransUnion 287, 314, 317, 327

trolls .... i, ii, 64, 153, 180, 181, 187, 197, 201, 226, 227, 228, 230, 232, 233, 302
Tumblr............... 185, 202, 214, 215
Twitch..................... 239, 240, 241
Twitter 54, 68, 70, 71, 78, 155, 172, 177, 178, 185, 187, 189, 192, 197, 199, 202, 218, 228, 229
U.S. Attorney's Office........ 260, 325
U.S. Constitution 112
U.S. Department of Defense 12
U.S. Department of Education . 324
U.S. Department of Health and Human Services 328
U.S. Pentagon............................ 12
U.S. State Department 320
U.S. Trustee 325
Uncleswagg 240, 241
University of Oxford.................. 68
unsolicited pornography 194
unsubscribe......................... 40, 41
unwanted sexualization 194
UrbanDictionary.com........ 47, 301
USB thumb drive 3, 11, 12, 13, 134, 143
Valenti, Jessica 199, 200
Verizon 25, 110, 111, 306
Verizon BlueJeans 306
Vermont Secretary of State 280, 281
video calls........9, 10, 122, 260, 301, 302, 306
Video Locker.................... 103, 256
virtual backgrounds 304
virtual waiting room................ 303
VirusTotal 95
VPN.............36, 146, 147, 148, 228
webcam...9, 10, 266, 303, 304, 305

West, Lindy 198	Yahoo ... 40, 81, 225, 247, 248, 253, 254
Western Union............................ 57	Yandex 231
whaling 34, 35	Yiannopoulos, Milo 197
WhatsApp 108, 185, 199, 306	YouTube 185, 186, 202, 220, 224
White House 12, 91	ZipRecruiter 298
Whois.net 247, 248	Zoom call 9, 38, 201, 301, 302, 303, 305, 306, 307
Wickr 106	
Without My Consent 245	Zoombombing 201, 301, 302
World of Warcraft............. 240, 241	Zscaler 36, 37
WPA2 encryption 20	

Made in the USA
Las Vegas, NV
25 August 2021